Origin of Woman

The Explanation, Volume 6

Sam Kneller

Published by Sam Kneller, 2020.

Also by Sam Kneller

The Explanation
Inventory of the Universe
Audit of the Universe
Origin of the Universe
Origin of Humankind
Origin of Woman

Watch for more at https://www.TheExplanation.com.

Table of Contents

Proprietorship

ORIGIN OF WOMAN

First edition. July 20, 2020.

Written by Sam Kneller.

---

1. https://theexplanation.com

2. https://mailchi.mp/theexplanation/7keystomasterbiblicalhebrew

Biblical Hebrew

Think about this:

Can you understand a document in a translated language?

If you haven't experienced the pleasure or hassle of learning and speaking a second language, you might not be able to do justice to the answer to that question.

My native language is English. I've now lived in France for the better part of my life, the last 40 years, since 1978. My French is pretty good, but I would in no way say I'm a French speaker. When it comes to colloquialisms, jokes, plays-on-words, and slang, leave me out. I don't know when to laugh, and I don't know what to answer. The simple evidence is that I don't understand what people are saying. Yes, I speak French, but to say I master the language like a French-person would be a gross exaggeration.

There's a lot of Bible-arguing going on based on one's native language. It's like fighting over bricks and forgetting about the house of which each one is a part.

Let me give you one example here. The original Biblical Hebrew word *commandment*, as in the *Ten Commandments,* is translated with over 50 (that's right, fifty) different English words by the translators of the King James Bible version. That's amazing when you think about it. I'll add that in Hebrew, this word *commandment* has only three letters: dbr. How can you get 50 different English translations out of that?

I won't get into a detailed explanation here of why this is so, but it should make you stop and think: How can this be?

If you start learning the Hebrew alphabet and vocabulary today, it'll take you forever to learn how to read and study the original language, and you'll still never be able to grasp the nuances of all those 50 shades of *commandment*.

That's why the **Annex** is devoted to *7 Keys to Master Biblical Hebrew–A Study Method to Unlock Bible Meaning, with no fuss*. There you'll find a summary of the free, acclaimed online course including all the freely accessible online Bible tools at UnlockBibleMeaning.com[1] for your study – even if you don't possess a Bible.

Let me say openly. You've never seen a method like this that will help you unlock Bible meaning so quickly and easily.

Hundreds of students have followed this course. Here are just a few reviews:

> The instructor was precise in his delivery and how to check the meaning. It was really helpful to learn the power of the Hebrew behind the words. Phyllis C.

> It's a SHAME!.. after many Bible translations, most people still have a blurred "understanding" of what Sam Kneller, so elegantly clarifies in this course. See it for yourself. This is a MUST TAKE COURSE for everyone, no matter their beliefs (or non-beliefs) are. Hey!, if you can't really comprehend the CLIMAX in 'the first story'...forget PhDs. Thanks! Jesse C.

> He explains in a very slow and concise manner. Allowing a student to keep up with the lesson. JoAnne J.

---

1. https://unlockbiblemeaning.com

I think it is well organized and very informative. I thought the instructor could be a little more enthusiastic but I think that might just be because everyone who teaches now acts as they have just won the lottery. Overall, I think it was great. Myrna P.

For someone so old willing to take his time to share his knowledge with the world, he deserves 5 stars. If the video you find it too long, doesn't matter, pay attention to the materials he has to share. In fact, the aim of this course is for him to enable you to self-learn independently. Shung J.

C'est concis, bien documenté, bien présenté verbalement. C'est vraiment superbe à tous points de vue. Bravo Viviane L.

I found this course to give a clear and useful example of using the website and tools mentioned. Need to be open-minded and willing to explore the Bible, rather than dogmatic, to get the most from this course. Thanks, Sam, for introducing me to these tools. I look forward to further explorations. Robin S.

Housekeeping Issues

Some links in this e-book connect you to websites on the Internet. Hence the need for an internet connection as you read. That said, the subject is understandable without navigating to those links. All links were correct at the time of publication. If you find an issue, let me know at sam@theexplanation.com Thanks in advance.

You will find all the Bible tools to follow along with this e-book at http://UnlockBibleMeaning.com

- The entire King James Bible online. Search by book, chapter, verse or word or phrase

- The Interlinear Bible with Biblical Hebrew, English, phonetics, Strong's numbers and link to his annotation and list of KJV translations

- Strong's Bible Concordance for each Hebrew and Greek word with its annotation and list of KJV translations

- The Hebrew-Greek Concordance. Also called Englishman's concordance. It gathers together all the Bible verses with the same original Biblical Hebrew and Greek words so you can study the various usages of each word in context.

At the end of each chapter of this e-book, there are ideas for *Further Study*. These are suggested exercises for your enrichment to dig for Bible Study gems to enhance your understanding. You can skip these and move on. I do suggest you peruse the content. Some comments complement the information in the chapter.

If you've come across this e-book for the first time, then please know that it is part of a much larger work: *The Explanation* series. See all the books[1].

www.TheExplanation.com

Join The Explanation Newsletter[22] no spam, total privacy. Receive Sam's latest blog post notifications and information about *The Explanation*

---

1. https://theexplanation.com/the-explanation-books-to-buy/

2. https://mailchi.mp/theexplanation.com/7keystomasterbiblicalhebrew

Preface

Given the social climate and the activity and talk that surrounds women's movements and women in general, some might consider this book controversial. The goal of *The Explanation* is not to participate, that is be for or against, in any movements or controversy. But rather to explain what the Bible indicates.

This book is simply the follow-on of *Origin of Humankind* (volume 5) which focused on Genesis 2:7; creation of the first man. In essence, the first human being of the world population. As such, the key is to understand what makes a human human. It is the *neshama*, the mind.

God placed that man with his mind in the Garden of Eden. But man, with mind, even in the Garden, is not good alone. Hence the creation of woman.

Her beginning occupies eight verses, whereas that of the man, only one. Straightaway, we realize there's something astonishingly special about her appearance on the scene.

Origin of Woman develops these telling details based on the meaning of the Biblical Hebrew words. The narrative is full of hidden gems. They enhance and complete the story of WHY God created humankind and what His plan is. And why the woman is a primary element in its accomplishment. The ending is magnificent, but you'll have to read the book to find out just how sumptuous it's going to be.

The story of the Universe, of which the man and the woman are key pieces, is the narrative of coherent completeness. Like an oversized jigsaw puzzle there's only one way to assemble it, to reveal the original picture. Likewise, with the roles of the man and the woman. *Origin of Woman* develops the mystery of man and woman. It explains WHY there are marked differences in their mindsets, WHY this is designed as it is by Yahweh, Himself.

The Explanation series answers the evasive question, "How can we bring peace and prosperity to humankind and Earth?"

Inventory of the Universe (volume 1) reveals just how interdependent, every single cog, all aspects of the Universe are. Space, atmosphere, water, land, flora, fauna and humankind, unique from animals, are the oh so complex, but oh so interconnected actors of our play. This book brings readers down to earth, away from consumerism and the daily hustle and bustle, back to our real roots. Focus on the big picture, the essentials.

Audit of the Universe (2) and *Audit of Humankind* (3) present an overview of how humankind has managed our planet. Is the half-full glass of peace and prosperity getting fuller or emptier? They focus on humanity's role in this equation. Humans are at the pinnacle of dominion over Earth, how are we faring in this role? It details the Singularities of Humankind, How Humans Function, Socialize, Govern, and Reason. What is the outcome of human relations and rulership?

Origin of the Universe[1] (4) unpacks popular ideas and shared beliefs in the light of Biblical Hebrew. For those not familiar with the Bible or Genesis, it includes preparatory material that answers fundamental questions: Why look for answers in Sacred Books[2], and in particular, the Bible? How to interpret the Bible[3], and what is real Theology[4]? It then jumps right into the thick of Genesis 1:1 and is a commentary on chapter 1.

---

1. https://theexplanation.com/read-content-origin-universe-online/

2. http://theexplanation.com/sacred-books/

3. https://theexplanation.com/the-sacred-book-if-it-exists-could-it-possibly-be-the-bible/

4. http://theexplanation.com/into-theology-a-fifth-approach-to-life-with-peace-and-prosperity/

This book, *Origin of Woman*, is the sixth book of *The Explanation series*.

Origin of Woman is a commentary on the end of Genesis 2. Learn what the Bible says about the rights and responsibilities of women.

There's so much polarized and conflicting information on this and so many other subjects today. It's can be a wearying task to differentiate fact from fiction. *The Explanation* will help in establishing groundwork benchmarks so you can measure the validity of circulating information. It will equip you with a robust grid onto which you'll be able to fit new pieces of the puzzle until you have a more focused and precise picture of the world in which we live.

Join Sam for a deep dive into a topic that concerns fifty percent of the world population. Seekers of answers to the big questions in life cannot skirt this issue. Such understanding is so much more than just information; it's fundamental knowledge. How and where do women fit in the puzzle of the Universe. Eight Bible verses you need to get right, to see how the female role fits into the puzzle of why Humankind is on Earth.

Jump into the narrative. The first man in on the scene (*Origin of Humankind*, volume 5). Next is the creation of the Garden of Eden, the sumptuous home, prepared like a diamond-studded jewel, for the arrival of the first woman.

1. In the Garden of Eden

Garden of Eden. Much More than a Garden.

Garden of Eden. Myth or reality? Imagination or Paradise? It is Bible reality, described from Genesis to Revelation in notable fashion.

The Garden of Eden and its creation was the immediate first act after creating the first man. Genesis 2:8 recounts this episode. Understanding the relationship of man, humans to the Garden of Eden, is comprehending the plan of God. Let's start by establishing some basics which mythology and religion have twisted out of shape. God made a neshama nefesh. A conscious being whom He houses in sumptuous surroundings. God alone, can insert and extract human beings from the Garden of Eden.

Genesis 2:8

And the LORD God *planted* (H5193) a *garden* (H1588) eastward in *Eden* (H5731); and there he put the man whom he had formed.

1. Technically it is not the Garden OF Eden. It's the Garden IN Eden. Eden is quite a vast territory, as I'll point out. Within is a relatively small space devoted to this Garden.
2. God had already created Eden. I would say on Day 3 when He created dry land and vegetation.
3. This Garden belongs to God. It's His abode on Earth. God is present everywhere in the Universe and beyond. But He has chosen and set up a particular and specific place as His dwelling. As unbelievable as it might sound, from every place He could prefer, He decided right here on our planet in a precise location we shall identify. It is more than a simple dwelling. I will show you this is God's Headquarters from where He rules Earth and beyond.
4. Remember, God gave humans dominion over Earth. He placed the man in the Garden, at Headquarters. Humans are going to rule in the company of God.
5. God is sharing His Rulership and His Headquarters with humans.

I used the analogy that the renewing of Earth was like preparing the room for baby[1]. In that case, you want to finish the room before the baby arrives. Why then does God first create Adam, and only AFTER that event, does He organize the Garden of Eden?

To answer that question, let's first take a closer look at what the Garden of Eden is. We are going to resort to the Biblical Hebrew[2] and Strong's

---

1. https://theexplanation.com/human-needs-basics-person-expect/

2. https://theexplanation.com/
   bible-tools-to-unlock-bible-meaning-using-biblical-hebrew-with-no-fuss/

concordance[3]. We need a deeper understanding of the vocabulary used here, starting with the word planted. What does that mean?

H5193

נָטַע nâṭaʿ new-tah'; a primitive root; properly, to strike in, i.e., fix; specifically, to plant (literally or figuratively):

KJV – fastened, plant(-er).

We think of planting seeds or flowers. This planting of the Garden carries major significance. This idea is solidly fastening, putting down (*striking in* as Strong expresses it, like with a hammer) deep roots. This Garden is firmly affixed. Once in place, it cannot be removed. Today, the Garden is nowhere in sight. Maybe that's why people read this as a myth. Notice that *nata – planted* is literal as well as figurative. That's the fourth key to master Biblical Hebrew[4]. See what else God plants figuratively. Here's a noteworthy related verse that Moses sang after passing through the opened Sea with the Israelites on their way to the Promised Land.

Exodus 15:17-18

17 You shall bring them [from the Egypt exodus] in, and *plant* (H5193) them in the mountain of your inheritance, in the place, O LORD, which you have made for yourself to dwell in, in the Sanctuary, O Lord, which your hands have established.

18 The LORD shall reign forever and ever.

---

3. https://theexplanation.com/strongs-concordance-demon-or-angel-which-will-it-be/

4. https://theexplanation.com/each-biblical-hebrew-word-is-a-precious-jewel-to-be-discovered/

All the elements of Genesis 2:8 are in these verses in Exodus. God's property is *the mountain of your inheritance*. There is the Sanctuary (Headquarters, referring to Jerusalem and specifically the Temple, this context is also prophetic), which God has built with His own hands and in which He dwells; this is analogous to God planting His Garden of Eden, His dwelling place. This mountain is God's inheritance, His estate, which He shares with[5] those of the Exodus, those who come out of Egypt, come out of sin, eventually all repentant human beings. How permanent is this planting of the Sanctuary, the Garden, and humans? Verse 18 answers unequivocally, forever, and ever.

When you can grasp the Biblical Hebrew and tell the story of just one word[6], to plant H5193, you can look into the depth of God's plan. You see the word garden and think of roses or vegetables. Yes, but in so doing, we've missed the entire figurative meaning.

H1588[7]

גַּן gan; from H1598 (גָּנַן); a garden (as fenced):

KJV – garden.

H1598

גָּנַן gânan gaw-nan'; a primitive root; to hedge about, i.e. (generally) protect:

KJV – defend.

---

5. https://theexplanation.com/

   god-to-do-with-his-work-to-make-them-on-7th-day-to-take-care-his-creation/

6. https://theexplanation.com/biblical-hebrew-roots-to-anchor-your-bible-comprehension/

7. http://www.unlockbiblemeaning.com/browse/

The Garden in Eden is fenced. Politically, today, walls have bad press, but they can fulfill a needed purpose. Here's a verse about a future Temple, a Sanctuary, with the explanation of why there's a wall.

Ezekiel 42:15,20

15 Now when he had made an end of measuring the inner house, he brought me forth toward the gate whose prospect is toward the east and measured it round about.

20 He measured it by the four sides: it had a wall round about, five hundred reeds long, and five hundred broad, to make a separation between the sanctuary and the profane place.

The Sanctuary and specifically certain parts like the Holy of Holies are holy. They are pure and dedicated for holy use ONLY by certain Priests. I can't get into the details here, but verse 20 reveals a WALL separating this holy area from the profane, which was all around; this is exactly the scenario and sense of the Biblical Hebrew word *gan – garden*. It is a protected area reserved for the holy. At their creation, Adam and Eve were holy, placed in a holy environment. You know the rest of the story and how they were ousted because they lost their holiness. They exited via the EAST gate. The whole plan of God consists of bringing humankind BACK INTO the Garden of Eden, this protected holy place, via the East gate.

Christ entered Jerusalem from the Garden of Gethsemane (East of Jerusalem). On His Return, He enters Jerusalem from the East. On His crucifixion, the curtain that was rent (Matthew 27:51), signifying the entrance to the Holy of Holies, RE-entry to the Garden of Eden, was on the EAST wall of the Holy of Holies. In ancient times and Biblically, the East was the main point of the compass, not the North. Once you've entered this Garden from the East, you're under the protection of the God of the Universe. This wall is not for belligerence, but rather a Sanctuary of Peace with an open gate on its Eastside. Yes, there are requirements to enter, to pass from the profane to the Holy, yes, there are other entry gates. But that's another aspect of our story.

A lot of people, even the religious, believe the concept that the Garden of Eden is a myth. Or, at best, it is the figment of the imagination of some author, based on an ancient myth, who wanted to transmit some hope or national nirvana to his people. *The Explanation* does not take this viewpoint. I'm presenting a theological point of view[8]. Taking God's Word as God's Word, as foolish at it might sound. Eden existed and is multi-symbolic of sacred places and worlds to come. Unfortunately, Strong's comments and even the translation do not give a hint of its majesty.

H5731.

עֵדֶן ʻÊden ay'-den; the same as H5730 (עֵדֶן) (masculine); Eden, the region of Adam's home:

KJV – Eden.-green

H5730.

עֵדֶן ʻêden ay'-den; or (feminine) עֶדְנָה; from H5727 (עָדַן); pleasure:

KJV – delicate, delight, pleasure. See also H1040 (בֵּית עֵדֶן).

These KJV words are an extremely pale representation of future reality. I realize, if you're reading this for the first time, it sounds very extravagant. But this presentation is based on mastering Biblical Hebrew and the roots[9] and stories[10] of the original language words.

---

8. https://theexplanation.com/foolishness-gods-word-true-theology/

None of this is hypothetical or mystical. It is coherent completeness[11] coupled with Biblewide corroboration[12]. In Genesis 2:7, God creates humans and then, in the very next verse, gives the ENTIRE plan, all the way through to the final accomplishment, Eden. It's magistral authorship by a majestic Author; we should expect nothing less of God.

Revelation 21:10-12, 24, 26-27

10 And he carried me [the Apostle John] away in the spirit to a great and high mountain (see the mountain of Ex. 15:17 above), and shewed me that great city, the holy Jerusalem, descending out of heaven from God,

11 Having the glory of God: and her light was like unto a stone most precious, even like a jasper stone, clear as crystal;

12 And had a wall great and high, and had twelve gates...

24 And the nations of them which are saved shall walk in the light of it: and the kings of the earth do bring their glory and honour into it.

26 And they shall bring the glory and honour of the nations into it.

27 And there shall in no wise enter into it any thing that defiles, neither whatsoever works abomination, or makes a lie: but they which are written in the Lamb's book of life.

---

9. https://theexplanation.com/biblical-hebrew-roots-to-anchor-your-bible-comprehension/

10. https://theexplanation.com/biblical-hebrew-roots-to-anchor-your-bible-comprehension/

11. https://theexplanation.com/coherent-completeness-is-the-logical-reasoning-of-the-ssource/

12. https://theexplanation.com/foolishness-gods-word-true-theology/

That's an introductory description of the future Garden of Eden. There's plenty more to add. Do you see the comparison? First, God prepares His people (like Adam) then comes New Jerusalem, (like planting the Garden). If there's not full righteousness, there's no Garden, that's why there's no Garden today. Verse 12 relates the walls that will protect the saved who walk in the light. The ungodly cannot enter this holy city, just like the two cherubim protected entry to the Garden of Eden.

Only those in the Book of Life are in New Jerusalem. These are all God's people who have the same pure nishmat chayim[13] the pure consciousness of life that Adam had, that God breathed into him at Creation. It's this entire process of the nations, all nations, all peoples who have ever walked the face of the Earth, receiving the opportunity to return to a pure nishmat chayim that is the story of the Bible. All people are equal before God, and all will have that opportunity. *The Explanation* tells the incredible story of the Garden of Eden inhabited by all those who will inherit Eternal Life.

This one verse, "God planted a Garden eastward in Eden," merits an entire book; maybe I'll write it. Because the Garden has multiple prefigurations in the Old and New Testaments with the Tabernacle, the Temples (plural), and the Church, the curtain was miraculously rent, from top to bottom, in the Temple when Christ died on the cross. That signified the removal of the two Cherubim from the entry gate to the Garden. For the first time since Adam and Eve were cast out, God's servants, Christ being the First, the Firstfruits, could enter the Holy of Holies, God's dwelling. For the first time, a human (the man, Jesus) had put on the FULL IMAGE and the FULL LIKENESS of his Father and entered the KINship of Elohim.

---

13. https://theexplanation.com/many-lives-you-i-bible-says/

The first man, upon his creation, was *put* into the Garden. The Second Man, upon His Spiritual Creational Resurrection, was *put* into God's Kingdom. What a story the Garden of Eden tells us.

Evil. God Allowed it in the Garden of Eden

First came the Tree of the Knowledge of Good and Evil, then Evil in the person of the Serpent. Understand the significance behind these seemingly incomprehensive moves by God Himself.

Evil, by whatever definition, is a phenomenon from which most of us would shy away. While some might revel in its devastation, I believe we can safely say, most wish to avoid evil. Why God planted it in the Garden and then sent in the fallen Archangel to contend with humans is one of the big enigmas of God's plan.

Let's comprehend this ambiguous piece of the Bible puzzle. This potent mixture of good and evil.

Genesis 2:9

> And out of the ground made the LORD God to grow every
> tree that is *pleasant* (H2530) to the sight, and *good* (H2896)
> for food; the tree of life also in the midst of the garden, and
> the tree of knowledge of good and evil.

We witness a special planting, separate from the Day 5 creation of
trees. Instant fully grown trees (I wonder about their dendrology) that
appealed to the human senses of sight and taste. We have already seen
the Biblical Hebrew good – tov – H2896. *It was good[1]* concludes each
day's creation. Better translations rendered by the KJV translators are
beautiful, precious, prosperity, ready, sweet, wealth, welfare. Both trees
were magnificent.

Pleasant, the second descriptive, warrants deeper study.

H2530

חָמַד châmad khaw-mad'; a primitive root; to delight in:

KJV – beauty, greatly beloved, covet, delectable thing,
([idiom] great) delight, desire, goodly, lust, (be) pleasant
(thing), precious (thing).

These trees evoked so much *delight* that they could lead to *coveting*. We
see the second key to master Biblical Hebrew[2]; words have opposing
meanings. Delighting in an activity should not cross the line into
covetousness. In Genesis 3, the man and woman crossed the line.

This garden has two centerpieces. The word *midst* is not chosen lightly
because there are two outstanding trees in the very center of the estate.
When you're in this garden, everything seems to draw your attention,
and your path leads inevitably to these marvels of nature. It's not just

---

1. *https://theexplanation.com/it-was-good-is-a-translation-fiasco-of-gods-actual-creation-statement/*

2. https://theexplanation.com/each-biblical-hebrew-word-is-a-precious-jewel-to-be-discovered/

their lusciousness; it's also their eye-catching and thought-provoking labels: *Tree of Life* and *Tree of Knowledge of Good and Evil*. In the midst of the garden, there's intrigue, what is *life*? What is *good*? What is *evil*? *Why two trees?*

Midst is significant. Let's grasp additional nuances of this word. They are enlightening.

H8432

תָּוֶךְ tâvek taw'-vek; from an unused root meaning to sever; a bisection, i.e. (by implication) the centre:

KJV – among(-st), × between, half, × (there-, where-), in(-to), middle, mid(-night), midst (among), × out (of), × through, × with(-in).

These definitions remind me of dividing between night and day[3]. There's a sheer separation between the two. The *midst* of the Garden designates a parting of the ways; a severance takes place. It's one way or the other. You can't take both roads. Indeed, when Adam and Eve took of one tree, they were severed from the other. What's pleasant to the sight and delectable to the taste (especially figuratively) is not necessarily the best path to take. It can sever a person from proper decision-making.

Do you see the story the Biblical Hebrew words are telling us? There's a choice here, despite no specific mention of free will choice. Let's focus on the two-tree-choice.

The Tree of Life (עֵץ הַחַיִּים – aits hachayim) which should be translated Tree of Lives, in the plural[4]. *The Explanation* discussed the nishmat

---

3. https://theexplanation.com/

   it-was-good-is-a-translation-fiasco-of-gods-actual-creation-statement/

chayim[5], the breath of lives (plural) God breathed into Adam in Genesis 2:7. It is the physical AND mental AND potential spiritual AND potential eternal LIVES; this is the reality and future of each human. I do not have the space to give a detailed explanation here, but in His conversation with Nicodemus, a religious leader who didn't understand the Bible teachings, Christ said,

John 3:15

15 That whosoever believes in him (Christ) should not perish, but have eternal life.

16 For God so loved the world, that he gave his only begotten Son, that whosoever believes in him should not perish, but have everlasting life.

Christ sent Nicodemus back to the clear-cut two paths of Genesis 2:9 symbolized by the two trees: Perishment and Eternal Life. A more significant severance of results is not possible. These are diametrically opposite goals set for each human being, immediately at the creation of the first man. God states his plan and purpose for humans in clear terms. Nicodemus didn't understand this, and I dare say, most people don't understand this today.

Likewise, it is challenging, even impossible to understand what Eternal Life is. Unfortunately, religion throws these two words around without grasping their significance. How can I affirm this? If they did, they'd better understand the real path that leads to eternal life. Many walk around with signs and quote, "Believe in Christ and you'll be saved" from John 3:15, which I quoted above. The fact is, demons believe and they will NOT be saved. James 2:19 states, "You believe that there is

---

4. https://theexplanation.com/many-lives-you-i-bible-says/

5. https://theexplanation.com/many-lives-you-i-bible-says/

one God; you do well: the devils also believe, and tremble." Not only do demons BELIEVE, but they KNOW who Christ is.

Matthew 8:28-29

28 And when he [Jesus] was come to the other side into the country of the Gergesenes, there met him two possessed with devils, coming out of the tombs, exceeding fierce, so that no man might pass by that way.

29 And, behold, they cried out, saying, What have we to do with you, Jesus, you Son of God? are you come here to torment us before the time?

They knew some main aspects of God's plan. Indeed, belief and knowing who Christ is are the pathway to eternal life, but they don't get you all the way there; otherwise, the demons would be partaking of the Tree of Life, which is not the case. There's more to it that needs to be understood.

The *more to it* that is misunderstood involves the Tree of the Knowledge of Good and Evil AND the Serpent being placed and allowed DIRECTLY in the Garden of Eden. We need to grasp WHY this seemingly counter-productive concept is a part of God's plan; this is where coherent completeness[6] plays a primordial role. Unless you can surmise a coherent answer to this question, you don't understand what God's plan is. The fact that evil was present in the Garden is a particular puzzle piece that must be turned right side up and perfectly assembled with all the other pieces.

Here's the million-dollar question: How can a *loving God* plant a *Tree of Death* in Paradise? The short answer is: To test human beings so each

---

6. https://theexplanation.com/coherent-completeness-is-the-logical-reasoning-of-the-ssource/

one makes a free will choice as to WHICH PATH they want to follow: Life or Death.

Let's step back an instant and summarize God's plan – Why He created humankind. He created us in HIS IMAGE[7]. Humans are of the GOD KIND[8]. Of course, we're on a much, much, much lower level but along with God, we humans alone possess neshama. **With our neshama, we can love, and we can hate.** He plans to give us Eternal Life. We have a minimal realization of what Eternal Life is; we know that it's going to last a long, long, long time.

BEFORE God gives us Eternal Life, He needs to know and be sure of ONE point; what we are going to do with our neshama, our consciousnes, and mind[9] for all of Eternity. Think of the person you least appreciate, someone who bothers you, maybe even drives you crazy. That's your neshama reaction to said individual. Now imagine you had to spend all Eternity with that individual with that same attitude! You might renounce Eternal Life because it would be more like hell. Granted, this is a simplistic example, but it's precisely what God wants to avoid among His kinship.

We have to *believe* God as we saw, but we have to *sort out our relationships*. Love God, love neighbor, love that bothersome person, love our enemies. God has no intention of allowing bickering people into the Garden of Eden. That's part of the reason Adam and Eve were ousted (I'll give you the surprising full idea later, and it's not what you think it is). How can God know if we can straighten out our relationships and problems?

---

7. https://theexplanation.com/humans-were-created-in-the-image-of-god-in-his-likeness/

8. https://theexplanation.com/were-humans-created-or-did-humans-originate-creation-day-6/

9. https://theexplanation.com/
consciousness-and-human-mind-you-cant-have-one-without-the-other/

There's only ONE WAY. PUT WRONG RELATIONSHIPS and PROBLEMS IN FRONT OF YOU and see how you're going to react with your neshama. That's why God put the Tree of Knowledge of Good and Evil in the Garden of Eden.

We put tests in front of babies, children, adolescents, and adults throughout their lives. Whether it's harder and harder games, homework exercises, exams, sports challenges, or business goals to reach, it's all to see how you're going to react and progress. The better you develop yourself, the harder the challenge.

The Bible refers to these challenges as, what I'd call, *neshama resistance*. In principle, the same Tree of Knowledge of Good and Evil is present today in the form of everything that can separate us from God. I can't go into all the details here. Even the serpent is present to lead us astray.

1 Peter 5:8-9

8 Be sober, be vigilant; because your adversary the devil, as a roaring lion, walks about, seeking whom he may devour:

9 Whom *resist* (G436) stedfast in the faith, knowing that the same afflictions are accomplished in your brethren that are in the world.

There's a New Testament verse that explains and corroborates Old Testament theology. We tend to use the word *trials* or *temptations* today, to refer to these afflictions. Eternal life is so mind-boggling in its vastness, not just time-wise but especially in what we're going to do with all that time, how we are going to allow our neshama to react during all that time. God must know the answers BEFORE He gives us Eternal Life. He has to know which path we've definitively decided to follow. And which path we've severed.

Lukewarm is abhorrent to God. One would think that God would approve an individual who walks down the median line between good and evil, leading a balanced spiritual life. But, look at what He says,

Revelation 3:15-16

15 I know your works, that you are neither cold nor hot: I would you were cold or hot.

16 So then because you are lukewarm, and neither cold nor hot, I will spue you out of my mouth.

This verse is the example of someone in the midst of the Garden of Eden looking at the two trees and NOT taking any action. *Not deciding* is a negative decision. Straddling two worlds is not what God has in mind regarding candidates for Eternal Life. He's looking for commitment. And the only way to see if someone is committed is to see how they resist. Believing is necessary, but it is not the only needed quality.

The Bible indicates that God placed the Tree of Knowledge of Good and Evil in the Garden of Eden and very soon afterward allowed the Serpent to enter the Garden. We all know the consequences. This same scenario is going to happen again in the future. Unfortunately, I cannot get into the prophetic details. But, following Christ's Return and after one thousand years of Godly reign on planet Earth, in a paradisiac landscape and atmosphere of peace, the Serpent will, for the last time, be permitted to stir up havoc. You should understand why God allows this.

Revelation 21:7

And when the thousand years are expired, Satan shall be loosed out of his prison,

At the end of this extended period of peace and prosperity established by God and His Kin, the Saints who have inherited Eternal Life, there will remain some humans on Earth who are lukewarm. At the end of the Millennium, the thousand years, some humans will take God for granted. They will NOT have made a clear-cut decision about following the path to Eternal Life or its alternate. Seeing whether they will RESIST or ACCEPT Satan will cause them to be hot or cold. Each person makes their own decision about the path they follow, life or death.

The way to help people make a decision is to see if they will resist or not. Eternal life is a serious matter, far beyond simple belief; this answers the question of why God allows trials and calamities. Notice, I didn't say causes trials and misfortunes. Yes, He can do that also, but we bring most of our woes on ourselves. We shall discuss the nature of the Tree of Knowledge of Good and Evil in a future chapter.

Further Study

I suggest you go over to UnlockBibleMeaning.com[10] and do a study on the word *resist* (1 Peter 5:9 - G436).

---

10. http://unlockbiblemeaning.com/

River of Living Water. The Deep Spiritual Meaning

A river that waters the ends of the known world flows out of Eden. Its significance is so much more than a description of the landscape.

A river of water flowed out of Eden and the Garden; it is a significant and essential element in this description of the first home of humankind. Rain is not sufficient. Here's why a continual flow of living water is vital.

God has planted the magnificent Garden of Eden. In its midst were two trees, pleasant to the sight and good for food. We have seen that this scenario is not only the physical reality of Paradise but the spiritual path to either Eternal Life or Death. It is a resume of the entire plan of God.

When we add the ingredient of God allowing the Serpent into the Garden to tempt Eve, from such a plot, we could conclude God is devious, cruel, and masochistic. As some have surmised, God was bored and took pleasure in seeing His created beings in pain. We have already seen why hardship is necessary[1] (1 Corinthians 3:13), but the very next verse reveals how to withstand this enmity. God does not leave His creation unprepared, having to face and fight evil unarmed.

Genesis 2:10

And a *river* (H5104) went out of Eden to *water* (H8248) the garden; and from thence it was parted, and became into four heads.

A quick read of this reveals a lushly watered garden, but it is far from the message of this verse. *The Explanation* can't emphasize enough how much the literal represents the figurative[2]. How the authors have included superlative meaning into this text. It is hidden, in the sense that God has saved it for those who have a desire to learn it (Matthew 11:25) and not for those who wish to remain blind.

River

Major cities of the world stride rivers. They add majesty and serenity as well as the practicality of transport, cleanliness, and water supply[3]. Originating in and flowing from Eden, the river carries all those notions and much more. Here's the meaning of the Biblical Hebrew.

---

1. https://theexplanation.com/evil-god-deliberately-allowed-it-in-garden-of-eden-heres-why/

2. https://theexplanation.com/each-biblical-hebrew-word-is-a-precious-jewel-to-be-discovered/

3. https://theexplanation.com/vital-water-transports-nourishes-cleanses-all-our-life-needs/

H5104

נָהָר nâhâr naw-hawr'; from H5102 (נָהַר); a stream (including the sea; expectation the Nile, Euphrates, etc.); figuratively, prosperity:

KJV - flood, river.

H5102

נָהַר nâhar naw-har'; a primitive root; to sparkle, i.e. (figuratively) be cheerful; hence (from the sheen of a running stream) to flow, i.e. (figuratively) assemble:

KJV - flow (together), be lightened.

A river is a place of gathering, of assembling in cheerfulness and prosperity. Psalm 46, below, is prophetic. God has a city with a holy place, His headquarters, we'll see its name. This river will contribute to the spiritual and physical qualities of *gladness* and *welfare* of its inhabitants.

Psalms 46:44

There is a *river* (H5104), the streams whereof shall make glad the city of God, the holy place of the tabernacles of the most High.

Psalms 36:88

They shall be abundantly satisfied with the fatness of your house; and you shall make them drink of the *river* (H5104) of your pleasures.

A river must have a source. Generally, it's the melting snow, rainy season, or underground aquifers. The source of the river flowing out of Eden is beyond the physical environment.

Jeremiah 2:13

For my people have committed two evils; they have forsaken me the fountain of living waters, and hewed them out cisterns, broken cisterns, that can hold no water.

Jeremiah 17:13

O LORD, the hope of Israel, all that forsake you shall be ashamed, and they that depart from me shall be written in the earth, because they have forsaken the LORD, the fountain of living waters.

The trees, not the river, drew Adam and Eve. Spiritually, our world today may live beside rivers and the sea, but the magnetic force of the Tree of Knowledge of Good and Evil still attracts us. Humankind has forgotten the Source, the fountain of living waters, of what not only nourishes us but participates in our peace and prosperity.

Throughout the Bible, we find references to this river and its implications. The story of the stream of flowing water reveals the history of humankind and God's continual presence to nourish His creation both physically and spiritually. It's another book, here's a snippet from Zechariah 14:8,9,11, "And it shall be in that day, that living waters shall go out from Jerusalem; half of them toward the former sea, and half of them toward the hinder sea: in summer and in winter shall it be. 10. All the land shall be turned as a plain... 11. And men shall dwell in it..."

The source is from Jerusalem (hint, hint! as to the whereabouts of the Garden of Eden). The water goes out East to the Dead Sea and West to the Mediterranean Sea. Both of these Seas are in dire straits right now. The Mediterranean is among the most polluted Seas in the World[4], and the Dead Sea is drying up[5] because of a cut-off water supply.

Humankind is physically wrecking the planet (the literal meaning) and spiritually destroying itself because it has turned its back on the river and its Source (the figurative meaning). But the Source has not forgotten its Creation and will heal the stupidity of humankind. Imagine North Africa, on the banks of the Mediterranean Sea and the deserted Dead Sea, turned into a populated plain with grazing animals and responsible farming. Living, regenerating water sourced at Jerusalem, watering the environs, all the way to the verdant Jordan Valley and the rich green coasts of North Africa and Southern Europe. Eden, in its splendor once again.

To Water

Together with air, water constitutes the principal ingredients for life. *The Explanation* elaborated on the physical necessity for water in section three[6] of *Inventory of the Universe*: cleansing, transport, and nourishment; this requires both living and flowing water, fresh and vibrant, devoid of harmful chemicals, and replete with natural minerals and magnetic alignment. Flowing, because stagnant water has none of the three key qualifiers.

H8248

---

4. http://panswiss.org/newsroom/the-7-seas-most-polluted-in-the-world/

5. https://www.weforum.org/agenda/2019/01/
   the-ambitious-plan-to-refill-the-dead-sea-just-got-the-go-ahead/

6. https://theexplanation.com/planet-water-our-cocoon-survival-beauty/

שָׁקָה shâqâh shaw-kaw'; a primitive root; to quaff, i.e. (causatively) to irrigate or furnish apotion to:

KJV - cause to (give, give to, let, make to) drink, drown, moisten, water. See H7937 (שָׁכַר), H8354(שָׁתָה).

The river and water are both literal and figurative, the fourth key to mastering Biblical Hebrew[7] to Unlock Bible Meaning. Without grasping what water represents in the spiritual world, you cannot understand either the Bible or God's plan or the Source of this pure water.

Understand the complementarity of the next two couples of verses. The first is an Old Testament verse that most understand only literally. The second is a New Testament text that indicates, without a doubt, the symbolic, spiritual nature of the OT verse.

Numbers 20:8

Take the rod, and gather you the assembly together, you [Moses], and Aaron your brother, and speak you to the rock before their eyes; and it shall give forth his water, and you shall bring forth to them water out of the rock: so you shall give the congregation and their beasts drink.

1 Corinthians 10:1-4

1 Moreover, brethren, I would not that you should be ignorant, how that all our fathers were under the cloud, and all passed through the sea;

2 And were all baptized to Moses in the cloud and in the sea;

---

7. https://theexplanation.com/each-biblical-hebrew-word-is-a-precious-jewel-to-be-discovered/

3 And did all eat the same spiritual meat;

4 And did all drink the same spiritual drink: for they drank of that spiritual Rock that followed them: and that Rock was Christ.

The Rock was Christ and the drink was spiritual. We'll see what this spiritual drink is in the next couple of texts.

Isaiah 43:20

The beast of the field shall honour me, the dragons and the owls: because I give waters in the wilderness, and rivers in the desert, to *give drink* (H8248) to my people, my chosen.

John 7:37-39

37 In the last day, that great day of the feast, Jesus stood and cried, saying, If any man thirst, let him come to me, and drink.

38 He that believes on me, as the scripture has said, out of his belly shall flow rivers of living water.

39 (But this spoke he of the Spirit, which they that believe on him should receive: for the Holy Ghost was not yet given; because that Jesus was not yet glorified.)

The spiritual drink is the Holy Spirit. The water that is provided by the Source, whether a Rock, Fountain or River, cleanses, transports, and nourishes. But, more importantly, it accomplishes these activities spiritually. It cleanses us of sin. It transports God's neshama to us[8]. It

8. https://theexplanation.com/human-software-god-breathed-neshama-adam/

nourishes us with the strength to resist the Tree of Knowledge of Good and Evil[9].

Genesis starts with a physical description of this watershed river that goes out to the known Biblical geographic world. The ultimate book of the Bible, Revelation, ends with a return to the spiritual narrative of the world encompassing effect of this river.

Revelation 22:1-2

1 And he shewed me a pure river of water of life, clear as crystal, proceeding out of the throne of God and of the Lamb.

2 In the midst of the street of it, and on either side of the river, was there the tree of life, which bare twelve manner of fruits, and yielded her fruit every month: and the leaves of the tree were for the healing of the nations.

The water of LIFE (Eternal Life) issues directly from God's throne (The Tabernacle, Jerusalem). God's nourishing Spirit along with the life-giving fruit of the Tree of Life, also symbolizing God's Spirit go worldwide to nourish all the nations. There's no Tree of Knowledge of Good and Evil; it's been eradicated. There's the river watering the New Earth and the New Heavens.

The River in the Garden of Eden expresses the entire plan of God

Further Study

---

9. https://theexplanation.com/evil-god-deliberately-allowed-it-in-garden-of-eden-heres-why/

Go to UnlockBibleMeaning.com[10] and look up Genesis 2:9. Switch to Strong's Concordance and verify *water* (H8248). See the symbolic meaning of well-being issuing from God, symbolized by *water*.

I have not developed the opposite theme directly related to water. You noted in the definition and KJV translations for H8248 the negative aspects of *water*. *Drown* reflects the 2nd key to mastering Biblical Hebrew[11] - having opposing usages. God uses water to both bless and chastise. He chastises to awaken people to their frailty, to open their eyes to other possibilities, to lead them back into the Garden of Eden to be watered by the Source of the river.

---

10. http://unlockbiblemeaning.com

11. https://theexplanation.com/each-biblical-hebrew-word-is-a-precious-jewel-to-be-discovered/

Four Rivers of Eden. World Geography Begins

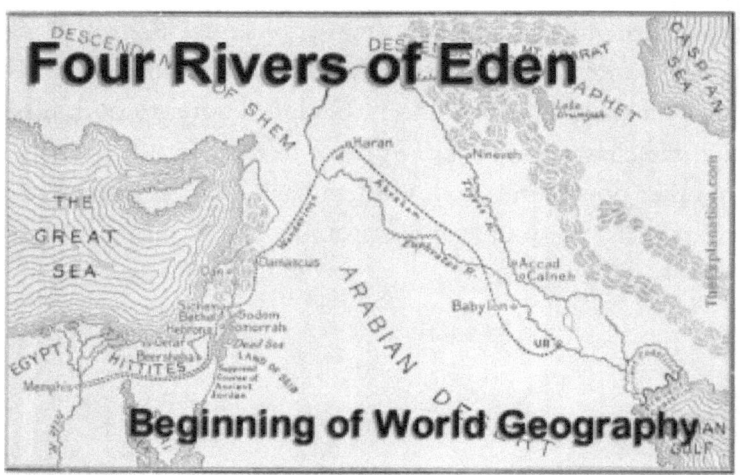

Four Rivers of Eden. The first geographic features establish the basis of the entire Bible narrative from Genesis to Revelation.

The four rivers of Eden sourced from the Garden of Eden reach the Western and Eastern limits of the key nations referred to in the Bible. God abundantly watered all the nations. What happened to these majestic waterways?

Genesis 2:10–14

10 And a river went out of Eden to water the garden; and from thence it was parted, and became into four heads.

11 The name of the first is Pison: that is it which compasses the whole land of Havilah, where there is gold;

12 And the gold of that land is good: there is bdellium and the onyx stone.

13 And the name of the second river is Gihon: the same is it that compasses the whole land of Ethiopia.

14 And the name of the third river is Hiddekel: that is it which goes toward the east of Assyria. And the fourth river is Euphrates.

These verses plunge us into yet another controversy regarding the Bible; the relationship between the Biblical narrative and certain historical events. Two of the rivers and place names above, although used elsewhere in the Bible, remain a mystery as to their origin and location. They are open to conjecture, and it is impossible to pin these narratives down one way or another. Are they figments of imagination or facts of geography and history?

Throughout the Bible, we find examples like Noah's worldwide flood, the Exodus with the parting of the Sea, and Joshua's long day with which debaters have a hay day. They point to Bible fables, not to say errors, to discredit this book. There are the uninitiated as well as diploma bearing scholars who are virulent detractors of the Bible. Where does The Explanation stand on this stage?

If you've been reading me for some time, you'll know. Faithful theology dictates that the Bible states the Word of God, how places exist(ed) and events took place. *The Explanation* does not have all the answers to all the questions, but it puts the Bible narrative first and foremost. In the last chapter, I expounded on the relationship between this river that waters Eden and the ultimate River that flows out of the Throne of God in Revelation[1]. Both the past and future events are UNprovable. The Explanations asserts both because these phenomena are part and parcel of the Bible narrative.

It comes back to assembling our puzzle pieces perfectly, what I'm calling *coherent completeness*. Nobody saw God take a part of Adam out of his side and form a woman. Whoever heard of a serpent talking to Eve? On paper, a lot, if not most, of these stories sound ridiculous, like living over 900 years. Belief or not, in God's Word, depends on how we approach these narratives. There are unknowns and mysteries as Paul said, "Let a man so account of us, as of the ministers of Christ, and stewards of the mysteries of God" (1 Corinthians 4:1). That is what *The Explanation* believes and is doing its best to expound.

There are still pieces of the puzzle, probably more than we realize, that are not entirely in place, for which we don't understand the contours. But there are enough pieces that we can assemble to see the mind of God; the what, how, and why of His Creation of the Universe and Humankind. And that is solely true because of understanding the Bible narrative.

So, let's move on with this first geographic description of the world of humankind. It is not intended to be an in-depth geography lesson where we visit and analyze all the referent verses. Suffice it to grasp an overview of the area involved. That's what Genesis 2 is anyway, a resume with sufficient information to give us a solid foundation.

Here are the four rivers of Eden. With key 5 of the Keys to Master Biblical Hebrew in mind, consider the significance of their names[2]. Like the Garden of Eden[3], these rivers have a past and future role to play in *breaking forth* and *gushing out* water to the world.

---

1. https://theexplanation.com/river-of-living-water-profound-spiritual-meaning/

2. http://theexplanation.com/each-biblical-hebrew-word-is-a-precious-jewel-to-be-discovered/

3. https://theexplanation.com/garden-of-eden-represents-much-more-than-a-garden/

1. **Pison**. Very enigmatic, impossible to pinpoint its whereabouts. From Strong's H6376, it means "dispersive from the root H6335 which the KJV translates: grow up, be grown fat, spread selves, be scattered." It refers to the result of all those who live beside the future resuscitated Pison. Havilah is an affluent area associated with gold, onyx stones, and bdellium[4]. It is not known for sure whether the bdellium in Genesis 2:12 is a metal or a resin. Havilah is variously associated with sub-Saharan Africa, Arabia, and the Far East; this is also the name of a son of Cush (of the lineage of Ham — Gen, 10:7) and a son of Joktan (of Shem — Gen. 10:29).

2. **Gihon**. Today, it is a spring in Jerusalem. From H1516 translated "break forth, labor to bring forth with the idea of water gushing out." The translation *labor to bring forth* is evocative of God's plan, bringing forth His sons and daughters. In verse 13, Gihon compasses the whole land of Ethiopia, giving us a reliable location for this river. It runs South-West of the Garden of Eden into Africa. Ethiopia in Hebrew is Cush, H3568, the name of one of Ham's sons. The correlation between Ethiopia and Cush is well documented; this is the identification of a geographic location both in the Bible and on today's map.

3. **Hiddekel**. Called *id Idikla* by the Accadians, the river of Idikla is associated with the Tigris which is the furthest Eastern point designated by these four rivers in Eden. It relates to Assyria, which we don't have to present; this is a well-known Eastern People and Empire referred to over 120 times in the Old Testament. It played a prominent role in the historical ups-and-downs that befell Israel. Strong's H804 points to Ashur, the name of a son of Shem with these

4. https://en.wikipedia.org/wiki/Bdellium

uplifting translations "*going, step* (H838) and (call, be) *bless*(-ed, happy), *go, guide, lead, relieve* (H833)."

4. The **Euphrates**. The most concise presentation. But, in the critical last position. Frequently in the Bible, the last mentioned in a series is the lead-in to the rest of the story. How so for the Euphrates which Strong's definition (H6578) refers to as "*to break forth; rushing*?" Because the infamous city of Babylon sits majestically astride this formidable river. There are 300 references to Babylon in the Bible, only surpassed by Jerusalem referred to over 800 times. Unlike any of the four rivers or associated cities, the book of Revelation pinpoints Babylon as symbolizing the archenemy of God Himself (Rev. 17:5). Babylon pictures the nations of the world, watered by the river Euphrates issuing from the Garden of Eden, God's Headquarters.

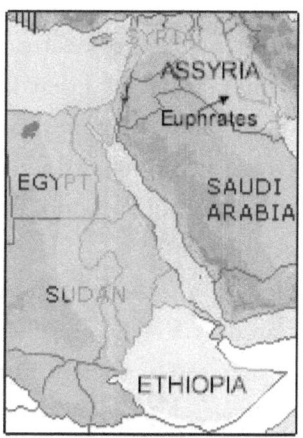

Branching out from Eden, there are enough known names here to situate Eden's approximate location. Toward the East, the Euphrates river, the former Empire of Assyria, and on the West, the horn of Africa, Ethiopia.

We have a western branch extended *Fertile Crescent* encompassing the Euphrates and Tigris rivers in the East. Then, up and around Northern Syria and down through Lebanon, Israel, further South to Egypt following the Nile down to Khartoum in Sudan. From there, via the Blue Nile, on to one of its sources at Lake Tana in the Ethiopian Highlands.

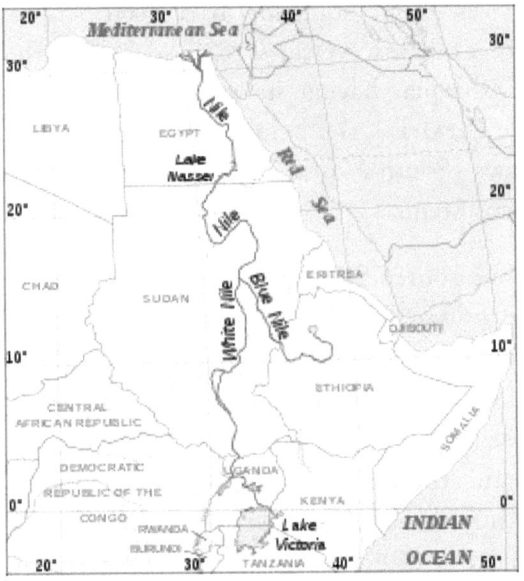

The other names in these verses are conjecture, and we cannot place them with any proven accuracy. I'm certainly not trying to identify the Nile with the Pison or Gihon. There are various indications that these rivers are in the *Fertile Crescent* region. We can reason that the location of the territory of Eden is unquestionably narrowed down to a specific area of the globe, and we will narrow it down further.

Eden, the watershed

These five verses in Genesis 2 spend time giving details about the four rivers in Eden and some details about the surrounding area, but we don't want to overlook the crux verse 10. It reveals the origin of the watershed: Eden. Today, as we've just seen, be it the Nile or the Euphrates, they have different sources. So, granted, we're talking about two different river patterns, I refer to the names solely to situate the tableau geographically. The original Eden, the Garden, the water source and head of the four rivers have all disappeared. That founding era is gone; today's rivers might somehow have been part of that watering system but are now just vestiges. Consider that the river Gihon encompassed Ethiopia, having its source in the Garden of Eden (Jerusalem, see Ezekiel 47:12 below) means it flowed North-South. The Nile flows South-North. These are two totally different hydrological ecosystems.

In Genesis 2, the source for all four rivers in Eden is Eden itself. It first waters the unique Garden God has planted and then spreads out to different points beyond Eden; bringing life-giving water to lands thousands of kilometers in all directions. Not only is there a *Tree of Life,* but there's a *River of Life* because wherever it goes, it brings fertility, food, and affluence. People flock to waterside communities for commerce, culture, livelihood, travel, and a better way of life. With the Hebrew meaning of Eden being *pleasure* and *delight*, it carries that implication, not only within its territory but through its waterways, it conveys this bountifulness far beyond.

These beginning chapters of Genesis are very intense in that they contain the most fundamental principles for the correct functioning of humankind both now and in the future. I can't move on without reminding us that the *physical* portrays the *spiritual*. We've seen this with the: light=truth[5], darkness=destruction[6], air=spirit/mind[7] etc.

These parallels continue. Water has many uses: drinking, washing, irrigation. The watershed's spiritual counterpart is the bountifulness spreading of spiritual washing, drinking, and irrigation to which the following two verses allude.

Psalm 104:13

He *waters* (H8248) the hills from his chambers: the earth is satisfied with the fruit of your works.

Isaiah 27:33

I the LORD do keep it (His people); *I will water* (H8248) it every moment: lest any hurt it, I will keep it night and day.

The four rivers of Eden are both real and symbolic. They portray God as Provider of both physical and spiritual benefits to ALL peoples around the world. Yes, individual people and nations are singled out, and we'll see why, but the end of the matter is God is Creator of ALL peoples and ALL nations.

Without establishing the timeline, here's a future Biblical scenario, after Christ's Return, revealing the physical benefits He will spread abroad. It's a glimpse of Earth during the Millennium. Notice, in verse 12, the source of this river is the sanctuary, the Temple of God, in Jerusalem. Engedi, mentioned in verse 10, exists to this day, I've been there on numerous occasions, on the Western shore of the Dead Sea. A desolation today, a paradise in the future.

Ezekiel 47:6–12

---

5. https://theexplanation.com/let-there-be-light-the-story-of-humankind-begins/

6. https://theexplanation.com/darkness-before-creation-wrecked-planets-asteroids/

7. https://theexplanation.com/human-software-god-breathed-neshama-adam/

6 And he [God] said to me, Son of man, have you seen this? Then he brought me, and caused me to return to the brink of the river.

7 Now when I had returned, behold, at the bank of the river were very many trees on the one side and on the other.

8 Then said he to me, These waters issue out toward the east country, and go down into the desert, and go into the sea: which being brought forth into the sea, the waters shall be healed.

9 And it shall come to pass, that every thing that lives, which moves, whithersoever the rivers shall come, shall live: and there shall be a very great multitude of fish, because these waters shall come there: for they shall be healed; and every thing shall live wherever the river comes.

10 And it shall come to pass, that the fishers shall stand upon it from Engedi even to Eneglaim; they shall be a place to spread forth nets; their fish shall be according to their kinds, as the fish of the great sea, exceeding many.

11 But the miry places thereof and the marishes thereof shall not be healed; they shall be given to salt.

12 And by the river on the bank thereof, on this side and on that side, shall grow all trees for meat, whose leaf shall not fade, neither shall the fruit thereof be consumed: it shall bring forth new fruit according to his months, because their waters they issued out of the sanctuary: and the fruit thereof shall be for meat, and the leaf thereof for medicine.

The four rivers in Eden, The river in Zechariah 14[8] and the one above in Ezekiel 47 are, in essence, the same river. It relays God's plan of spreading abundance throughout His Creation. The goal is established right from the start in Genesis, and its successful outcome is related in Revelation. We've come full circle. Here's the spiritual conclusion of the story of humankind. Let me add; this is NOT the end of the entire story!

Revelation 21:1–2, 16, 22:1–2

1 And I saw a new heaven and a new earth: for the first heaven and the first earth were passed away; and there was no more sea.

2 And I John saw the holy city, new Jerusalem, coming down from God out of heaven, prepared as a bride adorned for her husband.

16 And the city lies foursquare, and the length is as large as the breadth: and he measured the city with the reed, twelve thousand furlongs. The length and the breadth and the height of it are equal.

22:1 And he shewed me a pure river of water of life, clear as crystal, proceeding out of the throne of God and of the Lamb.

2 In the midst of the street of it, and on either side of the river, was there the tree of life, which bare twelve manner of fruits, and yielded her fruit every month: and the leaves of the tree were for the healing of the nations.

---

8. https://theexplanation.com/river-of-living-water-profound-spiritual-meaning/

See the parallel with Zechariah and Genesis. Here, the river proceeds out of God's Throne, before, the Sanctuary and the Garden of Eden. It's the same river but here, its spiritual with the same function of uplifting the nations. Notice the dimensions of New Jerusalem, twelve thousand furlongs, *stadion* in Greek (G4712). The length of a stadion[9] is between 177 and 192 meters. Therefore, New Jerusalem is a cube, each side is approximately 2400 kilometers! The distance, as the crow flies, between Jerusalem and Babylon is 1400 kilometers. I'm not establishing geographic references, but you can see that New Jerusalem encompasses a huge area that could easily reach to Babylon with the River of Life.

The significant nations (Egypt, Assyria, and Babylon) and their cities (Memphis (Cairo), Assur, and Babylon) with which the entire Bible history of Israel interplay are all built on major rivers. It is interesting to note that Jerusalem, the source of these rivers is perched on a mountain and has no river, not even close. This geography plays a vital role in the relationship of the people of Jerusalem, their God, and the three nations mentioned above. Just remember how the Israelites, via Jacob and his sons, went down to Egypt because there was famine in their land. Genesis 2 sets the geographic stage for our play. Today it is a rather harsh desertic area; tomorrow is another more glorious story.

We're far from done expounding the Garden of Eden and what it portends.

---

9. https://www.ancient.eu/Stadium/

Dress & Keep Garden of Eden. Are we Gardeners?

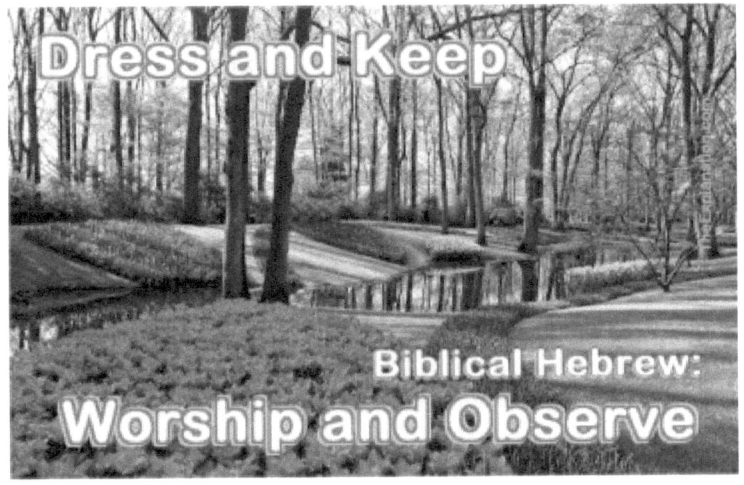

Dress and keep the Garden of Eden. In Biblical Hebrew, the verbs are worship and observe. That's what God desired of Adam.

Dress and keep the Garden of Eden has focused readers on the physical aspects of caring for a garden; that is secondary. Primarily, God's plan calls for Adam to worship Him and observe what He tells him; this is the all-important spiritual emphasis. God is not narcissistic; there's an excellent reason for this necessity.

A quick resume of Genesis 2. God creates man and endows him with consciousness and mind[1]. He puts him in the most splendid garden[2]

---

1. https://theexplanation.com/

consciousness-and-human-mind-you-cant-have-one-without-the-other/

beside a river of life[3] with a tree of life and one representing the knowledge of good and evil[4]. Then the Bible narrative tells us WHY God put the first representative of humankind in the Garden.

Genesis 2:15

And the LORD God took the man, and put him into the garden of Eden to *dress it* (H5647) and to *keep it* (H8104).

The scenario brings us back to the man in the Garden; this is one of these short verses that carry reams of overlooked meaning. To start with, an emphasis on a key element coupled with verse 8, God placed the first man specifically in the garden (not someplace in or out of Eden), why this repetition?

Because this is God's garden, His *House* on earth, which He shares with humans.

Previously we talked about parents preparing the room for baby's arrival[5], and that's what God did with the entirety of earth, except for this garden. He intentionally waits until after creating man, and He's personally and very directly implicated in that "... the Lord God planted a garden..." He was responsible for all the creation, but here it's as if He's doing it with His own hands. There's an extraordinary relationship between God and His hands-on planted Garden, precisely to place and situate man in this choice spot. Remember, God *with* man[6], we see this is a recurrent theme.

---

2. https://theexplanation.com/garden-of-eden-represents-much-more-than-a-garden/

3. https://theexplanation.com/river-of-living-water-profound-spiritual-meaning/

4. https://theexplanation.com/evil-god-deliberately-allowed-it-in-garden-of-eden-heres-why/

5. https://theexplanation.com/creation-environmentally-friendly-for-billions-of-humans/

6. https://theexplanation.com/
   god-pursued-his-work-resting-with-adam-and-eve-whom-he-created-to-make/

There are numerous references to the *Garden of Eden* in the Bible. In Ezekiel 31:9, referring to a magnificent kingdom, God says, "I have made him [Lucifer] fair by the multitude of his branches: so that all the trees of Eden that were in the garden of God envied him." Notice the use of the definite article, *the* garden, not just any garden; it's God's garden in God's location.

A few verses before the above, in Ezek. 28:13-14 discussing an *anointed cherub* (a high ranking angel - Lucifer), obviously, in an *out of this world* setting, we read, "You have been in Eden the garden of God; every precious stone was your covering, the sardius, topaz, and the diamond, the beryl, the onyx, and the jasper, the sapphire, the emerald, and the carbuncle, and gold: the workmanship of your tabrets and of your pipes was prepared in you in the day that you were created. You are the anointed cherub that covers; and I have set you so: you were on the holy mountain of God; you have walked up and down in the midst of the stones of fire."

For now, I draw your attention to *Eden, the garden of God* associated with *the holy mountain of God*. These are high-level quarters where God lives and governs. Just as we saw in Ezek. 1:10, some of our earthly animals were cast after heavenly forerunners[7]; likewise, the physical garden of Eden (and the precious stones in the land of Havilah), into which Adam was placed, is the physical counterpart of the spiritual Garden of Eden.

Remember, in Gen. 1:28; God told the couple to *subdue the earth*[8] *and have dominion over all creatures on earth*. God put the man in His garden to signify He's giving humans a seat, which is human HQ, from which to rule all the earth! As God rules the universe from His

---

7. https://theexplanation.com/humans-have-the-likeness-of-god-what-that-means/

8. *https://theexplanation.com/rule-earth-to-rule-the-world-is-gods-purpose-for-humans/*

heavenly Garden of Eden, so humanity is to *subdue and dominate* - rule - from His earthly Garden of Eden.

As we put the puzzle together, this concept of *man created to govern* is one of the critical pieces. How to govern one's own life[9], family, children, occupation, employees, business, association, organization, city, state, country, and all the different methods promoted to do this is the crux of learning to *live together in peace and prosperity*. The *garden of Eden* and *subdue and dominate* plunge us directly into one of the biggest challenges man has ever faced. What is more crucial to the 21st-century state of the world than the question of *government*?

The real question is, how is humanity going to govern? Are there prerequisites and rules? Is there a proper way to guide?

Dress and Keep

Step back a second for the overview. To this point in Genesis 2, it's been give, give, give. God has given it all; an incredible garden, a watering system, it's a little paradise. We could elaborate on the big lesson here about God's relationship with humankind.

Now, for the first time, God is going to ask something directly of the (hu)man; to dress and keep.

To be a gardener! Really! Is that all it is? Think. God created, God waters, God landscaped, He can weed and manicure the garden! And, in counterpart for all God's done, is His goal limited to creating professional gardeners?

Bible students and teachers tend to stop at that, with no further input. We read over this verse, grasping nothing of its vital importance; this is the FIRST verse where God asks Humankind, through Adam, to DO something. What is this something?

---

9. https://theexplanation.com/rule-life-responsibly-the-key-human-singularity/

We've already established God's goal for humankind: rulership and social relations[10]. Gardening is an itsy-bitsy part of rulership, but that would only be a minute part of the picture. Logic should tell you that.

What does *government* have to do with *gardening*?

At first glance, gardening is the reason God placed Adam in His Garden of Eden; maybe He needed a gardener! I have a garden, and I do agree, there's work to be done, but God had just recently planted this Garden, so it was proper and trimmed, and weeds (assuming that there were any!) don't grow that fast. Maybe this is referring to bamboo, which can grow 30 cm a day and needs constant tending, but I doubt that.

Think about it; God has just created man, He's planted a magnificent garden, He places man there and says, "put on your dungarees and clogs, here's a hoe, get to work," uh uh. The creation context, the opening scene of refurbishing earth and populating it with humans possessing a powerful, deep thinking neshama mind[11] calls for more. Also, consider the following verse 16, "And the Lord God commanded the man, saying, Of every tree of the garden you may freely eat"; the sole subject of *gardening* just doesn't fit in this context.

There's much more to this verse than the translations of dress and keep reveal. By now, you know how to dig it out: Strong's Biblical Hebrew over at UnlockBibleMeaning.com[12]. We are going to look at two words from verse 15, *dress* and *keep,* and see how other contexts render these same Hebrew words. First, *dress*.

H5647

עָבַד 'âbad aw-bad'; a primitive root; to work (in any sense); by implication, to serve, till, (causatively) enslave, etc.:

KJV - ✕ be, keep in bondage, be bondmen, bond-service, compel, do, dress, ear, execute, +husbandman, keep, labour(-ing man, bring to pass, (cause to, make to) serve(-ing, self), (be, become) servant(-s), do (use) service, till(-er), transgress (from margin), (set a) work, be wrought, worshipper,

H5648

עֲבַד 'ăbad ab-bad'; (Aramaic) corresponding to H5647 (עָבַד); to do, make, prepare, keep, etc.:

KJV - ✕ cut, do, execute, go on, make, move, work.

H5649

עֲבַד 'ăbad ab-bad'; (Aramaic) from H5648 (עֲבַד); a servant:

KJV - servant.

The basic comprehension of *abad* is work, of any nature, at the beginning of Genesis often associated with agricultural occupations (2:5, 3:23, 4:2) but when we dig a little deeper we also find *serve, servant,* and even *worshipper,* revealing an adjacent spiritual nature of this word; the figurative takes on a life of its own[13] and far outweighs the physical meaning. See the spiritual usage in these verses:

Zephaniah 3:9

---

13. https://theexplanation.com/each-biblical-hebrew-word-is-a-precious-jewel-to-be-discovered/

For then will I turn to the people a pure language, that they may all call upon the name of the LORD, to *serve* (H5647) him with one consent.

Joshua 24:14-16

14 Now therefore fear the Lord, and *serve* (H5647) him in sincerity and in truth: and put away the gods which your fathers *served* (H5647) on the other side of the flood, and in Egypt; and *serve* (H5647) you the Lord.

15 And if it seem evil to you to *serve* (H5647) the Lord, choose you this day whom ye will *serve*; (H5647) whether the gods which your fathers *served* (H5647) that were on the other side of the flood, or the gods of the Amorites, in whose land you dwell: but as for me and my house, we will *serve* (5647) the Lord.

16 And the people answered and said, God forbid that we should forsake the Lord, to *serve* (H5647) other gods;

In this short section of Joshua's discourse to the Israelites, *abad* is used eight times with the meaning of proper or improper *worship;* choosing whether to serve the right or wrong *god.*

Yahveh is NOT talking to Adam about gardening. He's instructing Adam about serving and worshipping. Doesn't that make sense?

You've already understood that an identical principle characterizes the second word in this verse, *shamar*: a physical and spiritual meaning with the translators emphasizing the former at the expense of the latter, far more important in the long run.

H8104

שָׁמַר shâmar shaw-mar'; a primitive root; properly, to hedge about (as with thorns), i.e., guard; generally, to protect, attend to, etc.:

KJV - beward, be circumspect, take heed (to self), keep(-er, self), mark, look narrowly, observe, preserve, regard, reserve, save (self), sure, (that lay) wait (for), watch(-man).

Shamar carries the meaning of *being circumspect, beware, taking heed to,* and *observing,* in the sense of keeping (not watching) something. In the Bible context, this refers to God's way,

Psalm 11:4-5 says, "You have commanded us *to keep* (H8104) your precepts diligently. O that my ways were directed *to keep* (H8104) your statutes!" This Psalm uses the Biblical Hebrew root *shamar* no less than 21 times.

Leading up to the giving of the Ten Commandments, in Deuteronomy 5:1, "Moses called all Israel, and said to them, Hear, O Israel, the statutes and judgments which I speak in your ears this day, that you may learn them, and *keep,* (H8104) and do them." Moses uses *shamar* in verses 10, 29, 32, and it's *doubled'* (denoting *emphasis* in Biblical Hebrew) in Deut. 6:17, "You shall *diligently* (H8104) *keep* (H8104) the commandments of the Lord your God..."

How can I emphasize to you the importance of what this physical orientation, incompletely translated verse, is telling us? Biblical Hebrew plays a capital role in understanding. Your native language renders only the surface aspects, hiding from view, the arch-important spiritual meaning.

I'm sure your mind is racing, mine certainly was when I understood the meaning of this verse. And then the realization sinks in; this is so simple and so clear.

We find both *dress and keep*, *abad* and *shamar* together in the same Ten Commandment context, "Then *beware* (H8104) lest you forget the Lord, which brought you forth out of the land of Egypt, from the house of bondage. You shall fear the Lord your God, and *serve* (H5647) him, and shalt swear by his name," Deut. 6:12-13. Let me add this thought. When you're in someone else's house, how should you act? Especially if it were God's House, His Garden? That's where the man was, and the premier point here is not gardening, it's being circumspect and serving the Master of the House.

In the New Testament, numerous Apostles like Paul, James, John never hesitated to refer to themselves as *servants of God* (Rom 1:1, James 1:1, Rev 1:1), this is anything but derogatory,

For those who might be a little turned off by concepts such as *keeping rules, sticking to the straight and narrow, being a servant*, this next verse brings together the cause and effect: "You shall *observe* (H5647) to do therefore as the Lord your God has commanded you: you shall not turn aside to the right hand or to the left. You shall walk in all the ways which the Lord your God has commanded you, that you may live, and that it may be *well* with you, and that you may prolong your days in the land which you shall possess," Deut. 5:32-33. *Well* is *tov* the same word pronounced by God on completion of the creation[14]; this is the state of peace and prosperity God and man are ultimately seeking.

The man was a guest in God's House, the Garden of Eden, he was to maintain the right relationship with his Host, and all would've been for *tov*, the best. The New Testament clearly states what God had in mind with *dress* and *keep*. Ephesians 6:1-3, "Children, obey your parents in the Lord: for this is right. Honour your father and mother; (which is the first commandment with promise;) That it may be well with you, and you may live long on the earth."

---

14. https://theexplanation.com/creation-day-5-and-6-god-created-fish-fowl-and-fauna/

There are other verses that present *abad* and *shamar* (dress and keep) together; see *Further Study* below. You understand the principle here.

Worship and serve God in the Garden; this is the first order of business God gave Adam. That is New Testament theology,

Christ said the First Commandment is to love God with all your heart and mind (Mark 12:30); this confirms what Yahveh had and has in mind for all humans in His Garden. The basis of the so-called Old and New Testaments and Covenants are identical; this is coherent completeness. Can you see the pieces of the puzzle coming together?

Further Study

How to find instances of *abad* **and** *shamar* together. Go to UnlockBibleMeaning.com[15] and locate Genesis 2:15. Switch to Strong's and click on H5647. At the bottom of Strong's entry, click on *Hebrew Concordance for H5647*. All the verses with abad - H5647 will display on the left. Now, do a search (ctrl + F in Windows) for H8104 (shamar). You'll find all the verses where these two words are associated: Deut. 13:4, Joshua 22:5, and many others.

The Hebrew letter *hay* - ה

I do not doubt the meaning of Genesis 2:15 and its spiritual nature of worshipping and serving. But I would be amiss not to point out a Hebrew particularity about this verse. See the image of the Biblical Hebrew.

Ge 2:15

H120	H853	H430	H3068	H3947
hā·'ā·ḏām;	'eṯ-	'ĕ·lō·hîm	Yah·weh	way·yiq·qaḥ
הָאָדָם;	אֶת־	אֱלֹהִים	יְהוָה	וַיִּקַּח
the man	-	God	the LORD	And took

H5647	H5731		H1588	H3240
lə·'ā·ḇā·ḏāh	'ê·ḏen,		ḇə·ḡan-	way·yan·ni·ḥê·hū
לְעָבְדָהּ	עֵדֶן		בְגַן־	וַיַּנִּחֵהוּ
to cultivate	of Eden	him into the garden		and put him
to dress (KJV)				

H8104
ū·lə·šā·mə·rāh
וּלְשָׁמְרָהּ
and to keep it

Genesis 2:15 dress and keep, worship and serve

In English, we read, "...put him into the garden of Eden to dress *it* and to keep *it*," and consider *it* refers to the Garden of Eden. However, if we use the translations *worship* and *serve* with *garden*, you see that it sounds strange and anti-productive.

Well, there's a twist with the grammar here. In Hebrew, every noun has a gender[16], as I've explained, it is either masculine or feminine. In Hebrew garden is masculine. However, *it* in Hebrew is *hay* (ה), which is feminine!

I asked my Hebrew teacher about this, and he replied that sometimes nouns change genders. I suppose that can happen, but this grammatical anomaly has always intrigued me. I offer you another viewpoint as an IDEA. Other words use the letter *hay* (ה) in an intriguing way.

Jonah's fish

16. https://theexplanation.com/human-beings-god-created-them-equal-but-different/

In Jonah 2:1 we see, "Then Jonah prayed unto the LORD his God out of the *fish's* belly," The word fish, הַדָּגָה, includes a ה at the end (on the left). However, the Hebrew word *fish* does NOT have an ending ה, as you can see in verse 10.

The ה is of special interest in particular in these three names.

Abram > AbraHam

H85 אַבְרָהָם ʾAbrâhâm ab-raw-hawm'; contracted from H1[17] (אָב) and an unused root (probably meaning to be populous); father of a multitude; Abraham, the later name of Abram:

KJV - Abraham.

There's no real indication as to the meaning of the new name with the additional ה. I submit to you that it might be showing the father of the faithful's relationship with God; this is just an idea.

Sarai > SaraH

H8297 שָׂרַי Sâray saw-rah'-ee; from H8269[18] (שַׂר); dominative; Sarai, the wife of Abraham:

KJV - Sarai.

H8283 שָׂרָה Sârâh saw-raw'; the same as H8282[19] (שָׂרָה); Sarah, Abraham's wife:

KJV - Sarah.

Aaron, as we say in English, is, in Hebrew, AHaron. You can see from H175 below Strong is UNcertain of its derivation.

17. http://www.unlockbiblemeaning.com/browse/

18. http://www.unlockbiblemeaning.com/browse/

19. http://www.unlockbiblemeaning.com/browse/

H727. אָרוֹן 'ârôwn aw-rone'; or אָרֹן; from H717[20] (אָרָה) (in the sense of gathering); a box:

KJV - ark, chest, coffin.

H717. אָרָה 'ârâh aw-raw'; a primitive root; to pluck:

KJV - gather, pluck.

H175

אַהֲרוֹן 'Ahărôwn a-har-one'; of uncertain derivation; Aharon, the brother of Moses:

KJV - Aaron.

I'm not able to go any further with this study at the moment. My theory is that the *hay* used in these instances represents YHVH. These events where we find the ה grafted to the vocabulary, are crucial moments in biblical history, associated with the direct intervention of God. I shall leave that idea with you for now. God does NOT want humanity worshiping and serving the Garden of Eden. On the other hand, it is clear; the first commandment is to worship and serve God which fits perfectly well with the *hay* (ה) at the end (left side) of לְעָבְדָהּ and לְשָׁמְרָהּ.

Trees in Eden - Significance of Hebrew "Tree"

The trees in Eden, particularly the two trees, have profound significance. But first, the Biblical Hebrew word for tree needs to be understood.

The trees in Eden are often depicted by Adam and Eve standing beside the *evil* tree generally with a serpent nearby. Such a caricatural image blurs our understanding. Not to say, enforcing the mythological side and obliterating meaningful comprehension of this all-important first encounter of humankind. Here's clarification.

Here's the story so far; the Creation is the quickest *room renovation* ever for a *newborn,* and what a makeover. God renovated the whole world; it was now ready for humankind. But rather than insert man in this global environment, God creates a spectacular, private Garden, with two meaningful trees, what a privilege. His *newly created guest,* this man, a full-blown adult with a developed mind, the neshama and ruach[1], was a neophyte in *living,* no experience whatsoever. His first encounter with his Creator is a solemn reminder of their relationship; that if the man wants all to go well (tov), he'd be wise to *worship* (dress) God and *observe* (keep) His recommendations[2] (Genesis 2:15).

In verse 16, we come back to the two trees in Eden. It seems to pick up the context from verse 9. As we develop the meaning of these trees, let's step back to the beginning. What is a tree? Just a wooden trunk with branches that bloom and give leaves and fruit? In English and probably most other languages that is the case, but not in Biblical Hebrew.

Genesis 2:9

And out of the ground made the Lord God to grow every *tree* (H6086) that is *pleasant* (H2530) to the sight, and *good* (H2896) for food; the tree of life also in the midst of the garden, and the tree of knowledge of good and evil.

Here's the origin of the word *tree.* not just from Strong's concordance, but from the different translations of the KJV scholarly translators. They're doing their best to capture the intent and meaning of the author. That's why many English words are used to render this one Biblical Hebrew word.

H6086

עֵץ 'êts ates; from H6095 (עָצָה); a tree (from its firmness); hence, wood (plural sticks):

---

1. https://theexplanation.com/neshama-ruach-make-humans-human/

2. https://theexplanation.com/dress-and-keep-garden-of-eden-man-gardener/

KJV - + carpenter, gallows, helve, + pine, plank, staff, stalk, stick, stock, timber, tree, wood.

H6095

עָצָה ʻâtsâh aw-tsaw'; a primitive root; properly, to fasten (or make firm), i.e. to close (the eyes):

KJV - shut.

A tree is not just a tree. In Hebrew, words have meaning that is often deeper than the visible appearance. H6086 is translated *gallows* in the book of Esther. A tree can give us positive shade, scent, leaves for healing, purification of the air, and wood for building purposes. But, negatively, *gallows* is another use for a tree. I'd invoke the second key of mastering Biblical Hebrew[3] in this instance. Two opposite outcomes for one word. The same word: two routes, two results. The root (maybe in this case literally) of the word tree is H6095 (עָצָה); this is enlightening given the two trees in Eden we're about to investigate. The first tree *opens* eyes to God's ways; the second *shuts* eyes to Godly thinking. Here's just one verse with the root of *tree*.

Proverbs 16:30

He *shuts* (H6095) his eyes to *devise* (H2803) *froward things*: (H8419) moving his lips he brings evil to pass.

There's no ambivalence in this verse. *Tree* leads to *shutting of eyes,* which leads to *plotting perverse things.* You can follow this trajectory by reading the meanings of a couple of the Hebrew words in Pro. 16:30.

H2803

חָשַׁב châshab khaw-shab'; a primitive root; properly, to plait or interpenetrate, i.e. (literally) to weave or (generally) to fabricate; figuratively, to plot or contrive (usually in a malicious sense); hence (from the mental effort) to think, regard, value, compute:

KJV - (make) account (of), conceive, consider, count, cunning (man, work, workman), devise, esteem, find out, forecast, hold, imagine, impute, invent, be like, mean, purpose, reckon(-ing be made), regard, think.

H8419

תַּהְפֻּכָה tahpukâh tah-poo-kaw'; from H2015 (הָפַךְ); a perversity or fraud:

KJV - (very) froward(-ness, thing), perverse thing.

H2015

הָפַךְ hâphak haw-fak'; a primitive root; to turn about or over; by implication, to change, overturn, return, pervert:

KJV - ✕ become, change, come, be converted, give, make (a bed), overthrow (-turn), perverse, retire, tumble, turn (again, aside, back, to the contrary, every way).

Partaking of the fruit of the wrong tree turns the mind upside down. That's the implication of the Biblical Hebrew; this is the effect of the Tree of Knowledge of Good and Evil.

In discussing the meaning of tree, I've emphasized the negative to show you how roots lead to deeper understanding. Of course, the Biblical Hebrew for *tree* has a positive meaning as well. This positive aspect is emphasized in Revelation 22:2 with the river flowing out of Eden, repeatedly highlighted with reference to trees and particularly the ultimate Tree of Life that brings healing to all nations.

Tree of Life

A quick summary to prepare us for the two trees in Eden. God has already told us **WHY** He created us (Genesis 1:26-27). Recollect, it is to become His kin. We've already received His image and likeness[4], with the hope of becoming His full sons and daughters[5]. God told the first human **WHAT** to do in Genesis 2:15, to worship and serve Him. Then He immediately follows with the **HOW** in verses 16-17; eat from ALL the trees, don't eat from just one tree. Pretty straight forward, right? Wrong! Humanity has not figured this out yet.

Frankly, in the 21st century with the Occidental environment of liberty, where *choices are primary and compulsory compliance is secondary* this kind of *hard, direct talk* is politically inappropriate. That said, it does have the merit of being clear. Well, this *direct talk* continues and before we get too negative about the approach let's see just how positive it is. The vista of well-being that this directive, decreeing God opens up is in verse 16.

Genesis 2:16-17

16 And the Lord God *commanded* (H6680) the man, saying, Of every tree of the garden you may freely eat:

17 But of the tree of knowledge of good and evil, you shall not eat of it: for in the day that you eat thereof you shall surely die.

---

4. https://theexplanation.com/humans-were-created-in-the-image-of-god-in-his-likeness/

5. https://theexplanation.com/yahweh-elohim-inseparable-relationship/

God reinforces this direct approach when He *commands* (vs. 16) the man to eat of every tree in the Garden.

H6680

צָוָה tsâvâh tsaw-vaw'; a primitive root; (intensively) to constitute, enjoin:

KJV - appoint, (for-) bid, (give a) charge, (give a, give in, send with) command(-er, -ment), send a messenger, put, (set) in order.

This *enjoining* order or *given charge*, as Strong's H6680 renders it, is generally only used by God Himself, God's servants, Kings, and high-ranking governmental officials. With authority, God says to the first man, he may eat from all the trees in the Garden.

Is this a positive or a negative command?

If you had a choice of dozens, maybe hundreds or thousands of luscious, delicious fruit, nuts, and berries for a meal, how would you feel? Just step up and pick your juicy, tasty lunch. Not only that, but amongst *every tree* was the *Tree of Life; man* could've eaten from that Tree at this point. Nowhere does it say he wasn't allowed that, to the contrary, access to the Tree of Life was open. The Hebrew for *freely eat* is *eat eat*, the doubling of words has the sense of *go ahead and feast*.

In verse 9, at the beginning of this chapter we saw that of all the flora, the trees in Eden are highlighted in relation to 2 human senses we are somewhat sensitized to when it comes to food. **Sight:** They are *pleasant* (H2530), as the KJV elsewhere translates: 'beauty, greatly beloved, covet, delectable, delight, desire, goodly, precious,' to the point that they could even evoke *lust* and *covetousness*. **Taste:** They are favorable, sweet, and precious for *good* (H2896) food. We'd go out of our way for a tasty fruit salad from this garden.

The reason I'm emphasizing this point is that many have the impression that God is austere, ascetic, and severe, depriving man of pleasure and the enjoyment of life. Not so, humans received all the beauty and practicality of creation, even the Tree of Life was readily accessible, Adam could've reached out and partaken of it.

Ponder this thought, since God has just given life to Adam; therefore, this Tree of *Life* must represent something beyond that, some benefit God was immediately ready to share with His physical creation; the importance of which the man failed to realize at that time. God had *good* in mind for humans, way beyond what they could and can even imagine. And God wants to share this goodness with humans so much, that He commanded man to partake of it, but God didn't impose the Tree of Life.

Further Study

Go to UnlockBibleMeaning.com[6] and do a study on H6086 (עֵץ) and H6095 (עָצָה) in Genesis 2:16. See where the first is translated *gallows* and the second *shut*.

Biblical Hebrew words tell stories. You'd never know it from the English word tree. For those of you who want to go further with this study, here's a clue. *Shut eyes* (H6035) has to do with spiritual blindness. That's what happened to Adam and Eve after they ate of the forbidden tree. We will develop this point.

---

6. http://unlockbiblemeaning.com

The Tree of Knowledge of Good and Evil

The tree of knowledge of good and evil impacts each of our lives. Four vital points to take away; this is not just symbolism; it's reality.

The Tree of the Knowledge of Good and Evil. Enigmatic, how can good lead to death? Let's understand. The Tree of the Knowledge of Good and Evil was highly discouraged, a massive penalty was attached to misconduct to dissuade the man from eating of its fruit. What was so negative about this tree, that eating its produce would bring death?

Death, yes, but this Tree of Knowledge of Good and Evil was not placed behind bars, made inaccessible, or protected in any way. The man could see it, as any of the other trees and had free access to it, just like the Tree of Life. The fruit was outwardly pleasing to the eye and fragrant to the nose; only the Godly interdiction gave away its harmful nature.

This sole *Tree of knowledge of good and evil* embodies four concepts we want to elucidate to understand what it signifies: Knowledge (H1847), Good (H2896), Evil (H7451), Death (H4191).

Genesis 2:15-17

15 And the LORD God took the man, and put him into the garden of Eden to dress it and to keep it.

16 And the LORD God commanded the man, saying, Of every tree of the garden you may freely eat:

17 But of the tree of the *knowledge* (H1947) of *good* (H2896) and *evil* (H7451), you shall not eat of it: for in the day that you eat thereof you shall surely *die* (H4191).

We've already seen the first two, which, due to the importance of this verse, I briefly remind you of here:

Knowledge

Knowledge is anything and everything that humans can acquire by themselves as a result of the neshama and spirit in man[1] that God had breathed into the first human. This ability to discover, attain, and accumulate knowledge is given only to humans as a result of their singularity[2]. As we've seen in *Inventory*[3] and *Audit of the Universe*[4] *and Humankind*[5], humanity has been able to obtain volumes of encyclopedic knowledge about ourselves and the surroundings in which we exist.

---

1. https://theexplanation.com/human-mind-mind-power-neshama-ruach/

2. https://theexplanation.com/rule-the-world-humankind-is-on-earth-for-that-purpose/

3. *https://theexplanation.com/inventory/read-all-the-content-of-inventory-of-the-universe-online/*

4. *https://theexplanation.com/read-content-audit-universe-online/*

5. *https://theexplanation.com/read-all-the-content-of-audit-of-humankind-online/*

When we use the term *knowledge,* we might tend to think of *physical* knowledge related to atoms, the sea, automobiles, flowers; but we must also include knowledge related to the social functioning of people like dating, sexuality, marriage, childrearing, leadership, and government. There are also the physical and mental aptitudes of humans that correspond to the medical and psychological disciplines, physical and mental health, all about the body and mind. In other words, *knowledge* encompasses all subjects, fields, branches, and twigs that observation and experience[6], science[7], philosophy[8], and religion[9] have investigated, probed and scrutinized, and which research continues to expand each day. Here's the Biblical Hebrew for *knowledge.*

H1847

דַּעַת da'ath dah'-ath; from H3045 (יָדַע); knowledge:

KJV - cunning, (ig-) norantly, know(-ledge), (un-) awares (wittingly).

H3045

יָדַע yâda' yaw-dah'; a primitive root; to know (properly, to ascertain by seeing); used in a great variety of senses, figuratively, literally, euphemistically and inferentially (including observation, care, recognition; and causatively, instruction, designation, punishment, etc.):

KJV - acknowledge, acquaintance(-ted with), advise, answer, appoint, assuredly, be aware, (un-) awares, can(-not), certainly, comprehend, consider, ✕ could they, cunning,

---

6. https://theexplanation.com/observation-first-way-human-reasoning/

7. https://theexplanation.com/science-world-savior-human-reasoning/

8. https://theexplanation.com/philosophy-love-wisdom-whose-wisdom/

9. https://theexplanation.com/religion-solution-world-peace/

declare, be diligent, (can, cause to) discern, discover, endued with, familiar friend, famous, feel, can have, be (ig-) norant, instruct, kinsfolk, kinsman, (cause to let, make) know, (come to give, have, take) knowledge, have (knowledge), (be, make, make to be, make self) known, + be learned, + lie by man, mark, perceive, privy to, ✕prognosticator, regard, have respect, skilful, shew, can (man of) skill, be sure, of a surety, teach, (can) tell, understand, have (understanding), ✕ will be, wist, wit, wot.

It is clear from the words above like *discover, instruct, perceive, understand* that only humans, and no other animate beings, can learn the knowledge referred to here. It is also evident that this knowledge, associated with the Tree that leads to death, is that which can be determined by the *neshama* and *spirit in man*. It is the comprehension that the human mind and brain can attain to, but limited to human intellectual capacity and understanding.

1 Corinthians 2:11 is very explicit in corroborating the origin and essence of human knowledge, "For what man knows the things of a man, save the spirit of man which is in him? even so the things of God knows no man, but the Spirit of God." Humans may like to think they are self-contained and limitless in their quest of knowledge, but that is not the case. The human defining singularity is the presence of this spirit coupled with the neshama[10] that confers on them their human capabilities. (If you're reading this for the first time. I insist you go and read both these links[11].)

We shall return to this crucial concept of knowledge. The other three elements: *good, evil,* and *death,* are all derivatives of this knowledge. We don't call our era the Information-Age for no good reason. Knowledge is at the core of all thoughts, activities, and decision-making. Now for the second aspect of the Tree of Knowledge of Good and Evil.

Good

This element of the Tree is, in my opinion, the most paradoxical and least understood component of this tree. We've already seen the Hebrew term *good* nine times before this verse, notably after creating the animals when God said, "it was very *good*." I devoted an entire chapter to explaining what a fiasco that translation is[12], the understatement of the year. And now, we see the same *good* associated with the Tree that leads to death. Explain! But, explain we must because it is a vital piece of the puzzle. If we can't understand the good of the *Tree of Death* then we can't assemble the jigsaw puzzle correctly, can we? Here's the Biblical Hebrew *good*.

H2896

טוֹב ṭôwb tobe; from H2895 (טוֹב); good (as an adjective) in the widest sense; used likewise as a noun, both in the masculine and the feminine, the singular and the plural (good, a good or good thing, a good man or woman; the good, goods or good things, good men or women), also as an adverb (well):

KJV - beautiful, best, better, bountiful, cheerful, at ease, ✗ fair (word), (be in) favour, fine, glad, good (deed, -lier, -liest, -ly, -ness, -s), graciously, joyful, kindly, kindness, liketh (best), loving, merry, ✗ most, pleasant, + pleaseth, pleasure, precious, prosperity, ready, sweet, wealth, welfare, (be) well(-favoured).

---

12. https://theexplanation.com/
it-was-good-is-a-translation-fiasco-of-gods-actual-creation-statement/

When we read *good and evil,* we tend to think of *good* from a *dictionary* point of view. Even Strong's and the KJV translations need to be put in perspective here.

In Genesis 2:17 the *good* **is associated with the Tree that leads to death.** We cannot overlook the precise shape of this piece of the puzzle otherwise it won't fit: even this *good* leads to death. We must answer the question: How can *good* lead to death?

We're talking about the human definition of *good.* For instance, in the name of *freedom,* we allow and condone *white lies,* foul vocabulary, suggestive images that characterize Top 10 songs and character assassination tidbits as headlines. That's the tip of the iceberg, and many will take a firm stance to defend such conduct. Some fundamental issues have become blurred; basic questions like, is there good? What is good? What is the Bible definition of good? Answers will be forthcoming, but, at this point, I reiterate that the *good* in this context leads to death. Hence, it's debatable as to how healthy this *good* is.

This idea impacts a significant concept that is widespread. It is held by what I call the spiritual philosophers[13] and secular religious[14]. These are two groups of people, the first for non-believers in God and the second for believers. The key defining characteristic is that both groups believe doing good is their salvation. Doing good, including being virtuous and loving your neighbor, no matter how it's expressed, allows these people to have a peaceful conscience. Please don't get me wrong; this is not a criticism. Doing good is 100% laudable. But the question is: To where does this good lead us? The Tree of Life or the Tree of Death?

Yes, that sounds horrible. To consider that devoting one's life to doing good, and even suggesting that it's partaking of the Tree of the

---

13. https://theexplanation.com/spiritual-philosophy-wisdom-spirituality/

14. https://theexplanation.com/religions-all-types-bible-quoters-pseudo-secular/

Knowledge of Good and Evil is outrageous. I will be giving you more details as we move forward with Genesis chapters 2 and 3. For now, ponder the words of Jesus, "...none is good, save one, that is, God" (Luke 18:19), and ask yourself, what is the reality of this *good* that is an integral part of this Tree of Death.

Look at it this way. Is doing *good* sufficient for God to attribute eternal life? The Bible answer is NO. You should be able to answer the next question. What supplementary necessity is needed to receive eternal life? Just think of the two commandments in the New Covenant. We shall be returning to this subject. The answer is in the previous verse, Genesis 2:15, God put the man in the Garden of Eden to _worship_ and _serve_ Him[15]. God answers the questions right in the context.

Evil

Evil leads to death. We'd agree on this even though some have deliberately chosen an evil way of life.

Since you've been reading this book, you know me and how I write. I get to the point. Well, correctly writing about evil isn't easy, but let's be open and do it. Here are three examples that illustrate the meaning of *evil*.

- Job was a servant of God. But he and his friends had a significant problem, self-righteousness. The whole book of Job expounds this self-righteous attitude. By the way, Job was the ultimate doer of good, and he used that to justify his righteousness and what he felt was God's unjust trial. In essence, Job says, "I don't merit this horrendous trial, I've done *good* all my life." As I said above, *goodness* is NOT the crux of the matter. The trial was to help Job learn the most crucial lesson a human being can learn. Job 42:5-6, "I have

---

15. https://theexplanation.com/dress-and-keep-garden-of-eden-man-gardener/

heard of you [God] by the hearing of the ear: but now my eye sees you. Wherefore I abhor myself, and repent in dust and ashes." This is _worship_ and _serve_[16] and seeing oneself through God's eyes. _Good_ is _a_ criteria, but not _the_ criteria when it comes to eternal life and death.

***

- Jordan Peterson is one of the most lucid public figures I know. His role as a clinical psychologist has brought him into contact with some of the most abject and degenerate types of people imaginable. At the same time, he's possibly one of the most profound thinkers alive today. He has insight, particularly into what is evil. Not evil in others, of which he is well aware, but evil in HIMSELF. Evil that he knows, that he's convinced, he could commit given the right circumstances. I've yet to hear it expressed in such a sincere and heartfelt way. Listen for yourself[17].   He realizes that he could've been a perpetrator in the Auschwitz concentration camp. That's serious-thinking about the potential evil lurking in you. Modern psychology and religion have hidden the realization of the depth and breadth of darkness in each of us. I'm generalizing, but the rampant idea today is that although humans can do bad things, humans are fundamentally good. That is diametrically opposite of what the Bible says. The example of Job and the words of Jesus Himself tell us otherwise.

***

- I evoked this earlier, but Jesus Christ, answering a rich man,

---

16. https://theexplanation.com/dress-keep-garden-of-eden-man-destined-to-be-a-gardener/
17. https://youtu.be/l7ufIBRZRKk

stated in Luke 18:19 "...Why call you me good? none is good, save one, that is, God." If none is *good*, then all are *bad,* and that includes you and me. We've all partaken of this Tree of the Knowledge of Good and Evil. We all are and carry evil; we all merit the results of this tree. Here's the Biblical Hebrew:

H7451

רַע ra' rah; from H7489 (רָעַע); bad or (as noun) evil (natural or moral):

KJV - adversity, affliction, bad, calamity, +displease(-ure), distress, evil((-favouredness), man, thing), + exceedingly, × great, grief(-vous), harm, heavy, hurt(-ful), ill (favoured), + mark, mischief(-vous), misery, naught(-ty), noisome, + not please, sad(-ly), sore, sorrow, trouble, vex, wicked(-ly, -ness, one), worse(-st), wretchedness, wrong. (Incl. feminine raaah; as adjective or noun).

Notice the translation, *wicked*, wretchedness. We have ideas about ourselves to the contrary. Are we delusionary? Isaiah 64:6, "But we are all as an unclean thing, and all our righteousnesses are as filthy rags; and we all do fade as a leaf; and our iniquities, like the wind, have taken us away." *Filthy rags* sums us up pretty well. *Audit of the Universe* was written to help us see what humans have done to Earth. The three major commodities have been polluted or depleted beyond repair: Air, water, land even space. Flora and fauna are paying a heavy price as species disappear. Our planet is dying. That's the result of partaking of the Tree of the Knowledge of Good and Evil.

Death

Both the Bible and real-life show us that death is real. As much as it's an enigma, we can't deny death in the Old Testament or the New Testament. God is love, but love includes death! I spent a lot of time explaining the meaning of the neshama that God breathed in Adam's nostrils. How neshama confers on humans their singularities[18] that make us what we are. At the time, I didn't emphasize a point regarding the Tree of the Knowledge of Good and Evil and death. It is necessary to return to the meaning of neshama and see an important aspect.

H5397

נְשָׁמָה neshâmâh nesh-aw-maw'; from H5395 (נָשַׁם); a puff, i.e., wind, angry or vital breath, divine inspiration, intellect. or (concretely) an animal:

KJV - blast, (that) breath(-eth), inspiration, soul, spirit.

H5395

נָשַׁם nâsham naw-sham'; a primitive root; properly, to blow away, i.e. destroy:

KJV - destroy.

The neshama of life is also that of death! The root of neshama includes *destroy;* this is the reason for the opposite meaning of the same Hebrew words[19]! You must be able to reconcile and explain this. Look at the Hebrew of Genesis 2:16-17. It doubles a couple of words *eat eat* (H398) and *die die* (H4191).

---

18. https://theexplanation.com/neshama-meaning-god-given-human-mind/

19. https://theexplanation.com/each-biblical-hebrew-word-is-a-precious-jewel-to-be-discovered/

"eat eat," "die die." In Biblical Hebrew, the doubling of words reveals that it will come to pass. Eternal Life and Eternal Death. Doubling a word is to emphasize the certainty of its outcome.

Eating of the Tree of Life means you will inherit *life forever* (Genesis 3:22). Eating of the Tree of the Knowledge of Good and Evil means death FOREVER.

There's no intermediary state. There is physical life and in the future eternal life forever. The alternative is death, destruction forever. I cannot develop this here, but you can pursue this study by looking at the Second Death in Revelation[20]. Some who don't understand this, think a *good God* would not tolerate eternal death. Again, it's a lengthy subject. Just think of the concept of what we do with a rotten apple. Those who persist in partaking of the Tree of the Knowledge of Good and Evil, and who do not come to see the rottenness of their ways; God removes them from the crate. The story of humankind reveals that the vast majority will live forever.

20. http://unlockbiblemeaning.com

God Created Evil. NO, God Only Creates Good

God Created Evil

Wrong!

God only creates Good

God created evil. We see evil all around us. The argument says, "God created everything, so it must include evil." Dead wrong. Here's why.

God created evil. How could have a good God created evil? A classic argument used to show how God is ambiguous, and belief in Him is senseless. There's even a Bible verse in Isaiah 45:7, where God says, "I create evil." Does He, or doesn't He? Here's the explanation.

We've already been introduced to a negative concept at the very outset of Genesis, *tohu, and bohu.* In this revitalization of planet earth from Day 1 of Creation, from the inanimate to the animate, including the final pinnacle of the creation of man, Earth is in a state of *light and virtue.* No vice whatsoever is present, not even in any nook or cranny.

It's an unknown, non-existent notion until it explodes onto the scene in the form of one word: evil.

God planted the Tree of the Knowledge of Good and EVIL in the midst of the Garden of Eden (Genesis 2:9). Here's the Biblical Hebrew for *evil*.

H7451

רַע raʻ rah; from H7489 (רָעַע); bad or (as noun) evil (natural or moral):

KJV - adversity, affliction, bad, calamity, +displease(-ure), distress, evil((-favouredness), man, thing), + exceedingly, ✕ great, grief(-vous), harm, heavy, hurt(-ful), ill (favoured), + mark, mischief(-vous), misery, naught(-ty), noisome, + not please, sad(-ly), sore, sorrow, trouble, vex, wicked(-ly, -ness, one), worse(-st), wretchedness, wrong. (Incl. feminine raaah; as adjective or noun.).

H7489

רָעַע râʻaʻ raw-ah'; a primitive root; properly, to spoil (literally, by breaking to pieces); figuratively, to make (or be) good fornothing, i.e. bad (physically, socially or morally):

KJV - afflict, associate selves (by mistake for H7462 (רָעָה)), break (down, in pieces), + displease, (be, bring, do) evil (doer, entreat, man), show self friendly (by mistake for H7462 (רָעָה)), do harm, (do) hurt, (behave self, deal) ill, ✕ indeed, do mischief, punish, still, vex, (do) wicked (doer, -ly), be (deal, do) worse.

The man must've gotten an earful. He heard about the *theory* of *calamity*, *distress*, *wickedness*, and *misery*. At this juncture, *evil* was nothing but a strange word of vocabulary. He had no experience, visibility, not even any conceivability, the very opposite of the world into which the man had been thrust. He could only look at the Tree and contemplate what evil was and its result: death.

God does NOT create evil

So why does Isaiah 45:7 state, "I form the light, and create darkness: I make peace, and create evil: I the LORD do all these things." The beginning of an answer is in Biblical Hebrew and the first key to master the Bible language[1]. As we can see from Strong's Concordance, the original H7489 here translated *evil* has many other translations and nuances. For instance, *adversity*, *affliction*, *calamity*, *displeasure*, and *distress*, among others. These words have very different connotations. I'm not saying they're comfortable, but they can all be a far distance from *evil*. The KJV translators made an unfortunate choice of word by insinuating God creates *evil* in this verse.

So, let's understand what God does and doesn't do. God allows and even inflicts suffering and even unnatural death on certain people. By unnatural death, I mean not under normal circumstances like sickness or old age. We have to call a spade a spade: God allows capital punishment. The Old Testament law provided for this, and there are multiple episodes where God orders His servants, like Joshua and Samson, to go into battle and kill people.

There are various reasons for this and why it is NOT evil. Is cleaning up a messy situation good or evil? When God annihilated 185,000 Assyrians in the time of the righteous King Hezekiah, He was

---

1. https://theexplanation.com/

your-native-language-does-not-render-the-fullness-of-biblical-hebrew/

protecting His city. You might say God only kills others. Well, during Moses' day, God's people rebelled against Him (episodes of the Golden Calf, Korah, rebellion in Numbers 21), and He allowed thousands of Israelites to die.

There are countless examples of God intervening to CLEAN UP messy situations. Cleaning up is GOOD, not evil. Humanly we might think that anything, at the expense of the life of another human, is evil. Unfortunately, it is precisely that reasoning, which is the knowledge of the tree of good and evil — thinking that NOT cleaning up a mess is GOOD. God does what has to be done; that's the first reason why *God created evil* is a wrong concept.

The second reason is God allows trials on His servants. And those tests can include suffering and even death; this can be, and is very hard, even impossible to comprehend by certain people, which is entirely understandable. When God tested Job, He used Satan to do it and gave him carte blanche, except for taking Job's life. Satan did take the life of Job's children. That sounds horrible, and indeed it is, but Job's trial was primary concerning other events.

I realize that some will be very upset by calling death and suffering other events. But you have to place yourself in God's shoes. I cannot explain all those details here. But whether it's God ordering the Israelites to eliminate the Canaanites or Abraham to sacrifice his son, a trial is involved, and the ULTIMATE results are primary.

There's one essential point that I must bring to the forefront, which most people, even Bible readers and scholars are not aware. Again, unfortunately, I do not have the space to develop this vital subject. This life that we are leading NOW is not the only life we'll have. Wow, Sam, what do you mean by that?! The Bible indicates that ALL humans, every single one of them, will be resurrected and given a REAL chance to KNOW GOD under GODLY CONDITIONS; this is part of

God's plan to SAVE ALL HUMANITY. That is God's goal; we should expect nothing less. See *Further Study* below to pursue this eye-opening subject.

Is God responsible for Evil?

In this 21st century, in our Western world and I'd say worldwide, there are many moral issues; sex outside of marriage, distributing the *pill* in school, adoption of children by same-sex couples, mediatization of kids, money in sports, harassment in the workplace, immigration, building of walls, abortion with debates giving conflicting views as to which way to turn. Situation ethics, right and wrong. Fundamental issues have become blurred. Basic questions go unanswered, like, is there evil? What is evil? What is the Bible's definition of sin? Hence the misunderstanding that God created evil.

Let's take a closer look at the meaning of Knowledge of Good and Evil.

Humans have spent their time and energy accumulating *knowledge; we've* looked into, analyzed every practice, and examined every way of thinking under the sun. Having access to this knowledge is a prerogative of human being; this is one of the reasons God gave us a neshama-mind[2]. And empowered with those cognitive powers of logic, rationale, and interpretation, humans have reasoned and justified taking a stance and applying all the extremities of every controversial subject that has ever hit the headlines: abortion, liberty of speech, guns, euthanasia, socialism or liberalism or conservatism, political or religious extremism, death penalty, leniency for criminals, genetically modified organisms.

It is not only the knowledge of each issue that can lead to death. Knowledge, of and by itself, is not the sole problem, but it is what we do

---

2. https://theexplanation.com/human-mind-mind-power-neshama-ruach/

primarily with the knowledge. It is when some think abortion is right while others think it is wrong, and this controversy comes to a head that we get into hot water. It is when one religion or one philosophy or one government decides it is so *right* that it begins to put down, eliminate, and exterminate opposing concepts that it leads to very ugly dilemmas.

When individuals and peoples take sides convinced that their particular knowledge brand is the ultimate and only way to go, that others *must* follow that *way,* even imposing that way against other people's desires, that it can lead to hideous attitudes, heinous acts, and horrid death.

It's the disagreement as to what's *good* and *evil,* the divergences of what's virtuous or depraved; it's the *I decide what's good and bad for me and others* and the defense and imposition, by any means, of *my* principles as *the* principles to be followed, that leads to death.

If I had to use one word to summarize this unhealthy state of affairs, I'd choose *confusion, where* everyone has their own opinion about everything based on their *own* knowledge, thoughts, and self-wisdom. Everyone is voicing their views, debates are the primary method of communication, where everyone is entitled to their point of view, and where there is a heap of knowledge. But, there's no basis, no foundation, nothing to *measure* that knowledge by, no *consensus of basic rules*. Everyone is just evaluating and proposing and doing whatever they feel is right in any particular situation.

Yes, I've taken a few paragraphs to expound this concept. Because, from our 24/7/365 practically instantaneous world-girdling official and people newscasts via TV, radio, and social networks on the internet, we're getting a continual stream of suffering and death that *The Explanation* expounded in *Audit of the Universe*[3] and *Humankind*[4].

---

3. *https://theexplanation.com/read-content-audit-universe-online/*

Before you think we're getting too gloomy and doomy, yes, in *Audit*, I also enumerated good news, excellent initiatives, and accomplishments.

That's the whole point: This mixture of humankind's extensive KNOWLEDGE + the resultant GOOD news + the resultant BAD news is what the Tree of the KNOWLEDGE of GOOD and EVIL is all about.

We've got precisely the *mixture of good and evil*, conceived by humans, that is being discussed in this verse. Each one with their *solution* to hunger, war, poverty, economic woes, violence, each one thinking *their solution* is the answer. It is the *proper* way to go, of course, no one thinks their way is the *evil* way to go but, in the end, are we flushing out more confusion or more real solutions?

This indiscriminate application of *good and evil* is what God wanted humanity to avoid precisely. He clearly stated, "... you shall not eat of it..." of this potent brew of humans thinking they can come up with all the knowledge and collectively decide how to apply it for the real good of humankind.

We might not realize it, but in the few introductory verses we've read here in Genesis, God gave man clear indications of what is *good* and what is *evil*. These fundamental elements are not left *up in the air* as points of conjecture and speculation.

A very short **resume of** *Good* is *serving* God and respecting His directives which include correctly *dominating* and subduing the earth (at least the part for which each of us has responsibility), *respecting* the mutual relationships and *multiplying* as a husband-wife, father-mother couple in marriage and even *eating* of the Tree of Life which is accessible today as we shall see.

---

4. *https://theexplanation.com/read-all-the-content-of-audit-of-humankind-online/*

Evil is when we ultimately look to our own, human wisdom, be it in psychology, moral education, employer-employee, and many other types of relationships to decide what is the basis of life. It's when we do our *own thing* regardless of what Godly knowledge shows us.

These two showcase Trees represent God's way of doing things and humankind's way of doing things. God *forced* neither on Adam and Eve, clear instructions - eat/don't eat - were given and the ultimate destiny - life/death - for their conduct was clearly stated. They were put before a choice which sooner or later they would make.

Either they would accept God's way of avoiding what He considers *evil*, doing what He considers right. OR they would reject God's way and not do what they decided was *evil* and do what they decided was right.

God gave humans a clear, straightforward direction in the form of a command, an order, and an authoritative rule. God knew what would happen if humanity took ultimate decisional power upon itself, allowing itself the luxury of differentiating between what is right and what is evil. He knew that self-determination of right and wrong would lead to death, death, yes *death,* repeated twice in this verse to indicate its certainty.

So, if God knew this atrocious outcome, why didn't He, at least, put a fence around the Tree of knowledge of good and evil? Why did He even place this wretched Tree in the Garden? Is He some sadistic God, who enjoys watching humans destroy themselves? Not only that, but it appears contradictory, God just gave man *life* and immediately He's telling him he can *die die.*

Is this some game? See how long humans can last before game over. And now comes the punch line: delivery of an exquisite package - woman.

Further Study

The subject of every human being getting a SECOND life is, very controversial, not to say, ridiculous, in the eyes of the vast majority. *The Explanation* resorts to the Bible and turns the Bible pieces of the puzzle right side up, and places them in their proper position in the entire picture.

Go to UnlockBibleMeaning.com[5] and read Revelation 20:11-13. It's an exciting subject. God's justice involves judging people ONLY after those people have learned about God and His ways. Since humankind has been on Earth, the vast majority has NOT learned about God, nor known His ways. A just God will neither bless nor condemn such people. He will FIRST give them a real chance to know Him and let them decide for themselves of which Tree they will partake. As Rev. 20:12-13 states, ALL these people will be resurrected and be involved in that process of free choice. Then, and only then will they be judged. That is the plan of a just God.

---

5. http://unlockbiblemeaning.com

2. The Creation of Woman

Women in the Bible, the Strangest Creation story

Women in the Bible starts as the strangest Creation story of all time. So many mysterious details. Why?

Women in the Bible is a controversial subject. The Creation story fills her beginning with mysterious and unexplained details. Until now. The female presence completes the story of creation. It's the final crowning piece. Without the woman, God's plan is impossible. Start to understand why.

The last eight verses of Genesis 2, verses 18-25, are what I consider some of the most fascinating verses in the Bible. We are going to take our time to dig out Bible meaning. The reason being, these verses present a scenario so out of sync, so strange, that it's no wonder Bible readers have difficulty understanding them and Bible critics have a heyday pointing out the ambiguities.

Genesis 2:17-18

17 But of the tree of the knowledge of good and evil, you shalt not eat of it: for in the day that you eat thereof you shall surely die.

18 And the LORD God said, It is not good that the man should be alone; I will make him an help meet for him.

These verses, about the creation of woman, the beginning of the story of women in the Bible, explain the capstone of God's creation. They represent the WHAT, the HOW, and the WHY for His creation. And these verses are skimmed over with practically no thought given to the depth of their teachings. We are going to stop and learn.

Creation of Woman Context

The first aspect of learning is their context. And that is what this chapter is devoted to; to explaining the incongruencies that most have not noticed here. We're going to look at how jumbled and incoherent this context appears to the casual Bible reader. Here are some questions to ponder.

I've often compared the Universe to a puzzle with millions of pieces. The Bible is one huge section with thousands of pieces. In the story of the creation of woman, each issue is like an individual, separate piece of the puzzle. Your goal is to assemble them flawlessly!

- Why is it recorded that God gives clear instructions to the man, Adam, regarding worshipping and serving Him[1] and eating from the Two Trees, and NOT to the woman, Eve? Eve could've used this as an excuse, "God, You never told me I shouldn't eat from that tree."

---

1. https://theexplanation.com/dress-keep-garden-of-eden-man-destined-to-be-a-gardener/

- Why is there such a contrast, a break in subject matter between verses 17 and 18? The former relates dying if one eats from the Tree of the Knowledge of Good and Evil, while the latter does a volte-face into "It is not good that man should be alone." What if any is the relationship between these contrasting subjects? Remember, each is a puzzle piece, verses 17 and 18 follow each other, so how do we assemble these two pieces for coherent completeness?
- Why is there another total flip-flop of subjects in verses 19-20? God creates animals and parades them in front of Adam for him to name them! What's the point? Why doesn't God get on with it and create the woman?
- All the other living things were all created together, male and female. In Genesis 1:27, "male and female created he them," God gives the impression He created the male and the female together. Here, at the end of Gen. 2, it's the opposite, first the man, then the woman, WHY? Bible detractors have a heyday with this one. Can you fit these two pieces together?
- Why does God put Adam to sleep? All, the other elements of creation were SPOKEN into existence, "let the(re be)." Yahveh is The Word, all He has to do is "say," and it's done.
- Why such a vivid, detailed description of this surgical operation performed by Yahveh? Did God need a rib? Why not a kidney?
- God formed man from the dust, WHY did He form woman from a bone? And why, was it the bone of the man specifically? These questions may sound dumb, but you know some detractor is going to ask this. Perhaps you've never asked yourself these questions, that's why I'm doing it.
- Why is this operation on Adam performed by Yahveh and not by Elohim? Is there any significance to that?
- "Bone of my bones, flesh of my flesh"; is this only a physical

remark? "She shall be called Woman because she was taken out of Man." Does that make the woman inferior?

- "A man should leave his father and his mother, and shall cleave to his wife." Generally, we think of the woman leaving home and going where the man goes. Why the emphasis on the man doing the *leaving*?

Women: Contemporary Answers and Bible Confirmation

As we move into the final episode of the Creation story, which ends Genesis 2, we will have a complete tableau of God's plan. All the characters of our Universal Play will be on stage, and their roles will be clear. In this chapter, we've stepped back to grasp an overview. This conclusion broaches two global subjects.

Firstly, with the creation of the woman does her role coincide with what we find in contemporary life? Many have the impression that the Bible, in particular, Genesis, written some 3500 years ago, has no relevance for our modern world. Today, if there's a controversial subject, it is women in society. What their role is and how to treat them make daily headlines. There is relevance between women in the Bible and women today.

Here's a list of deplorable but prevalent crimes against women. We even find them committed against women in the Bible. The authors did not hide crime; it's there in black and white for our improvement. One of the reasons is that humanity does not know what the role of a woman is. And, certainly doesn't respect that role. Women's movements, women's rights, #metoo, gender issues. Harassment, Violence against women: Acid throwing, Breast ironing, Dating abuse, Domestic violence (pregnancy), Eve teasing, Female genital mutilation (Gishiri cutting, Infibulation).

Footbinding, Force-feeding, Forced abortion, Forced marriage, Forced pregnancy, Marriage by abduction, Raptio, Witch trials, Bride burning, Dowry death, Honor killing, Femicide, Infanticide, Matricide, Pregnant women, Sati, Sororicide, Uxoricide, Sexual assault and rape, Sexual assault, Campus sexual assault, Mass sexual assault, Sexual violence (Congo Papua New Guinea South Africa), Child sexual initiation, Rape (and pregnancy laws). Types of rape (by deception, corrective, date, gang, genocidal, in war, marital, prison, statutory), Forced prostitution, Sexual slavery, Sacred prostitution, Devadasi, Fetish slaves, Human trafficking, Violence against prostitutes, Widow cleansing.

The Explanation has discussed the basis of these issues in *Audit of the Universe*, I devoted a chapter to *How Humankind Socializes*[2], and pulled together a few articles with the hashtags [3]**#AuditWomen #AuditFemale #AuditGirls.**

We are going to see that Genesis 2 establishes the basis of what a woman is and her vital role in every aspect of society.

Secondly, in today's atmosphere of biting criticism and controversy that surround God and the Bible, the context about the creation of woman is evidence that this Book is a Sacred Book. It contains jewels of information that you cannot find anywhere else. The Bible narrative, written 3,500 years ago, is contemporary and reveals a story flow from Genesis to Revelation.

We're not discussing a "bunch of fabulated memories thrown together and pawned off as something divine." It is the Word of God, our Creator, Who establishes and transmits to us His plan from the beginning (Genesis) to the end (Revelation). This context about the creation of woman encompasses the entire plan of God, the whole

---

2. *https://theexplanation.com/read-content-audit-universe-online/*

3. https://theexplanation.com/audit-of-the-universe-hashtags-that-corroborate-the-explanation/

history of humankind, past, present, and future. Of and by itself the creation of woman is coherent completeness.

In the next chapter we will get right into this fascinating story of women in the Bible. *The Explanation* will answer ALL the above questions and show you how ALL the pieces in the puzzle assemble perfectly.

Further Study

For those who want to meditate on the above questions and how to give Biblical answers, not human conjectures, here's the clue. One of the keys to mastering Biblical Hebrew is the literal represents the symbolic[4]; the physical represents the spiritual. The man and the woman prefigure Christ and the Church. You can use the free Bible tools at UnlockBibleMeaning.com[5] to see the meaning of the Hebrew words in the Genesis 2 context. But, primarily focus on the relationship of Christ to the Church. The Preeminent to the Eminent.

---

4. https://theexplanation.com/each-biblical-hebrew-word-is-a-precious-jewel-to-be-discovered/

5. http://unlockbiblemeaning.com

One of a Kind: Woman, Man, Church, Elohim

One of a Kind. The Creation of Woman is unique, likewise with Man, the Couple, the Spirit, Yahveh, Elohim.

One of a kind is the description not only of the creation of the woman but of the woman herself. This uniqueness is a vital point God impregnates on the mind of Adam. To be always remembered. Have we forgotten?

In the three verses, Genesis 2:17-19 of the Bible narrative, the author abruptly changes subjects THREE times. Why, what's the common denominator that glues this heterogeneity together? Here's the clue; to save humankind from sure death, we need a woman who is unique. Let's talk about this uniqueness.

Genesis 2:17-19

17 But of the tree of the knowledge of good and evil, you shall not eat of it: for in the day that you eat thereof you shall surely die.

18 And the LORD God said, It is not good that the man should be alone; I will make him an help meet for him.

19 And out of the ground the LORD God formed every beast of the field and every fowl of the air; and brought them to Adam to see what he would call them: and whatsoever Adam called every living creature, that was the name thereof.

In Genesis 1:24, following the creation of the animals, on the sixth day, God saw, *that it was good*. In Genesis 1:31, after the creation of man in His own image, male and female, also on the sixth day, God beholds, *it was very good*. Yet, in Genesis 2:18 Yahveh Elohim (Lord God) states it is NOT good. The identical Hebrew word, *tov* (H2896), is used in these three contexts. Putting these three events in sequential order reveals the following. Yahveh created the animals, that was good. Then Yahveh first created man alone; that was NOT good. Finally, Yahveh created the woman, and then it was VERY good. ONLY the couple, man and woman, together are VERY good. Separately, they are good BUT incomplete. To be VERY good, the man needs a *helpmeet for him*. *Meet* is an old English term meaning suitable, appropriate, or fitting. We are going to see that Yahveh makes the man a mate who is tailor-made, custom-fashioned physically, mentally, psychologically, and spiritually.

Before this exquisite creation, Yahveh has the man do a specific exercise to teach him a lesson about the magnificent and superb partner he was about to receive. Without her, the man was not good enough.

Genesis 2:9

And out of the ground the LORD God formed every beast of the field, and every fowl of the air; and brought them to Adam to see what he would call them: and whatsoever Adam called every living creature, that was the name thereof.

20 And Adam gave names to all cattle, and to the fowl of the air, and to every beast of the field; but for Adam there was not found an help meet for him.

This strange exercise is interjected before the creation of the woman. Two verses out of a narrative of 7 verses for such a banal episode appears disproportionate. There's a foremost reason for this.

Firstly, Adam does the naming of the animals. In Gen. 1:5, 8, 10, God named: day, night, heaven, earth, seas. Now, God gives this prerogative of *naming* to the man. The responsibility of naming is also part of the injunction to have dominion and subdue the Earth (Gen. 1:28); we continue to name our houses, boats, pets, dolls, and fossils. The importance of *naming* is the fifth key to mastering Biblical Hebrew[1] because names are not merely dog tags for ID. Names identify the characteristics and character of living beings. In the Bible, the Biblical Hebrew expresses the personality, mentality, and heart of an individual. A person doesn't get any name; a name finds a person. Later the man (Biblical Hebrew: *ish*) names the woman (*isha*). The man's name naturally gives rise to the woman's name; just as the man gave rise to the woman. You've noticed that it's the man who does the naming, he was on the scene first. We'll see why he has the prerogative of *naming*.

Secondly, when the scripture says, "there was not found..." it's NOT talking about a two-legged, upright being that could walk, talk and

---

1. https://theexplanation.com/each-biblical-hebrew-word-is-a-precious-jewel-to-be-discovered/

have sex, or who could be mistreated and used as a submissive instrument. It's referring to a *helpmeet* who would be physically, mentally, psychologically, and spiritually identical and compatible with the man. I'll show you that *helpmeet* means all of those distinctive characteristics. God had the man perform this naming ceremony because He wanted this realization to sink into Adam's mind; the animals have nothing in common with humankind. A profound truth that Adam would never forget. Remember, masculine (zachar H2145), in Biblical Hebrew, also means, remember[2]; this is a self-evident truth God wanted and wants men and humanity to understand. In the 21st century, we've forgotten this truth; that's the story of *Audit of Humankind*[3].

Naming, Identifying and Designating Uniqueness

This naming is to contrast the creation of animals while focusing the man's attention on the uniqueness of his helpmeet, his partner, the woman. Verse 9 is a bit ambiguous. It says God formed the animals and brought them to Adam. Well, the animals were created earlier on the sixth day BEFORE the creation of Adam. Verse 9 indicates the opposite; this is the kind of *anomaly* discreditors want to get into, which is not my intention. God could've taken the animals He ALREADY had created and brought them to Adam. Or, I think it possible that God MAY have formed animals right in front of Adam to reinforce the *one of a kind* helpmeet He was going to create for the man. One way or another, don't get side-tracked by chronological trivia; the key here is the woman is a unique custom-made specimen.

The singularity of the woman is capital to the rest of the Bible story, as we can gather from these two verses. I want to stay with this puzzle piece to elaborate its contours and we'll see how it fits perfectly into the

---

2. https://theexplanation.com/creation-week-reveals-gods-plan-remember-it/

3. *https://theexplanation.com/read-all-the-content-of-audit-of-humankind-online/*

entire puzzle. Here's the principle: Everything about the woman and everything related to the woman is *one of a kind.*

God has never ceased to remind humankind so that we REMEMBER. When it comes to God and His Creation, whether it is the Universe, Earth, Man, Woman or Animals, it is all Unique. This concept of uniqueness, concerning God and His Creation, is so vital that He makes Adam perform this first *do-and-tell* example, naming the animals, in the Bible.

One of a kind is a recurring theme in the Bible. God, Himself is Absolute. When God established His unique nation, Israel, He told them, "Hear, O Israel: The LORD our God is **one** LORD" (Deuteronomy 6:44). There is only ONE Lord; this flies in the face of "as long as you're worshipping *god*, that's fine." Humankind doesn't get to decide who God is and how to revere Him. Here's another poignant example to underscore how *one of a kind* Yahveh is. Elijah was a prophet of God who also performed a do-and-tell example to reinforce the uniqueness of God.

1 Kings 18: 24-25

24 And call you [the false prophets] on the name of your gods, and I will call on the name of the LORD: and the God that answers by fire, let him be God. And all the people answered and said, It is well spoken.

25 And Elijah said to the prophets of Baal, Choose you one bullock for yourselves, and dress it first; for you are many; and call on the name of your gods, but put no fire under.

The false prophets prayed to their multitude of gods, and nothing happened. Elijah prayed to his single God, and the sacrifice on his alter was immediately consumed by fire. "And when all the people saw it, they fell on their faces: and they said, The LORD, he is the God; the LORD, he is the God" (verse 39). Elijah identified and designated the One Single Lord.

This one of a kind principle is clearly stated and corroborated in the New Testament. The Apostle Paul tells the Church in Ephesus.

Ephesians 4:4-6

4 There is one body, and one Spirit, even as you are called in one hope of your calling;

5 One Lord, one faith, one baptism,

6 One God and Father of all, who is above all, and through all, and in you all.

One is mentioned seven times in these three verses. Each of these seven elements is one of a kind. There's something severely wrong with religions and oecumenism; that is comparable to the cacophony of the gods of the false prophets above. Elijah demonstrated, or rather, God did, that He is the One and only.

A little further on in Ephesians 5:31-32 Paul adds the significance of ONE man joined to ONE woman. "... a man ... shall be joined to his wife, and they two shall be one flesh. This is a great mystery: but I speak concerning Christ and the church." The ONE husband joined to the ONE wife represent the ONE Christ joined to the ONE church. This ONE couple with their children represents the ONE Elohim family.

I realize if you're reading this for the first time, it's a mouthful. Remember, "man is made in the image of God[4]" (Genesis 1:27) That man includes the woman and children. The couple, the husband and wife union, is the image of Christ and the Church. As the couple

---

4. https://theexplanation.com/humans-were-created-in-the-image-of-god-in-his-likeness/

engenders and gives birth to human children, so does the Christ-Church union engender and give birth to God's spiritual children.

Adam, without Eve, is the same as Christ without the Church. Like the cornerstone (1 Peter 2:6, Ephesians 2:20 read these passages at UnlockBibleMeaning.com[5]) without all the other stones that form the spiritual building (1 Peter 2:5). Like a Brother without any other brothers and sisters, which doesn't make any sense. You can NOT have one without the other. You have to understand the complementary roles of each! Which we will see. Each is UNIQUE, but each is NOT a STAND-ALONE. The two stand together.

A final thought about the one of a kind woman, the unique creation, especially the particular sequential diverse events in Genesis 2:17-19. Here's why. The two partial verses below are only excerpts to focus on the point at hand; the chronological events in this Genesis context. I'll explain the other aspects of these verses in Timothy a little later.

1 Timothy 2:14-15

14 ... the woman being deceived was in the transgression.

15 Notwithstanding she shall be saved in childbearing ...

The transgression of the woman is the equivalent of the "surely die" (Gen. 2:17). Immediately followed by a woman's unique (Gen. 2:19-20) capacity to bear children, namely, the Savior, Christ, through Whom, the woman and all her descendants can be saved by "freely eating" of the Tree of Eternal Life. The sequences of both Genesis 2 and 1 Timothy 2 summarize the whole plan of God; the creation, transgression, and redemption of humankind.

---

5. http://unlockbiblemeaning.com

The six "*one of a kind*" players of the cast presented in Genesis 1 and 2 (man, woman, couple-family[6], Yahveh-Christ[7], Church, Elohim[8]) play out the strangest scenario in verses Gen. 2:21-24 that explain the entire plan of God; this is so much more than just the creation of woman. It certainly includes that, but the entirety of the Gospel is present in this short narrative.

6. https://theexplanation.com/yahweh-elohim-inseparable-relationship/

7. https://theexplanation.com/yahweh-yahveh-meaning-identity-gods-name/

8. https://theexplanation.com/yahweh-elohim-inseparable-relationship/

God Created Woman Showing Humankind's Future

God created woman. The drama surrounding this breath-taking event is prophetically stupendous.

God created woman. He told Adam He was going to create a *helpmeet* for him. Adam has named all the animals, and there's not one that could serve as his mate. Here's the narrative of her creation.

Did you realize there are more verses devoted to the creation of the woman than to the man (7 to 1)? Why? Among other reasons, her creation represents the spiritual creation of the Church[1] (Ephesians 5:32 as I've explained[2]). It's also an enactment of the plan of God to save

---

1. https://theexplanation.com/one-of-a-kind-woman-man-couple-yahveh-elohim-lesson/

2. https://theexplanation.com/one-of-a-kind-woman-man-couple-yahveh-elohim-lesson/

humankind. It's the Gospel, the Good News, preached on the sixth day of Creation, four thousand years before the First Coming of Christ.

Personally, it is one of the most poignant testimonials to the inspiration of the Bible. This narrative has been sitting in front of us for six thousand years, 560 years since Gutenberg printed the first Bible, 111 years since Gideon started distributing them free around the world. And, to my knowledge, the meaning of the creation of woman has not been fully understood.

Its simplicity and parallel with New Testament events have escaped the most critical Bible scholars. Beyond the incredible Creation story of woman, here is evidence of coherent completeness of this sacred book as you've never seen before. The Bible tells the same story in both the Old and New Testaments. Written 1400 hundred years apart by authors who had never met and never concerted to write the plot together. Here it is, in plain BIBLICAL HEBREW. NOT in your native language. That's why we have to get into the original language.

Genesis 2:21-22

21 And the LORD God caused a *deep sleep* (H8639) to fall upon Adam, and he *slept* (H3462): and he took one of his ribs, and *closed up* (H5462) the flesh instead thereof;

22 And the rib, which the LORD God had taken from man, made he a woman, and brought her to the man.

Question: God could have instantaneously and painlessly removed the man's rib? Why plunge him into a deep sleep? Question: Since God did plunge the man into a deep sleep, why does it have to reinforce this point with *he slept*. After all, if God causes you to sleep, it will happen. Readers don't ask such *silly* questions. Well, you should.

Here's the kicker. The words sleep/slept, identical in English are TWO DIFFERENT WORDS in Biblical Hebrew. Yes, I put that in full caps to emphasize this point that it is IMPOSSIBLE to see in English. That's why we're using the original language as the basis for our study. What's the significance of using two different words for *sleep*?

Before I answer those questions, I want you to realize that something prodigious is occurring here. A disproportionately large space is devoted to when God created woman AND mysterious details light up the narrative. Here are the two Biblical Hebrew words translated *sleep* in English.

Exercise: What do these two Biblical Hebrew words have in common? Notice how the King James (KJV) translators rendered the Biblical Hebrew word root[3] (the basis), H7290, of the first word.

H8639 – deep sleep

תַּרְדֵּמָה tardêmâh tar-day-maw'; from H7290 (רָדַם); a lethargy or (by implication) trance:

KJV - deep sleep.

H7290

רָדַם râdam raw-dam'; a primitive root; to stun, i.e. stupefy (with sleep or death):

KJV - (be fast a-, be in a deep, cast into a dead, that) sleep(-er, -eth).

H3462 - slept

יָשֵׁן yâshên yaw-shane'; a primitive root; properly, to be slack or languid, i.e. (by implication) sleep (figuratively, to die); also to grow old, stale or inveterate:

KJV - old (store), remain long, (make to) sleep.

These two words have DEATH in common; this is a symbolic representation of sleep. The figurative meaning is one of the keys to master Biblical Hebrew[4]. God did not need to put the man to sleep! The author of Genesis did not need to use two different words for sleep to get the point across. I hope you're able to put two and two together. The sole reason for this staging is to show that symbolically the man DIED. Are you understanding? The *first* man died to prefigure the Second Man, Jesus, who would die 4000 years later!

Next, God took a rib. No, he did something BEFORE that. God first cut open the man's flesh. How do we know this? Because it says, God *closed up the flesh*. To close up, you first have to open up. Look at the Biblical Hebrew for *close up*.

H5462

סָגַר çâgar saw-gar'; a primitive root; to shut up; figuratively, to surrender:

KJV - close up, deliver (up), give over (up), inclose, ✕pure, repair, shut (in, self, out, up, up together), stop, ✕ straitly.

After removing the rib, God *repaired* the wound. Again, God could've taken a rib withOUT opening up the man's side. What does this signify?

---

4. https://theexplanation.com/each-biblical-hebrew-word-is-a-precious-jewel-to-be-discovered/

I consider that *The Explanation* has demonstrated from the Bible that the Old Testament Yahveh God creating the woman, prefigures the New Testament Christ creating the Church[5]. The first man *slept*, the Second Man died. What happened immediately AFTER the Second Man's, Christ's death by crucifixion?

John 19:30-37

30 When Jesus therefore had received the vinegar, he said, It is finished: and he bowed his head, and gave up the ghost.

31 The Jews therefore, because it was the preparation, that the bodies should not remain on the cross on the sabbath day, (for that sabbath day was a high day,) besought Pilate that their legs might be broken, and that they might be taken away.

32 Then came the soldiers, and brake the legs of the first, and of the other which was crucified with him.

33 But when they came to Jesus, and saw that he was dead already, they brake not his legs:

34 But one of the soldiers with a spear pierced his side, and forthwith came there out blood and water.

35 And he that saw it bare record, and his record is true: and he knows that he says true, that you might believe.

36 For these things were done, that the scripture should be fulfilled, A bone of him shall not be broken.

---

5. https://theexplanation.com/one-of-a-kind-woman-man-couple-yahveh-elohim-lesson/

37 And again another scripture says, They shall look on him whom they pierced.

Christ died and the very next event was a soldier pierced His side. Once again, Christ was already dead. Was there any need to *pierce His side*? From a prophetical and spiritual point of view, the answer is yes and yes. Prophetically, Yahveh opened up the side of the first man, and the soldier opened up the side of the Second Man. Notice that both were dead BEFORE the opening up. Christ GAVE His life for us; Nobody TOOK Christ's Life! The debate about who killed Christ, the Romans or the Jews, is a moot point.

While we're in the context, John 19:34 states that blood and water issued from Christ's side. Let me ask you. If an individual were pierced, what would YOU see coming out of the side? You'd see blood; you would not be able to distinguish water. So why is water mentioned? Let me first mention another significant event that took place at the same moment; the ripping open of the entrance curtain (Matthew 27:51) to the Holy of Holies in the Temple. The significance of this miraculous event is the ability to REenter the presence of God. Christ's death removed that barrier.

Spiritually, people could now REENTER the Holy of Holies, which symbolizes the Garden of Eden[6]. Those people are the ones who ENTER the CHURCH that God established by His death. HOW do you ENTER God's CHURCH? You REPENT of your sins which are paid for by the BLOOD of Jesus Christ. And you are BAPTISED in WATER for the washing away of those sins. BLOOD and WATER (Acts 2:38[7]). Christ's death and the outflowing of *blood* and *water* demolish the wall, the curtain, the gate that separated humankind from the spiritual Church, the Holy of Holies, and the Garden of Eden.

---

6. https://theexplanation.com/garden-of-eden-represents-much-more-than-a-garden/

7. http://unlockbiblemeaning.com

When God created woman, He enacted the saving of Humankind. God wrote and exposed His entire plan from the foundation of the world. The book of Revelation is the fulfillment of the book of Genesis. Christ is the Alpha and the Omega, Adam, the first man, the Savior, the Second Man. But He does NOT do it ALONE. Christ is the FOUNDER of the CHURCH; it's CORNERSTONE. That's why the first man was created FIRST and afterward, the woman. It has NOTHING to do with superiority and inferiority. It has to do with the order of things. "But every man in his own order: Christ the firstfruits; afterward they that are Christ's at His coming" (1 Corinthians 15:23).

Christ died so the Temple curtain could be ripped open; that act signified the founding of the Church. It is through Christ's blood and water that we have remission and cleansing of our sins and can enter the Church and, at His Coming, the Holy of Holies, the Garden of Eden, the Kingdom of God.

Remember, "the wages of sin is *death*; but the gift of God is eternal life through Jesus Christ our Lord" (Romans 6:23). That *death* is the *surely die; the* die die from eating of the Tree of the Knowledge of Good and Evil[8] in Genesis 2:17. That is why the one-of-a-kind sleep/death of the first man/Second Man, Adam/Christ, and why God created woman immediately follows. God's focal point is the Tree of Eternal Life. It's only through Christ dying and the establishment of His Church that this goal is attainable. That's why the narrative of God created woman is lengthy.

The whole plan of God was on stage when God created woman. This surprising narrative holds many more revelations about the Gospel, as we will see.

---

8. https://theexplanation.com/the-tree-of-knowledge-of-good-and-evil-the-meaning/

Helpmeet, the God Given Role of Woman

Helpmeet is a strange word for the unique and vital role God specially designed women to play. It isn't what you think.

Helpmeet is an old English KJV (King James Version) translation. A modern definition of *helpmeet* would be *suitable help*. Before you go scurrying off thinking this refers to a maid or doormat (not that there's anything wrong with either of those!) let me assure you *helpmeet* and *suitable help* include the highest level of positive characteristics you can image. We will devote several chapters to detailing the beauty and valor of a helpmeet.

This chapter will limit itself to the elaboration of help; we'll discuss meet a little later on and, of course, *The Explanation* will show the relationship between *suitable* and *help*.

To start, I realize I'm on touchy ground. Feminist movements are clamoring for equal rights as women around the world live under very harsh conditions and treatment. All around, gender has become an issue, and it seems no matter where you position yourself, you can come under fire. *The Explanation* is not against anyone. It tries to raise issues to a higher level of explanation based on Biblical Hebrew. Beyond that, everyone exercises their free will, and so be it.

This chapter, with the first part of *helpmeet*, the word, *help*, is the foundational role of the woman. To be realistic, we have to talk about the pros and cons of women and men. Not everything is rosy with gender, no matter which it is. Always keep in mind the initial and ultimate roles of women (and men) and realize we're now in a very tumultuous intermediary time.

Here's the Bible verse, and we immediately want to note the contrast of ideas in the vocabulary. Can you spot it? I ask you this because we tend to read words, which we understand, but not the deeper meaning of what they are conveying. Take time and meditate on this.

Genesis 2:18

And the LORD God said, It is not good that the man should be *alone* (H905); I will make him an *help* (H5828) meet for him.

Alone and *helpmeet* are in complementary opposition. We'll scrutinize *alone*. But first, I want to remind you that the Hebrew word for *male* (zachar) includes the concept of *preeminence*[1]. Please go to the link[2] if you haven't heard this before. Don't be jaded by preconceptions; this is not to show that he has all the rights. We have seen and shall see that this preeminence has responsibilities and obligations[3]. Here I want to

---

1. https://theexplanation.com/male-gender-its-significance-and-why-god-created-it/

2. https://theexplanation.com/male-gender-its-significance-and-why-god-created-it/

show you that preeminence ALONE is NOT GOOD. The man lacks something essential.

H905

בַּד bad bad; from H909 (בָּדַד); properly, separation; by implication, a part of the body, branch of a tree, bar for carrying; figuratively, chief of a city; especially (with prepositional prefix) as an adverb, apart, only, besides:

KJV - alone, apart, bar, besides, branch, by self, of each alike, except, only, part, staff, strength.

H909

בָּדַד bâdad baw-dad'; a primitive root; to divide, i.e. (reflex.) be solitary:

KJV - alone.

Alone can be good, but it is not complete. In the desert, God gave the people ONLY ONE dish of food, manna, for 40 years for a lesson. This type of bread had no accompaniment; it was ALONE.

Deuteronomy 8:33

And he humbled you, and suffered you to hunger, and fed you with manna, which you knew not, neither did your fathers know; that he might make you know that man does not live by bread *only* (H905), but by every word that proceeds out of the mouth of the LORD does man live.

This manna was sufficient to keep them alive. It had all the nutrition they needed (don't ask me what its composition was). It was good. But

3. https://theexplanation.com/male-gender-its-significance-and-why-god-created-it/

the manna ALONE was not good. It was a reminder that something important was missing, God's Word, which is the bread of spiritual life. The physical bread needed a spiritual complement.

Alone is also translated *strength* in the KJV (see above); this appears strange until we realize the relationship in the verse below, Bildad, one of Job's friends, talks about how wickedness demolishes strength.

Job 18:13

13 It [wickedness] shall devour the *strength* (H905) of his skin: even the firstborn of death shall devour his *strength* (H905).

Man, men tend to rely on their strength. I'm generalizing, but men gravitate to being islands of strength unto themselves. Being strong is a good quality, but an individual cannot, particularly a man, should NOT be a solitary strength. It is NOT good to be a strength unto himself. Hence the need for help. Hence the need for female help; this is the contrast in the verse, the insufficiency of *solitary strength* and the complementary need for *help*.

Help

This help is not a cry for help, like that of a drowning person. It is not from an inferior position. Remember, the male is preeminent, but, in his preeminence, he is INcomplete. Let me ask you a question. If you have a problem with configuring Excel or installing some plumbing you look for help, right? Do you want your help to be MORE ADVANCED and BETTER EQUIPPED than you? Of course, you do, there's no point asking help from someone with LESS or even EQUAL capacity compared to you. They must have MORE, BETTER know-how than you do. Then, and only then, can they help you. Conclusion, this woman helper is BETTER EQUIPPED in certain areas to HELP the man than the man ALONE is. That's why the man needed and needs a woman, a *helpmeet*.

H5828

עֵזֶר 'êzer ay'-zer; from H5826 (עָזַר); aid:

KJV - help.

H5826

עָזַר 'âzar aw-zar'; a primitive root; to surround, i.e. protect or aid:

KJV - help, succour.

Our keyword H5826 is unique in that it only has one English KJV translation for the 21 times it appears in the Old Testament. As you know, most Biblical Hebrew words have multiple translations. The first couple of times, it is used as *helpmeet* referring to the first woman. The third time, below, it talks about the name of Moses' second son, *God my Help*.

Exodus 18:4

And the name of the other was Eliezer; for the God of my father, said he, was my *help*, (H5828) and delivered me from the sword of Pharaoh:

Deuteronomy 33:7

And this is the blessing of Judah: and he said, Hear, LORD, the voice of Judah, and bring him to his people: let his hands be sufficient for him; and be you an *help* (H5828) to him from his enemies.

In Deuteronomy, like in Exodus, help refers to GOD! Sixteen of the twenty-one verses with *ezer* (H5828) refer to God as the help. Do you make the connection?

The woman, created for the man, is comparable to God. She's a helper like God is a helper. The help-ezer is an extraordinary and elevated role; this is not a lowly, subservient, spiritless, subdued blob of a human being in man's shadow.

The Biblical Hebrew juxtaposes the woman with God. Realize also that Moses and Judah were preeminent figures in the Bible story. I don't have space to develop that. In Deuteronomy above, the blessing is that Judah's hands be sufficient. Check that word at UnlockBibleMeaning.com[4]. It means *plenteous* and *mighty*. So, as preeminent, plenteous, and mighty as Judah was, he still needed an ezer. All men need an ezer. And that ezer has superior qualities than what the man possesses to help him meet his challenges.

You cannot find a higher and more eloquent and marked comparison than God. Anyone God compares to Himself is in an excellent spiritual state. Read Exodus 7:1, God says to Moses, "I have made you a god to Pharaoh." The Hebrew does not say "a god," it says Elohim, "I have made you GOD..." When you understand the symbolism here, it is indeed God. Even with that preeminent status, Moses needed ezer-help. He knew the value of the assistance he requested from God, and never forgot it. He even named his son Eli-ezer, God, my help.

The woman was created to be man's helpmeet.

Humankind cannot decide what the *value* or *role* of a woman is, no more than that of a man, or God. When God created the UNIQUE characters and characteristics that animate each aspect of His Creation, He SET the VALUES. He decided what the *pieces of the puzzles* are, and

---

4. http://unlockbiblemeaning.com

He placed them in their appropriate positions in the overall picture. Humankind and each one of us have the right to accept or reject what God has established; that's free will. In dismissing the originally named values, we are putting the cart before the horse. We think humankind can decide the role of a woman (and man) in society; we're the horse. Or, we can see the value God has placed on a woman (and man) and accept and do our utmost to respect His pieces in the puzzle: God is the horse, and each of us is the cart.

Jordan Peterson, in his many videos, refers to his helper. He has the exact right approach. Like all men and women, we often fall short of the standards we should respect; however, we should at least know what they are and be doing our utmost to strive for them.

Here are his words of wisdom starting around the 81-minute mark[5]. "I've been fortunate in my marriage because I have someone to contend with. You know we have our discussions, and they're not easy. Partly because we have hard problems to solve because life is full of hard problems. I want someone who stands up, you know, and has her say even if it's not what I would say and maybe I'm even willing at times because she's quite intuitive and a good dreamer, and I'm more facile verbally, and so we have to be careful in our relationship because if I'm in a particularly ornery mood and she has something to say I can usually slice up her arguments verbally..."

Let me be frank. Some might think taking *helpmeet*, looking up *ezer* (H5828), and comparing a woman's role to God, as blasphemous. Imagine men looking on women, not just their wives, as representing God. How many inter-gender problems would vanish?!

Let's refer back to Genesis 1:27, "So God created man in his own image, in the image of God created he him; male and female created he them." Both genders have the identical image of God. In that, the

5. https://youtu.be/MnUfXYGtT5Q?t=81

preeminent and the helper are fully equal. Please go back and read How Humankind Socializes: Gender Equality, Gender Inequality, or Gender Compatibility?[6] Men and women have the same spiritual potential, "For whosoever shall do the will of my Father which is in heaven, the same is my brother, and sister, and mother" (Matthew 12:50). To be a helper is to be Christ's sister. That is a lofty ideal for all women.

6. https://theexplanation.com/gender-equality-gender-inequality-or-gender-compatibility/

God Made a Woman. The Feminine Moment.

God made a woman. This phrase encloses the entire reason for being of women; all women, worldwide. Finally, we can understand their destiny.

God made a woman. Learn the depth of understanding in this statement; in the one Biblical Hebrew word *made*. A must-read for every woman who wants to discover the real reason for her existence. And men, especially, need to grasp the calling of half the world population.

The English translation *made*, is incomprehensible, and hides the depth of comprehension that *The Explanation* will make crystal clear. Here's the Bible context.

Genesis 2:22

And the rib, which the LORD God had taken from man,
made (H1129) he a woman, and brought her to the man.

The Biblical Hebrew word for made (H1129) is *banah*. This verb is
used for the FIRST time in the context when God made a woman;
this is significant when it comes to creation which is the general subject
of Genesis 1-2. Let's quickly look at verbs used for preceding creation
events.

Four different verbs refer to events of Creation, three of which we've
seen and elaborated.

1. **Bara** - The first and best-known meaning creation ex nihilo[1],
   from nothing
2. **Asa** - A general term[2], *to make;* this is the regular verb used in
   umpteen circumstances
3. **Yatsar** - Formed. Used in Gen. 2:7 (for man) and verse 2. (for
   animals). A short meaning is made for a specific purpose[3].
4. **Banah** - Its first use is in the context of God *made* a woman;
   this is different from the creation of *man, animals, and the
   entire Universe.* When God created a woman, it was a unique
   act. The Biblical Hebrew begs us all to understand why.

God built an ezer[4] (help) for the man. We saw that this ezer has Godly
characteristics of the highest nature[5]. Let's be more specific and see
what these BUILT-in characteristics are. Here's the first definition of
banah.

1. http://theexplanation.com/genesis-creation-starts-off-with-a-surprise-how-about-a-big-bang/

2. https://theexplanation.com/day-4-of-creation-sun-and-moon-establish-calendar/

3. https://theexplanation.com/god-created-man-bible-god-formed-man/

4. https://theexplanation.com/helpmeet-the-surprising-god-given-role-of-woman/

5. https://theexplanation.com/helpmeet-the-surprising-god-given-role-of-woman/

H1129

בָּנָה bânâh baw-naw'; a primitive root; to build (literally and figuratively):

KJV - (begin to) build(-er), obtain children, make, repair, set (up), ✕ surely.

Banah contains all the basic and essential ingredients that characterize the ezer when God made a woman. Banah is translated over 350 times with the word *build* and only three times with the word *made*. Biblical Hebrew is not a question of statistics but of meaning. *Banah* means to build; the other translations are derivatives related to ways to build like *set up* and *repair*. A figurative counterpart is building a family by *obtaining children*.

Genesis 4:17

And Cain knew his wife; and she conceived, and bare Enoch: and he *builded* (H1129) a city, and called the name of the city, after the name of his son, Enoch.

Genesis 16:2

And Sarai said to Abram, Behold now, the LORD has restrained me from bearing: I pray you, go in to my maid; it may be that I may *obtain children* (H1129) by her. And Abram hearkened to the voice of Sarai.

2 Chronicles 33:16

And he *repaired* (H1129) the altar of the LORD, and sacrificed thereon peace offerings and thank offerings, and commanded Judah to serve the LORD God of Israel.

Ezekiel 39:15

And the passengers that pass through the land, when any sees a man's bone, then shall he *set up* (H1129) a sign by it, till the buriers have buried it in the valley of Hamongog

Banah (H1129) is a Biblical Hebrew *root*, the sixth key to master Biblical Hebrew[6]. Roots are the most basic form of a word. We should say, the most fundamental form of a concept. Why? Because with the usage and meaning of *banah* we've already seen that there's a universe of difference between the English, *make*, and the Hebrew *build* (this is a common modern Hebrew word). There are derivatives of the root that bear additional meaning. Look at this one, which is very well-known.

H1121

בֵּן bên bane; from H1129 (בָּנָה); a son (as a builder of the family name), in the widest sense (of literal and figurative relationship, including grandson, subject, nation, quality or condition, etc., (like father or brother), etc.):

KJV - + afflicted, age, (Ahoh-) (Ammon-) (Hachmon-) (Lev-) ite, (anoint-) ed one, appointed to, ([phrase]) arrow, (Assyr-) (Babylon-) (Egypt-) (Grec-) ian, one born, bough, branch, breed, + (young) bullock, + (young) calf, × came up in, child, colt, × common, × corn, daughter, × of first, + firstborn, foal, + very fruitful, + postage, × in, + kid, + lamb, ([phrase]) man, meet, + mighty, + nephew, old, ([phrase]) people, + rebel, + robber, × servant born, × soldier, son, + spark, + steward, + stranger, × surely, them of, + tumultuous one, + valiant(-est), whelp, worthy, young (one), youth.

---

6. https://theexplanation.com/biblical-hebrew-roots-to-anchor-your-bible-comprehension/

H1122

בֵּן Bên bane; the same as H1121 (בֵּן); Ben, an Israelite:

KJV - Ben. [/box]

Ben, a common name, known to all. In many languages *ben-...* or *bin-...* means *son of.* What people don't realize is that this harks back to the very creation when God made a woman and inaugurated her role, her piece in the coherent, complete puzzle. When Yahweh BUILT the woman, He was building future sons through her. One of the main titles to designate ALL humans in the Bible is the *sons of God.* Whether they are for-or-against God, a human being is a *son of God.* It is thanks to the woman that the world population can be fruitful and multiply with sons and daughters. The way God *made* and *built* the woman incorporates one of the meanings and purposes for her creation.

Maybe you're thinking, Sam Kneller has twisted scripture. It says God *made,* (*built*). You can't apply what God built to the woman; the built refers to God's qualities, not the woman. That's a legitimate query. Let's answer it. To do so, we have to refer back to Genesis 1:27, "So God created man (this is a generic term referring to ALL humans[7], NOT the male gender) in his own image, in the image of God created he him; male and female created he them." God embodies BOTH genders[8]. God has the perfect male and female characteristics.

When He *formed* (yatsar) the male gender, He endowed them with His MALE qualities. When He *built* (banah) the female gender he endowed them with His FEMALE qualities. The verbs *yatsar* and *banah* embody these qualities. Both males and females are in the IMAGE of God in that EACH carries the specificities of EACH of God's characteristics. Without going further here (I will later), that's

---

7. https://theexplanation.com/human-beings-god-created-them-equal-but-different/

8. https://theexplanation.com/humans-were-created-in-the-image-of-god-in-his-likeness/

why COMBINED (not ALONE, it is NOT good that the man be alone.) they better represent the WHOLE IMAGE of God.

I don't have space here but, go over to UnlockBibleMeaning.com[9] and do a study on some of the translations of H1121, ben/bane. Look at: *branch, firstborn, lamb, worthy*. If you even have a cursory knowledge of scripture, just those four words make your mind jump to WHOM it's referring, Christ. Remember the seventh rule to master Biblical Hebrew; each word tells a STORY[10]. *Banah* tells the story of the entire plan of God which centers on His Son who is the Branch, the Firstborn, the Lamb, "Worthy is the Lamb that was slain to receive power, and riches, and wisdom, and strength, and honour, and glory, and blessing" (Revelation 5:12).

When God made a woman, when God *banah* a woman, for the first time, He uses a verb that incarnates His entire plan of Salvation. It is only through this *Building of a Woman* that all humankind can attain salvation.

Here is another in-depth look at the meaning and relevance of *build, banah*. It is in the form of a related word. Strong's does NOT show any relationship between these words. I do not consider that a problem, simply because Strong did incredible research in looking at the ORIGIN of words, but not necessarily, the relationship of words BEYOND their ROOTS.

Biblical Hebrew words with the SAME ROOT letters might not be related grammatically, but they can and do RELATE in meaning and significance. I've already discussed this point, read the significance of *shevet*[11]. *Banah* is another of those words. We have seen the root in H1129 and a related word in H1121. The word H995, below, has

---

9. http://unlockbiblemeaning.com

10. https://theexplanation.com/biblical-hebrew-roots-to-anchor-your-bible-comprehension/

11. https://theexplanation.com/biblical-hebrew-roots-to-anchor-your-bible-comprehension/

identical consonants as H1129. These consonants are ב (beth) and נ (nun), this changes to a final nun (ן) when it's the last letter of a word, hence ן = נ). All the other letters, the hay (ה), and the yod (י) are vowels and interchangeable and not part of the root. Let's see another word with the same consonants that Strong does not associate with *banah*, erroneously, in my opinion.

H995

בִּין bîyn bene; a primitive root; to separate mentally (or distinguish), i.e.(generally) understand:

KJV - attend, consider, be cunning, diligently, direct, discern, eloquent, feel, inform, instruct, have intelligence, know, look well to, mark, perceive, be prudent, regard, (can) skill(-full), teach, think, (cause, make to, get, give, have) understand(-ing), view, (deal) wise(-ly, man).

You immediately see the root letters (ב and ן). Do all those KJV translations reflect God? Yes, yes, yes. By this word's root construction, it is related to *banah*. God built the woman with ALL these attributes. An incredible woman you'd want to have as an *ezer*. A help every man should want by his side.

Strong adds *to separate mentally*. In brackets, he adds *distinguish*. I'll explain why he pinpoints these words. Leading from this idea, a woman has a SEPARATE MENTALITY compared to a man; A DISTINGUISHABLE, different mindset, and outlook than man. There's no question about superiority or inferiority involved here. We've already discussed the equality of the male and female[12] in that both possess the image of God. We shall be taking a closer look at some of the KJV translations for בִּין bîyn. But, diligence, eloquent,

---

12. https://theexplanation.com/female-gender-significance-why-god-created-it/

intelligence, thinking, understanding, wisdom are all highly positive qualities for any person. These qualities characterize the woman Yahveh created.

Man is *preeminent*[13] but woman is *distinguishable*. Equal, but different[14], both genders have outstanding and complementary roles.

That's why the creation of woman receives so much attention and leads to the climactic conclusion of the creation narrative in Genesis 2:25. That verse is particularly difficult to understand, and *The Explanation* will explain it in due course. Without Woman, we are ALL lost, With Woman, there's hope and a future. Men, it is not good to be alone, we owe everything to women.

We are not finished with *banah*. In the next chapter we'll see another dimension of the scope of this word, this exciting piece of the puzzle.

---

13. *https://theexplanation.com/male-gender-its-significance-and-why-god-created-it/*

14. https://theexplanation.com/human-beings-god-created-them-equal-but-different/

I will Build My Church = Yahweh Built the Woman

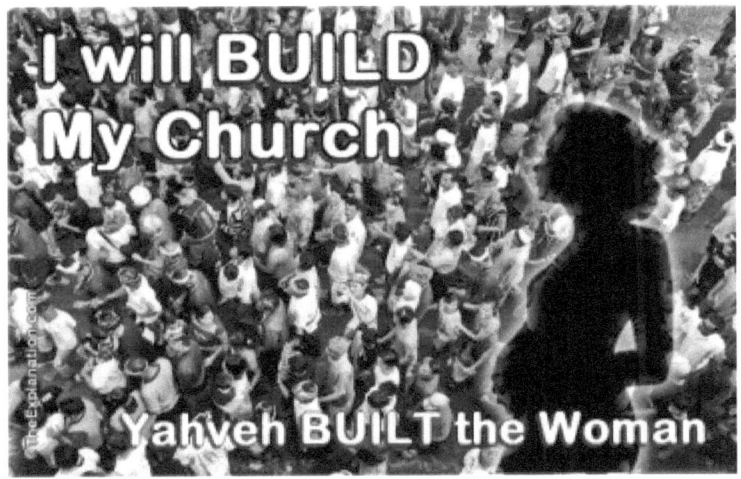

"I will build My Church," are the Words of Jesus Christ. Four millennia earlier, Genesis 1:22 says the Lord God *made* a woman. The *building* (Biblical Hebrew word translated *made*) of the woman forecast the building of the Church. Only the woman can give birth to sons and daughters, who become the Sons and Daughters of God. Here's the captivating story.

In the last chapter we discussed the meaning of the Biblical Hebrew word for *made* in Genesis 2:23, "Lord God *made* ... a woman." God *built* a woman[1]. Build, *banah* in Biblical Hebrew has to do with building a family to *obtain children* as we see below in H1129.

H1129

---

1. https://theexplanation.com/god-made-a-woman-the-feminine-moment-discover-the-meaning/

בָּנָה bânâh baw-naw'; a primitive root; to build (literally and figuratively):

KJV - (begin to) build(-er), obtain children, make, repair, set (up), × surely.

We will discuss the figurative meaning of *banah*. God is a Builder. The first structure (if I may call it that) He built was a Woman. Within the Biblical Hebrew term, *banah* (build) is the expression *ben* which means son. Through the woman, God built sons (all of humanity, sons, and daughters). But it goes much further than just physical sons. God's goal is to build spiritual sons, His divine sons. There's only one place where His children can be built. It is in His Church.

God built the woman. God built and continues to build His Church. The woman, figuratively, represents this Church. Ephesians 5:31-32, "...shall a man leave his father and mother, and shall be joined to his **wife**, and they two shall be one flesh. This is a great mystery: but I speak concerning Christ and the **church**." The entire story of this Church is somewhat enigmatic, Paul (author of Ephesians) classifies it as a mystery. There are plenty of questions that still need answers. In essence, it is a group of worshippers of God. This assembly or congregation is associated with and composed of direct descendants of the *wife*, the *woman*.

The *woman* that Yahveh built in Genesis 2 prefigures what Christ said in Matthew 16:18, "I will *build* my *Church*." Jesus ended that affirmative statement with, "and the gates of hell shall not prevail against it." In other words, if there's something sure, it's the existence of His Church.

One of the themes and constants of the Old Testament is the building and presence of the Tabernacle followed by the Temple. Immediately at the Exodus, right after giving the Ten Commandments and the Law,

God gives instructions for BUILDING the Tabernacle. Exodus 25-31, seven full chapters are devoted to this subject. Unfortunately, most readers focus on the physical building and surrounding objects. In reality, its primary use was a place of gathering in the presence of God, "... that I (the Lord) may *dwell* among them" (Ex. 25:8).

Further, in the same context, God adds, "And there (at the Tabernacle) I will *meet* with the children of Israel, and the tabernacle shall be sanctified by my glory. And I will sanctify the tabernacle of the congregation, and the altar: I will sanctify also both Aaron and his sons, to minister to me in the priest's office. And I will *dwell* among the children of Israel, and will be their God (Exodus 29:43-45).

These edifices represented the Old Testament Congregation, the place of assembly, where God dwelt with and instructed His people. He had His servants, Moses, David and in particular, Solomon BUILD these assemblies and the places where they were to meet.

The affirmation, *I will build My Church*, is an ongoing endeavor even after Christ's Second Coming. It would probably be better to say, especially after His Second Coming. Why? Because today, by God's will and plan, the assembly is a small minority. But after His Return, it will be the vast majority of humanity. Look at Christ's declaration.

Acts 15:14-18

14 Simeon [the Apostle Peter] has declared how God at the first did visit the Gentiles, to take out of them a people for his name.

15 And to this agree the words of the prophets; as it is written,

16 After this I [Christ; the Lord, verse 17] will return, and will *build again* (G456 from G3618) the tabernacle of David, which is fallen down; and I will *build again* (G456 from G3618) the ruins thereof, and I will *set it up*:

17 That the residue of men might seek after the Lord, and all the Gentiles, upon whom my name is called, says the Lord, who does all these things.

18 Known to God are all his works from the beginning of the world.

Building the woman represents building the human spiritual family. All of humanity becomes holy and meets God at His Holy Place, the Tabernacle, the Temple, the Church. After Christ's Return, there will be the Temple, as a point of reference. Physical people need physical reminders of spiritual truths. This vast assembly is the spiritual fulfillment of what God told the male and female, "Be fruitful, multiply and replenish the earth..." (Genesis 1:28). They were to grow the physical family, the sons, and daughters of God. After Christ's Return, He and His Wife, the Second Man and the Church, The Woman will grow God's Family, the Sons, and Daughters of God. That's the reference to *all the Gentiles*, in verse 17 above. In general, we'll have a converted world population living in harmony and meeting with Christ. What a contrast with today's world.

Notices verse 18, *known, from the beginning of the world* Yes, known from Genesis 1 and 2. The Creation of the man and the woman prefigured the salvation and growth of God's Family. The building process started with the woman in the Garden of Eden. And later on, the Tabernacle, and Temple, specifically the Holy of Holies represented God's Assembly and New Jerusalem. *The Explanation* has taken the symbolism from Genesis to Revelation. The entire plan of God symbolized by the building of the woman.

Here's the New Testament verse and verb recorded for when Christ said He would build His Church.

Matthew 16:18

And I [Jesus] say also to you, That you are *Peter* (G4074 - Petros), and upon this *rock* (G4073 - Petra) I will *build* (G3816) my church; and the gates of hell shall not prevail against it.

G3618

οἰκοδομέω oikodomeō oy-kod-om-eh'-o; From the same as G3619; to be a house builder that is construct or (figuratively) confirm:

KJV - (be in) build (-er -ing up) edify embolden.

Matthew 16:18 is a controversial verse because of the relationship between the Greek words Peter (G4074) and Rock (G4073). Strong makes an important distinction. *Peter* is a *piece* of rock; *Rock* is a *mass* of rock. Since we now understand the relationship between the man and the woman, the husband and wife, Christ and the Church, the understanding of Rock, Petra, a mass of rock, should be clear. Christ is the Rock of this Union. He built the Woman. He builds the Church.

There's another building analogy to drive the point home, using the same Greek word for build. Detractors regarded the *building stone* as worthless, unsuitable for construction; it became the very cornerstone of the edifice Christ is building

1 Peter 2:7

To you therefore which believe he is precious: but to them which be disobedient, the *stone* (G3037) which the *builders* G3618 disallowed, the same is made the **head of the corner**,

1 Peter 2:5

You also, as lively **stones**, are *built up* (G3618) a spiritual house, an holy priesthood, to offer up spiritual sacrifices, acceptable to God by Jesus Christ.

Christ is the Rock-solid Cornerstone and Foundation of the Church. Notice the building analogy continues referring to *you,* those who are true believers and part of the assembly as *lively stones.* They are the completion of the spiritual house. That is the spiritual accomplishment of building the woman in Genesis 2:22.

The spiritual implication of *build.*

The act of *building* is not just construction and then, abandonment. Building involves repair, maintenance, improvement, embellishment. It is an ongoing process. Both physically and spiritually. Spiritually that was the role of the Priests in Old Testament times with the rituals associated with their assembly. Later, that role fell to the Apostles and now to the ministry and the brethren and spiritual activity, like charity, as we see from the following verses.

Acts 9:31

Then had the churches rest throughout all Judaea and Galilee and Samaria, and were *edified* (G3618); and walking in the fear of the Lord, and in the comfort of the Holy Ghost, were multiplied.

1 Corinthians 8:11

... we know that we all have knowledge. Knowledge puffs up, but charity *edifies* (G3618).

1 Thessalonians 5:11

Wherefore comfort yourselves together, and *edify* (G3618) one another, even as also you do.

Paul praised the Church for its edification, its continued building process. Notice in Acts 9:3 that the churches were *multiplied*. That vocabulary reminds us of what God told the male and female, "Be fruitful and multiply." In all these ways, the building of the woman (the Church) is the piece of the salvation puzzle that, together with the work of the male (Christ), can bring about the multiplication of God's sons and daughters.

Further Study

You can go over to UnlockBibleMeaning.com[2] and visit Matthew 16:18, "I will build my Church." By checking the verses with *build* (G3618), you'll find a couple of interesting points. Firstly, the negative side when the Pharisees built and garnished tombs (Mat. 23:29). Then the positive side, Luke 7:55, "For he [a centurion] loves our nation, and he has *built* (G3618) us a synagogue (G4864)." There are other lessons from studying the word *build*.

It's also interesting to look at the meaning of *Synagogue*. It closely resembles that to do with the *Tabernacle* — a place of assembly. Please realize I'm talking about the meaning of the word. I'm not suggesting the place to assemble is in a Synagogue.

G4864

συναγωγή sunagōgē soon-ag-o-gay'; From (the reduplicated form of) G4863; an **assemblage of persons**; specifically a Jewish synagogue (the meeting or the place); by analogy a Christian church: - assembly congregation synagogue.

G4863

συνάγω sunagō soon-ag'-o; From G4862 and G71; to lead together that is collect or convene; specifically to entertain (hospitably):

KJV - + accompany assemble (selves together) bestow come together gather (selves together up together) lead into resort take in.

Proverbs 31, Feminism and Women's Rights

Proverbs 31 in the Bible focuses on women. It is in the Old Testament. Is it harsh and male dominant? What is God's viewpoint?

Proverbs 31 is one of the Bible perspectives of women. Many God-seeking women look to these words of wisdom for inspiration on how to live their lives. Can we look to this passage to draw the ultimate picture for a woman's calling?

We are pursuing our study of Genesis 2:22, where God said it is not good that the man be alone[1]. Then, He puts Adam to sleep[2], removes a part of his side, and builds a woman[3]. This woman is to be a helpmeet[4]

---

1. https://theexplanation.com/helpmeet-the-surprising-god-given-role-of-woman/

2. https://theexplanation.com/god-created-woman-and-reveals-humankinds-future/

by his side. Let's summarize what the Bible has already revealed about this woman and every woman worldwide, regardless of religion or creed. In the beginning, at Creation, there was neither religion nor racial identity. It is essential to understand the foundation.

Both Genesis 2 and Proverbs 31 are NOT the foundation. Genesis 1 is the departure for understanding both the male and female identity and roles.

If you happened to open this book at this page, I request you take a minute and go to the couple of following links for the basis of *The Explanation*. ALL men and ALL women are EQUAL before their Creator God[5]. The male and female genders are DIFFERENT from each other[6]. Please lock those two keys into your mind. Keep it simple. Twins are EQUAL, but one came out first. Whether you have a boy and girl, two boys or two girls, EACH individual twin will be DIFFERENT from the other. EQUAL and DIFFERENT are complementary ideas[7] that you have to be comfortable with if you wish to have cohesion and not an opposition between men and women.

There are maybe as many definitions and opinions of feminism and women's liberation as there are women. Women's **rights** fight for the freedom to be appropriately treated sexually and otherwise. To obtain an education, own property, vote, earn a fair wage, live free from discrimination, violence, slavery, and many other rights. All of those attributes are commendable, worthwhile, and necessary. *The Explanation* has to step back and look at the overall picture from a different perspective; from a Godly point-of-view. What does His word

---

3. https://theexplanation.com/i-will-build-my-church-yahweh-built-the-woman/

4. https://theexplanation.com/helpmeet-the-surprising-god-given-role-of-woman/

5. https://theexplanation.com/gender-equality-gender-inequality-or-gender-compatibility/

6. https://theexplanation.com/female-gender-significance-why-god-created-it/

7. https://theexplanation.com/human-beings-god-created-them-equal-but-different/

say about womanhood? We live in a world and society that is questioning everything. Nothing seems to be sacred anymore. Nothing seems to be basic, sound, and foundational knowledge. That's what *The Explanation* searches for, that's why we look into God's word to seek what He says, get His mix on feminism.

Let's take a closer look at how God *made* the woman and the Biblical Hebrew construction of this word.

Genesis 2:22

And the rib, which the LORD God had taken from man, *made* (H1129) he a woman, and brought her unto the: man.

H1129

בָּנָה bânâh baw-naw'; a primitive root; to build (literally and figuratively):

KJV - (begin to) build(-er), obtain children, make, repair, set (up), ✕ surely.

Now I need you to follow the Biblical Hebrew and the relationship between words. Look at this next word and compare it with H1129 above.

H998

בִּינָה bîynâh bee-naw'; from H995 (בִּין); understanding:

KJV - knowledge, meaning, ✕ perfectly, understanding, wisdom.

H995

בִּין bîyn bene; a primitive root; to separate mentally (or distinguish), i.e.(generally) understand:

KJV - attend, consider, be cunning, diligently, direct, discern, eloquent, feel, inform, instruct, have intelligence, know, look well to, mark, perceive, be prudent, regard, (can) skill(-full), teach, think, (cause, make to, get, give, have) understand(-ing), view, (deal) wise(-ly, man).

The only difference between H1129 (בָּנָה) and H998 (בִּינָה) is the presence of the yod (י) which, in this instance, is a vowel. Other than that, the letters are identical. Although Strong makes no relationship between these words, Sam Kneller is taking the liberty to make that connection. When you understand Biblical Hebrew, there is grammar, and also poetic comparisons that play a role in revealing comprehension.

When YHVH BUILT (בָּנָה - H1129 banah) the woman He built her with WISDOM (בִּינָה - H998 binah). She is an ezer, a help[8]. We already discussed that when you need help you search for someone WISER than yourself to solve problems; you can't figure it out ALONE. The point is, YHVH built a knowledgeable, understanding, intelligent, prudent skillful, eloquent, instructed, thinking woman to fill that role.

Notice H995 (the root of H998) *to separate mentally (or distinguish)* I point this out, mainly because previously, in reference to the man, we saw *preeminent*[9]. He has his responsibilities and obligations. The woman has a distinguished mentality. She is not less nor more important than the man. He and she are different but complementary.

---

8. https://theexplanation.com/helpmeet-the-surprising-god-given-role-of-woman/

9. https://theexplanation.com/male-gender-its-significance-and-why-god-created-it/

All the characteristics in H998 and H995 are qualities that characterize women and that any wise man would cherish to have by his side.

Building with Wisdom. That's what a woman is and does. The man ALONE, without the woman, was INcomplete. The woman ALONE, without the man, would've been INcomplete. Only together do they make a whole.

The woman is the binah-ezer, the wise-help

The principles of the woman of Proverbs 31 conform to the binah-ezer, the wise-help God built for man. A wise, strong, and independently successful, fully family devoted, Godly woman.

"Who can find a virtuous woman? for her price is far above rubies." So starts the description in Proverbs 31:10. I suggest you follow along in your Bible or click on UnlockBibleMeaning.com[10] and read the verses online. You'll have a clear picture of the combination of qualities of a Proverbs 31 woman.

Fear of God

Verse 30 says, "beauty is vain: but a woman that fears the LORD, she shall be praised." Beauty depends on the eye of each of us. My philosophy is everyone is beautiful to someone. But the first requisite of a Proverbs 31 woman is the reverence of God. Trying to learn and do it His way. Of course, this applies to men as well, but here we're focusing on the woman. Remember, binah-ezer = wise-help. Interestingly, a woman personifies wisdom. Pro. 1:20, "Wisdom cries without; she utters her voice in the streets." Pro. 1:7. "The fear of the LORD is the beginning of knowledge."

The virtuous woman starts from that foundational beginning.

---

10. http://unlockbiblemeaning.com

Family first

We shall see, she is extremely active. But they are never detrimental to her family relations. Her husband, children, and household have the priority. After the initial question about a virtuous woman, the very next section focuses on her husband, "She will do him good and not evil all the days of her life" (11-12). We will discuss this more in the next chapter.

Verse 27, "She looks well to the ways of her household, and eats not the bread of idleness." Read verses 21, 23, 27, 28. Her children are well taken care of and lack for nothing, as is indicated.

Her Myriad Attributes

She is a woman displaying **leadership** (15, 26), **vision** (21, 25), **reflection** (16), **entrepreneurship** (16, 24) and **strength** (25) among others.

The woman knows and has developed her **talents**. She is skillful with her hands (16, 19-20, 31) and is happy in her undertakings (13). There are specific tasks that are more apt and appropriate for women. Just as there are for men. It is not my intention to name them here. The point is, it is unrealistic to think, let alone impose a 50/50 requirement in equality of jobs. It is also out of place to state that there are positions of employment that cannot be fulfilled by women, as with men. Some women are better and more qualified to accomplish certain tasks and occupy certain positions than their masculine counterparts. We can say the same of men.

ALL women can fill big shoes. The story of Katherine Johnson and NASA[11].

---

11. https://youtu.be/5wfrDhgUMGI

The Proverbs 31 woman has her eyes **open to the needs of others**, beyond her family (15, 20). Women are particularly sensitive in this domain.

She is animated by a **positive attitude** (13, 18); this is probably the most encouraging quality of women. They are sympathetic, outgoing, and ready to show it in the right way. The Proverbs 31 woman is a busy-bee who uses her resources correctly and in the most complimentary way. She is considered a *hard worker* by all who know her. Here's a short video about women in Rwanda[12] who particularly stand out as an example because of the hardships the country has experienced.

Down through history and today, there are many wonderful women. Sure, they may not know who God is, and yet, they fulfill the entire list of qualities in Proverbs 31. How many men think about this? We men, all come up short in some ways, but this should not take away from female accomplishments. And especially the will to move forward physically, mentally, and spiritually. The binah-ezer, the wise-helper, never finishes growing and perfecting her art. One hundred women who changed the world[13].

"Every wise woman builds (H1129) her house: but the foolish plucks it down with her hands" (Pro. 14:1).

God built the woman to build. The virtuous woman is a wise-builder. She is a *banah-banah* the double meaning of the word *banah* (H1129).

For that, the Proverbs 31 woman is loved, praised, and recognized by her husband, her children, and indeed, the entire community. "Her children arise up, and call her blessed; her husband also, and he praises her, let her own works praise her in the gates," (verses 28-31). The

---

12. https://youtu.be/DWo6GfY4IQE

13. https://youtu.be/HgFRabY2TAE

gates are where the wise elders gather to administer the city (23). Her accomplishments attest to her values and value (31). A wise woman is an asset to all.

Song of Solomon, Friends & Lovers, Love & Sex

Song of Solomon, a tale of love and sex. A married couple of friends and lovers.

Song of Solomon, one of the most enigmatic books in the Bible. It's about an intimate relationship, but is it only on a physical level of Solomon and the Shulamite woman? Or, is it on a spiritual plane of Christ and the Church? It's the only book in the Bible with no direct reference to God.

The Explanation broaches this subject because we are in Genesis 2:21-24, discussing the creation of the woman. In Genesis 1:27, we discussed the meaning of the Biblical Hebrew words zachar (male)[1] and nekava (female)[2]. The names of the genders have significant sense: preeminence[3] and hole[4]. Please revise those chapter for details, or you

---

1. https://theexplanation.com/male-gender-its-significance-and-why-god-created-it/

2. https://theexplanation.com/female-gender-significance-why-god-created-it/

will not grasp the deeper meaning of these terms. They are used both figuratively and literally. Literally, concerning the sexual act.

I pointed out that human genitals are the prominent, visible identifier of gender and reproduction. But reproduction and particularly sex, which we shall be discussing here, begin way before and end way after the climactic act itself. Human behavior, feelings, emotions, and body functions come into play long before sexual intercourse; this is what the Song of Solomon is all about.

I think that poetically, the Song of Solomon mentions the sexual act or, at least, we can imagine it. In the excerpt below, I have added various translations of the Biblical Hebrew from Strong, which you can verify, study, and enhance using UnlockBibleMeaning.com[5]. Here's a provocative lover's scene with the mutual triggering of sexual desire.

Song of Solomon 1:9, 2:3-10

1:9 I have compared you, O my love, to a company of horses in Pharaoh's chariots. (HE pulls, motivates, goes in the right direction...)

2:3 As the apple tree among the trees of the wood, so is my beloved among the sons. I sat down under his shadow with great delight, and his fruit (literal or figurative) was sweet to my taste. (Open to interpretation)

4 He brought me to the *banqueting* (H3196, effervescence-intoxication) house, and his banner over me was love.

---

3. https://theexplanation.com/male-gender-its-significance-and-why-god-created-it/

4. https://theexplanation.com/female-gender-significance-why-god-created-it/

5. http://unlockbiblemeaning.com

5 *Stay* (H5564, take hold, lie hard) me with *flagons*, (H809, something closely pressed together) comfort me with apples: for I am sick of love.

6 His left hand is under my head, and his right hand does *embrace* (H2263 to clasp) me.

7 I charge you, O you daughters of Jerusalem, by the roes, and by the hinds of the field, that you stir not up, nor awake my love, till he please.

8 The voice of my beloved! behold, he comes leaping upon the mountains, skipping upon the hills.

9 My beloved is like a *roe* (H6643, prominence) or a young hart: behold, he stands behind our wall (denoting a mutual possession, their home, hence a married couple), he looks forth at the windows, shewing himself through the lattice.

10 My beloved spake, and said to me, Rise up, my love, my fair one, and *come away* (H3212 to spread).

God built the woman[6] with the attractiveness to arouse a man. From her feet to her legs, hips, breasts, lips, eyes, hair, face, men can and are aroused by various aspects of the female anatomy. Women can use their attributes to gain just about anything they want in this way. I believe we'd all agree on this point.

In the original order of books in the Old Testament, the Song of Solomon follows Psalms, Proverbs and, Job. These four books have been called the Wisdom of God, the Wisdom of Life, the Wisdom of Suffering, the Wisdom of Love. Indeed, the latter focuses on love, both physical and emotional. I mention these other Wisdom books because

---

6. https://theexplanation.com/i-will-build-my-church-yahweh-built-the-woman/

the Song of Solomon does not say everything about love. But we know Solomon had 700 wives and 300 concubines (1 Kings 11:3). That's a lot of women! They were his demise; because of them, Solomon turned his heart away from God. These wisdom books and Genesis 1 and 2 indicate that one man should have one wife, that was God's design from the start. In the next chapter we will focus on that and explain why.

Song of Solomon highlights the love of two human beings, one of which is undoubtedly King Solomon (Song. 8:11). The other being his dove, his beloved, "I am my beloved's, and my beloved is mine" (Song of Solomon 6:3, 9-13). It extols desire, longing for the welling-up of emotions. It is explicit in men and women knowing not only their physical attributes but the power they have and can wield. They are fully aware of the pleasure they can give and procure. They are not prudes; between them, there's consent in sexual desire, craving, play, and love.

Song of Solomon 8:10-11, 14

10 I am a wall, and my breasts like towers: then was I in his eyes as one that found favour.

11 Solomon had a vineyard at Baalhamon; he let out the vineyard to keepers; every one for the fruit thereof was to bring a thousand pieces of silver.

14 Make haste, my beloved, and be you like to a roe or to a young hart upon the mountains of spices.

Some commentators say that the Shulamite woman was his first love. I don't know; there could be other explanations. That said, the other wisdom books, as well as elsewhere in the Bible, make it clear that marriage is with one wife.

It needs to be made clear that God created the woman with all her attractiveness, charms, prettiness, desirability, and persuasiveness. That's why I decided to bring in Song of Solomon during this presentation of the creation of the woman. Every single one of those attributes is pleasurable excitation for both parties when deployed and made available under the proper circumstances.

They are devastating when used under improper circumstances, both for women and men. Just so we understand and keep the books straight, we can say the identical for men. They exude strength, muscular bodies, power, and status. Likewise, these positive attributes, under proper circumstances are assets, but misused, they too are devastating. I'm not pitching for females or males. But this chapter is about females and their attributes.

A woman's charms are for her man (singular) in private. That's the bottom line from a Bible point of view. Song of Solomon shows us that a woman can and should go all out to stay attractive and rightfully seductive for her husband. Her body sways with her movements; her silhouette has golden proportions, and her style is unique. She is made to keep her husband's eyes, mind, desires, and cravings focused on her. Everything about her and every part of her are a sight to behold.

Vine, fragrance, fruit, banqueting, sweet to my taste are poetic ways of discussing the most intimate parts of her body. Her *hole* is not just men's pleasure or for reproduction, as some would have us erroneously believe. Female sexuality is an extraordinary phenomenon. It is a biological marvel that God incorporated into the woman at creation. It is designed for her physical, emotional, and psychological pleasure and enrichment. It is a feminine aspect that starts way before intercourse and lasts a long time after intercourse.

The act, needless to say, impacts males, but not in any way like a female. She is deeply touched emotionally by the physical contact and the bonding relationship; her physical and mental throbbing go far beyond that of a man. Women have an enticing, immensely powerful tool, if I may call it that; it both procures for themselves heightened pleasure and serenity and for their partner both physical and emotional contentment. The song of Solomon openly displays, encourages, and promotes female sexiness and sexuality.

All the wisdom books and all the books of the Bible make it clear that this God designed sexuality is for heterosexual couples within marriage. I'm fully aware of the rules of polygamy in Exodus 21:10 and will explain that a little later in Genesis. The long and the short of it is God ALLOWED multiple wives because of the hardness of human hearts (Mark 10:5-6). But it was NOT intended that way at all from the beginning, as Christ made clear. The Bible teaching is one husband for one wife with sexual relations delighted in, to the fullest, by this couple.

Female attributes are an integral and vital component of all healthy women. They have a desire and need to both give and receive sexuality.

From a Bible point of view, this give-and-take is only within a specific environment. That context is marriage and nothing else. In today's modern progressive society and world of moral freedom, such a statement sounds prude and out of place. Be it as it may, the public exhibition of sexuality is one of the causes of the deep malaise we witness in the relationships between men and women today.

Internet, TV, movies, magazines, media, social networks, publicity, clothing, anything that can display women's attributes are doing so. The Song of Solomon's sexuality should be exercised in private; instead, it is on public display. What should attract a husband now attracts hordes of men; this is not to remove blame from men and the negative roles of many. Both parties are responsible for this degraded situation.

There are all sorts of arguments, the pro and con supporters can invoke to bulwark their case. And I have no intention of getting into such a debate. Song of Solomon reveals the goodness of feminine sexuality. The creation of women endowed with their warmth, charms, and delights in Genesis 2 is a given. In the same light, Genesis 2:24 clearly states that sex between a man and woman is reserved for a married couple in their private quarters. I shall expound on this over the next couple of chapters in the context of the creation of women. *The Explanation* will explain why it is for a married couple alone. And why friendship is vital before getting married and a basic value for a happy marriage.

Public Sexuality - Audit

It so happens that last night I watched a TV documentary and commentary on pornography. Its ready availability with ease, via the internet, is hallucinating. In spite of laws, at least in France, that order adult sites to warn potential viewers about the nature of what they're about to see, there's little compliance. A search on a cell phone in Google with even anodyne keywords can give a seven-year-old access to porn sites. They come unrequested and unbeknown to kids.

Youngsters are getting their sex education from pornography. Sex acts by paid actors with *perfect* erect genitals have become the norm by which youngsters measure themselves, coming up very short. Girls are requesting plastic surgery to correct their genitals, and boys learn that women are objects at their disposal. One of the panel members who works with youth said, 100% of youngsters had seen pornography at a very young age, around ten-years-old. And the situation is worsening, if it can. Teachers and schools, those dealing directly with kids and young people, are pulling their hair out, many are overwhelmed by the state of affairs.

This situation is far from limited to our youth. I discussed the adult scene[7], which is, unfortunately, no better. The point isn't whether we're pessimistic or optimistic; it is to see why we are in this situation and what we can do to improve this gap between males and females.

The answer is simple: its application difficult. I'm calling a spade a spade. The model for youngsters now is the internet and society replete with their immodest video clips, publicity, exhibitionism, music lyrics, Hollywood, twerking, and nudity. Even comedy plays on sex nowadays, the provocation of female and male stars to outdo each other in trashiness, and the inuendoes, and sexual intrigue in sitcoms.

The real model needs to be PARENTS. Kids should grow up with their MOTHER and FATHER[8], a female and a male. Girls should see and learn what masculinity[9] is by the way their father treats their mother and herself as a daughter. Boys should learn what femininity[10] is by the way their mother treats their father and himself as a son. HOME is where kids go through critical periods[11] when first impressions, emotions, gender biases embed themselves in their minds for life. Youth, adolescence, teenage years, and young adulthood are all the continuum of what society built at the earliest age.

It should not be the role of schools, associations, clubs, organizations, the police, or the army to instill respect for an individual's sexuality and that of the opposite sex. That is the role of the home and parents. Society should conform to home values. And therein lies today's problem. Society has shattered the family and installed its own values: sexual abuse and deviation batter parents and kids day-in, day-out.

---

7. https://theexplanation.com/women-in-the-bible-the-strangest-creation-story-why/

8. https://theexplanation.com/parenting-father-mother-have-essential-complementary-roles/

9. https://theexplanation.com/parenting-father-mother-have-essential-complementary-roles/

10. https://theexplanation.com/parenting-father-mother-have-essential-complementary-roles/

11. https://theexplanation.com/critical-periods-when-babies-and-children-learn/

The more deviation we see and hear, the more it affects our minds and becomes the norm. And we pay the ugly price. Men and boys who want to be *decent* are old-school, and they are often bullied and strong-armed. Women and girls who want to be decent are harassed and badgered, intimidated, and seduced.

The wrong pressure being exercised on men and women today is nearly impossible to withstand. It takes a woman, a massive amount of strength, courage, and endurance to stand up for her virginity, respect of her body, and integrity of her mind. Same with men.

The only way to turn this careening beast around is for adults, all adults, to start or continue a modest way of life. One where they keep their bodies, minds, tongues and acts off of a public sexual agenda. With their life-partner, both can exercise their sensuous sexuality. In the public light, restraint and self-discipline are the order of the day in how to conduct oneself. Will it happen?

The Song of Solomon is an ode to femininity. It reminds us of the attractiveness and sensuality of the feminine gender. Even if God is not mentioned, Solomon, notwithstanding all the mistakes he made, including his womanizing, was in his right senses with this inspiring message. Maybe before his degradation, maybe after learning the lessons from his degradation. Whatever, it is the record of how God built the woman. It is the record of the beauty, the desire, the attractiveness, the loving-kindness, the pleasurable sensations that every woman should be able to identify with, feel, and experience.

Proverbs 31[12] is the woman in public. Song of Solomon is the woman with her husband in private. Both descriptions go together to build the female gender and make her what she is and can be.

---

12. https://theexplanation.com/proverbs-31-feminism-and-womens-rights-what-mix/

3. Ultimate Coherent Completeness

Bone of my bones. Relationship to Womanhood.

Bone of my bone, flesh of my flesh. So said Adam to Eve when he saw the woman God had built for him. Unusual response. Why?

Bone of my bone, flesh of my flesh is not what you'd expect to hear from a man who's just met his bride-to-be. I doubt that Adam could even see any of his future wife's bones. Maybe her cheekbones?! this unlikely statement carries much more meaning than the English translation reveals. We have to delve into the original language, Biblical Hebrew.

To start with, we have to go back to the previous verse, where the text uses the word *rib*. That's a bone.

Genesis 2:22-23

22 And the *rib* (H6763), which the LORD God had taken from man, made he a woman, and brought her to the man.

23 And Adam said, This is now bone of my bones, and flesh of my flesh: she shall be called Woman, because she was taken out of Man.

Physical Woman

Did you know that in the entire Bible, this is the only time the English translation *rib* appears? Yes, undoubtedly, God did take one of Adam's ribs, since it was a *bone*. But there is a more significant meaning here.

H6763

צֵלָע tsêlâ' tsay-law'; or (feminine) צַלְעָה; from H6760 (צָלַע); a rib (as curved), literally (of the body) or figuratively (of a door, i.e. leaf); hence, a side, literally (of a person) or figuratively (of an object or the sky, i.e. quarter); architecturally, a (especially floor or ceiling) timber or plank (single or collective, i.e. a flooring):

KJV - beam, board, chamber, corner, leaf, plank, rib, side (chamber).

H6760

צָלַע tsâla' tsaw-lah'; a primitive root; probably to curve; used only as denominative from H6763 (צָלַע), to limp (as if one-sided):

KJV - halt.

Go over to UnlockBibleMeaning.com[1] and find Genesis 22:22. Verify the word *rib* (H6763), and you'll find it's translated *side* about 40 times.

Adam's *rib* was on his *side*, just like your ribs are. Here's the sleuth work. How can Strong affirm that the root, H6760, of *rib* is to *limp* or *one-sided*? The translators never use the word limp in the Bible! I've given you a clue in Further Study below. It has to do with an essential episode in the life of Jacob.

The point is, Adam's removed side-rib, which figuratively denotes him being one-sided, unbalanced, or limping, was built into a beam, a board, a plank, a side, other nuances of this word *tsala* (H6760). Put in other terms, they SUPPORT the structure, just as the woman was built to support the man. They are to support each other, but in this context, we are explicitly talking about womanhood and her role. The rib, part of the rib-cage, supported Adam. Upon removal, he was lop-sided. God built this same rib into a supportive woman.

After her creation, Adam declared about his rib-woman, you are "*bone* (H6106) of my bone, flesh of my flesh." Look at the Biblical Hebrew meaning of **bone**, especially its *root*, (H6105) or basic construction.

H6106

עֶצֶם 'etsem eh'tsem; from H6105 (עָצַם); a bone (as strong); by extension, the body; figuratively, the substance, i.e. (as pron.) selfsame:

KJV - body, bone, × life, (self-) same, strength, × very.

H6105

עָצַם 'âtsam aw-tsam'; a primitive root; also denominatively (from H6106 (עֶצֶם)) to bind fast, i.e. close (the eyes); intransitively, to be (causatively, make) powerful or numerous; to crunch the bones:

KJV - break the bones, close, be great, be increased, be (wax) mighty(-ier), be more, shut, be(-come, make) strong(-er).

Bone of my bone is expressing a symbolic truth, *strength of my strength*. We, often pejoratively, refer to women as the weaker sex. The Bible refers to the woman as *my strength*, man's strength. Did you notice the translation of H6105, *selfsame*?, this indicates that woman has the SAME strength as man. We're not talking about physical strength here, that's obvious. We're talking about mental strength. So many women are so much stronger than many men. A one-sided man needs a strong woman to lean on. He shouldn't push her over, and she shouldn't have to carry all the weight. The one supports the other. They carry the load together.

Now let's look at the Biblical Hebrew deeper meaning of *flesh*, in the term *flesh of my flesh*.

H1320

בָּשָׂר bâsâr baw-sawr'; from H1319 (בָּשַׂר); flesh (from its freshness); by extension, body, person; also (by euphemistically) the pudenda of a man:

KJV - body, (fat, lean) flesh(-ed), kin, (man-) kind, + nakedness, self, skin.

H1319

בָּשַׂר bâsar baw-sar'; a primitive root; properly, to be fresh, i.e. full (rosy, (figuratively) cheerful); to announce (glad news):

KJV - messenger, preach, publish, shew forth, (bear, bring, carry, preach, good, tell good) tidings.

Likewise, *flesh* is not just pointing us to the outer layer of skin over the skeleton of a human being. H1320 reveals a clear notion of *kin* and *(hu)mankind*. The woman is kin to the man. Physically, they are the same, certainly with different functions and attributes, but the same, nonetheless.

Did you also notice that *basar* (H1319), figuratively, means *rosy* and *cheerful, tell good*. Ask any man if he'd like a cheerful woman by his side. Basar characterizes BOTH the man and the woman. We should have both a cheerful man and a cheerful woman. When one is down, the other should be able to cheer their partner up. Adam states she's bone of MY bone; they are both bone and flesh; this is the mutual support one for the other.

Adam's statement, *bone of my bones, flesh of my flesh*, goes far beyond the physical. The material is even less critical than the immaterial implication. In essence, he's giving the metaphorical reason for her creation, when one is lop-sided and down the other is there, as a beam, to support them. She is bringing her strength and cheerfulness to bear on her husband, and it's reciprocal.

In Genesis 2:20, we read, "but for Adam there was *not found* an help meet for him." With his statement, "this is *now* (H6471) bone of my bones," he's declaring, "wow, this *time* (another translation of H9471) I've found a perfect helpmeet for me." God built him the superb counterpart support.

Spiritual Woman - The Church

Readers of these passages in Genesis 2, like *bone of my bones and flesh of my flesh,* focus on the physical implication. But this refers to a much higher level of spirituality. We've already discussed that implication in Ephesians 5:31-32 "...a *man* shall leave his father and mother, and shall be joined to his *wife*... This is a great mystery: but I speak concerning

Christ and the *church*. The statement *bone of my bones and flesh of my flesh* is New Testament theology directly referring to the Church being part of Christ's bones and flesh. Meditate on the following verse in this light. It precedes the above verse and IS THE GREAT MYSTERY.

Ephesians 5:30, "For ***WE ARE MEMBERS OF HIS BODY, OF HIS FLESH, AND OF HIS BONES.***" I have put that in capitals, italics, and bold because it is the focus and ultimate purpose for the creation of the woman. It is also the primary reason for the way and method of her creation[2] as expounded in these nine verses in Genesis. Yes, it refers to the woman, but even more so, to the Church. The New Testament refers to this overall understanding as WE ARE MEMBERS OF HIS BODY. The body incorporates the flesh, the bones, and the blood of Christ.

Here are some corroborative contexts to drive this point home. I'd say this relationship of "bone of my bones, flesh of my flesh," related to Christ's body, is a new concept for many readers. Take time to study and meditate on this.

- **Hebrews 10:19-20**

19 Having, therefore, brethren, boldness to enter into the holiest by the blood of Jesus,

20 By a new and living way, which he has consecrated for us, through the *veil*, that is to say, his *flesh*; (Sam: we become *flesh of His flesh* joined to Him).

- **Colossians 1:21-22**

21 And you, that were sometime alienated and enemies in your mind by wicked works, yet now has *he reconciled*

---

2. https://theexplanation.com/i-will-build-my-church-yahweh-built-the-woman/

22 In the *body of his flesh* through death, to present you holy and unblameable and unreproveable in his sight:

- **John 6:51, 56**

51 I am the living bread which came down from heaven: if any man eat of this bread, he shall live for ever: and the bread that I will give is my *flesh*, (Sam: Adam gave of himself for the life of Eve) which I will give for the life of the world.

56 He that eats my flesh, and drinks my blood, *dwells in me, and I in him*. (Sam: do you see the union of Christ and His people? That's *flesh of my flesh*)

- **Luke 22:19**

And he took bread, and gave thanks, and brake it, and gave to them, saying, This is my *body* which is *given for you*: this do in remembrance of me. (Sam: the act of communion portrays that we are spiritually the flesh of the Second Man's flesh which He gave for us).

- **Ephesians 5:30**

For we are members of his *body (G4983), of his flesh, and of his bones*. (Sam: this is the meaning of *bone of my bones*. In the New Testament body is associated with flesh and bones).

I've repeated this last verse in Ephesians. Notice below in G4982, the origin of the word *body*, its relation to *helpmeet*, in Genesis. There it refers to *support; here* it is to *heal, preserve, save, do well, make whole*. Those are all roles of both the help-meet-woman and the Church.

G4983

σῶμα sōma so'-mah; From G4982; the body (as a sound whole) used in a very wide application literally or figuratively:

KJV- bodily, body, slave.

G4982

σώζω sōzō sode'-zo; From a primary word σῶς sōs (contraction for the obsolete σάος saos safe); to save that is deliver or protect (literally or figuratively):

KJV - heal, preserve, save (self), do well, be (make) whole.

The man and the woman prefigure Christ and the Church. We find the spiritual counterparts of the physical right here on earth. As God is and does, so humankind is and does. God equipped man to be and do as Himself, in His Image, in His likeness[3]. Man, woman, marriage, children, the Garden of Eden, and even Earth are physical counterparts of God and God's spirit environment. The very brief chart below extrapolates this point and merits a few chapters that we don't have space to cover here, but we will revisit these concepts as we develop *The Explanation*.

---

3. https://theexplanation.com/humans-were-created-in-the-image-of-god-in-his-likeness/

Christ left the Father to establish the Church	as	The man leaves his father to set up his new family	Gen. 1
Christ loves the Church	as	Husband is to love and bind to his wife	Eph.5:25, 33
The Church is to respect Christ	as	The wife is to respect her husband	Eph. 5:33
Christ and the Church are one	as	Christ and those in Christ are one	Eph. 5:30
Christ marries Church	as	Husband marries wife	Rev. 19:7
The Church has (multiplies) children	as	The woman has (multiplies) children	Gen. 1
Jesus and the Church, of which He's the Head, nurture God's children	as	The family composed of the father, who's the head, and mother nurture their children	Eph. 5:29
Jesus and Church *dominate and subdue the earth*	as	Husband and wife *dominate and subdue* their environment. In the proper sense. They have the responsibility to govern.	Gen. 1

One cannot comprehend the *why* of humankind, man, woman, and children nor the fundamental relationships between these members of a family[4], unless we understand that man is in the image of God, how He works, and how He set out His plan for humankind in Genesis chapters 1 and 2.

The primary worldwide human institution of marriage[5] sets the stage for all other types of organizations where government (*dominate* and *subdue* in the proper sense of the terms) is involved.

Christ, Cornerstone of the Church's Stones

4. https://theexplanation.com/family-the-cornerstone-of-human-society/

5. https://theexplanation.com/couple-relationship-binding-husband-and-wife-in-marriage/

We already saw the verb used in Genesis 2: Yahveh *built* the woman[6]. It's the first time in the Creation story that the text uses this verb. It signifies something unique: God *builds* His Assembly, His Church, His Ekklesia. Christ said, "upon this rock I will *build* my church; and the gates of hell shall not prevail against it (Matthew 16:18). You might wonder why there's so much emphasis on the Tabernacle and the Temple in the Old Testament? Why did God instruct such precision building and beauty? They represent the building of the woman; they prefigure the Spiritual Temple, the Church, the spiritual group of God's people. The Woman represents the Church. Her destiny is to give birth to physical children.

The destiny of the Church is to give birth to spiritual children. The Church is a composition of God's people.

Christ is Founder and Cornerstone of the Church

I Peter 2:6

6 Wherefore also it is contained in the scripture, Behold, I lay in Sion a *chief cornerstone*, (Sam: the Husband, the Second Man, Christ) elect, precious: and *he that believes* (the Woman, Wife, Church members of His Body) on him shall not be confounded.

5 You also, as lively stones, are built up a spiritual house... (Sam: God's people are the Church, this is bone of Christ's bones, flesh of Christ's flesh, body of Christ's body).

The Preeminence of Christ and the eminent supporting role of the Church. Christ the Cornerstone and all the other stones built to form a solid spiritual building. It is the combination of the two, the Man and the Woman, the Husband, and the Wife, Christ, and the Church, that

---

6. https://theexplanation.com/i-will-build-my-church-yahweh-built-the-woman/

engender and nurture children to adulthood and triumph. With Christ and the Church, it is victory over *you shall surely die*. It is partaking of the *Tree of Eternal Life*.

Remember **H1319 above,** בָּשַׂר bâsar baw-sar'; a primitive root; properly, to be fresh, i.e. full (rosy, (figuratively) cheerful); to announce (glad news): KJV - messenger, preach, publish, shew forth, (bear, bring, carry, preach, good, tell good) tidings.

Isn't it amazing that flesh carries the meaning, *preach good tidings*!! It is the Woman, the Church, and her role! Of course, it's Christ's role too. Biblical Hebrew word relationships never cease to amaze me. Why would *flesh* mean *good tidings*? Now we know. There's no way to see this in a translation. And there's no way to understand this without comprehending the mystery the Apostle Paul refers to in Ephesians 5.

The Garden of Eden narrative reveals all this basic life knowledge, the first five minutes of the Story of humankind. The plot is right there from the start.

That is the reason this section of the creation of the woman follows *die die*[7] (Genesis 2:17). It is the only remedy to turn the situation around. The Savior and the Church are the only way to save the family of humankind. Their collaboration allows humanity to recover from the tree of death, which all humans merit. Only this way, can we eat of the Tree of Life. From *die die,* God has a plan, via Christ and the Church, to advance humankind to *eternal life*. He has assembled the pieces of the puzzle perfectly. Not one is missing; not one is out-of-place — what a message of good tidings.

Further Study

---

7. *https://theexplanation.com/the-tree-of-knowledge-of-good-and-evil-the-meaning/*

How can Strong, in his concordance, affirm *rib* means *to limp* and *one-sided*?

Understand the beauty of Biblical Hebrew, how the vocabulary, how the words interplay with each other. These are the sixth and seventh keys to mastering Biblical Hebrew[8] to unlock Bible meaning; the usage of roots and individual words that tell stories.

Strong draws this conclusion from the episode about Jacob. Genesis 32:31, "And as he [Jacob] passed over Penuel the sun rose upon him, and he *halted* (H6760) upon his thigh.

H6760. צָלַע tsâla' tsaw-lah'; a primitive root; probably to curve; used only as denominative from H6763 (צֵלָע), to limp (as if one-sided): KJV - halt.

The angel with whom Jacob wrestled all night, until the sun rose, dislocated his thigh joint to end the contest. As a result, Jacob halted, he suffered on *one-side*, causing him to *limp*. I don't know about you, but each time I see this interplay of words, based on the root-meanings, their various nuances, I'm amazed. These are the word stories that open-up insight into Bible meaning.

Man & Woman. In Front, Beside, or Behind?

Marriage relationship. The most challenging relationship between two people. It can be heaven or hell. Here's why.

Traditionally, the marriage relationship is two people of the opposite sex living together for life. Biblically, this is the case. Marriage is the ultimate, the epitome of relationships. Humans are relational beings, and society stands or falls based on relationships.

The Explanation is expounding the eight verses in Genesis 2:18-25 regarding the creation of woman. I've recounted how God took the side of the man[1] and built the woman[2]. How the man declared she is bone of my bones and flesh of my flesh[3]. I could add, *And, then there were TWO*. In an instant, the world population doubled! There were a

---

1. https://theexplanation.com/god-made-a-woman-the-feminine-moment-discover-the-meaning/

2. https://theexplanation.com/i-will-build-my-church-yahweh-built-the-woman/

3. https://theexplanation.com/
   bone-of-my-bone-flesh-of-my-flesh-whats-the-relation-to-womanhood/

man and a woman. There were TWO, and they had to live together for probably 50 years or more (no precision in the Bible) before they gave birth to Cain, their first child.

Like living with someone of the opposite sex for 50 loooooooong years on a big prosperous island. Do you think a marriage relationship is important? And other human relationships? They are vital. Here's what the marriage relationship is.

Genesis 2:18

And the LORD God said, It is not good that the man should be alone; I will make him an *help* (H5828) *meet* (H5048) for him.

A marriage relationship is a man and his female helpmeet. The word *helpmeet* is a bit strange for us today, so let's break it down. We have already looked at help, which is azer (H5828)[4], and is translated by the King James translators with the variants: *help*, and for the root (H5826), *succour* with the idea of *surround* and protect. I pointed out that if you want help, you obtain it from someone BETTER than you are, otherwise, what's the point? At her creation, this *help* is the side taken[5] from the man who describes her as, bone of my bones[6]. She is his mutual support, being better than him in certain domains, that's *azer*.

The woman completes the man just as the man completes the woman. Only as a paired twosome, are they one whole. That is the marriage relationship.

---

4. https://theexplanation.com/helpmeet-the-surprising-god-given-role-of-woman/

5. https://theexplanation.com/
   bone-of-my-bone-flesh-of-my-flesh-whats-the-relation-to-womanhood/

6. https://theexplanation.com/
   bone-of-my-bone-flesh-of-my-flesh-whats-the-relation-to-womanhood/

In Strong's presentation of Genesis 2:18 and *help meet,* there is one Biblical Hebrew word missing, *meet. Meet* can change everything in a marriage. For whatever reason, the online Strong's concordance at UnlockBibleMeaning.com[7] doesn't display this reference. But it does in the Interlinear where we find H5048 based on the root H5046. In the online Interlinear, the word *neged* is translated *suitable*, which I think is quite appropriate.

H5048

נֶגֶד neged neh'-ghed; from H5046 (נָגַד); a front, i.e. part opposite; specifically a counterpart, or mate; usually (adverbial, especially with preposition) over against or before:

KJV - about, (over) against, ✕ aloof, ✕ far (off), ✕ from, over, presence, ✕ other side, sight, ✕ to view.

H5046

נָגַד nâgad naw-gad'; a primitive root; properly, to front, i.e. stand boldly out opposite; by implication (causatively), to manifest; figuratively, to announce (always by word of mouth to one present); specifically, to expose, predict, explain, praise:

KJV - bewray, ✕ certainly, certify, declare(-ing), denounce, expound, ✕ fully, messenger, plainly, profess, rehearse, report, shew (forth), speak, ✕ surely, tell, utter.[/box]

Please take a little time to read the translations of H5048 carefully. This Biblical Hebrew word jerks you into the second key of mastering Biblical Hebrew[8]; the SAME word can have different, even opposite,

---

7. http://unlockbiblemeaning.com

meanings. *Neged* is translated, *about* (with the idea of *round about*) *over against, presence*. This female *help* is present, round about. Strong's definition clarifies with *counterpart, opposite, over against*, and *before*. The Biblical Hebrew word *neged* reflects all these differences and contrasts of meaning. Impossible to know in English, hence the lack of understanding.

I entitled this chapter, Man & Woman. In Front, Beside, or Behind? The idea is, to try and make it clear WHERE the position of the woman can be with regard to the man, and the man in relation to the woman. One word, *neged*, projects all these positions.

When you have two people in movement, there's always a relative position between them. One is either in FRONT of, BESIDE or BEHIND the other. Three-dimensionally, they could also be OVER, BESIDE, or UNDER one another. The Biblical Hebrew word allows for ALL these scenarios. And therein lies the answer to both the tranquility and the turmoil we find in the marriage relationship. As well as any relationship between two or more people: in business, child-parent, student-teacher, gangs, workplace, or other relational situations.

Where are the players (the husband and wife), one in relation to the other? Are they *in front, beside* or *behind*? Each should be OCCUPYING the CORRECT POSITION at the RIGHT MOMENT. Then there is harmony and proper support. If not, there's chaos and confusion.

The passing skills and soccer moves of the Barcelona football team beautifully illustrate such positioning in this video[9]. Even if you're not a soccer player, watch the first minute or two with the exchanges between the two players as they pass the ball between themselves.

---

8. https://theexplanation.com/each-biblical-hebrew-word-is-a-precious-jewel-to-be-discovered/

9. https://youtu.be/NpdQADW0WXk

Notice that one is BEHIND, BESIDE, and then IN FRONT of the other. What's important is the coordination so that EACH can SUPPORT their partner.

When the *behind, beside, in front* works, it's perfection. Each player is sometimes behind, beside and in front of the other, they coordinate their movements. If one player is out of place, there's IMbalance. If one player is playing selfishly by holding on to the ball, there's IMbalance. Do you see the relationship with a married couple?

God created woman to be a help, a support, beside her husband. Sometimes, she has to be OUT FRONT to motivate, encourage, show and give him what he does NOT possess (understanding about relationships or emotional empathy, etc.). Sometimes she has to be BEHIND him and receive instruction (to bear her up when under duress, or face a difficult decision, etc.). Sometimes she has to be BESIDE him with a frank exchange. This *NEGED* is her FEMININE EMINENT role toward her husband. Likewise, this *NEGED* is his MASCULINE EMINENT role toward his wife.

It's like juggling with the husband and wife as you can see in this video[10], each carrying the ball and knowing how to pass it and receive it. Correct positioning, balance, and equilibrium are vital. Each has a specific role; each must play THEIR role and NOT the part of the other.

It is not my intention to get into the details of what a woman's forte is and what a man's forte is. We have already seen that God set two significant goals for humankind. Rulership and relationships[11]. The GENERAL sharing of these roles puts the men more on the RULERSHIP side and the women more on the RELATIONSHIP side. It's equality with different purposes[12].

---

10. https://youtu.be/PZ4s_bvUGA4

11. https://theexplanation.com/genesis-1-reveals-basics-social-relations-rulership/

Absolutely keeping in mind that you can NOT RULE WITHOUT RELATIONS and you can NOT have RELATIONS WITHOUT RULE. That is where the balance comes in.

All of the above is theory. But if we translate it into practical reality, we can express it this way. A family has a preeminent leader, the husband, with an eminent relational helper, his wife. He cannot rule without the relational help, and she cannot be relational without proper rulership.

Mutual LOVE between a man and a woman is striving for that balance. When two players are in perpetual movement, it's hard to reach that equilibrium. When both are pulling together, there's a likelihood that the balance can be struck. That is a beautiful marriage union. When one or the other of the twosome is playing solo, or not at all, then everything is out of sync. That is a disastrous marriage.

Below are the different balls EACH partner, the husband, AND the wife constantly juggle in their *ruling* and *relational* marriage union. I've highlighted them in italics, that's a lot of balls to keep up in the air!

I Corinthians 13:4-7

4 Charity (Sam, this is *love*) *suffers long*, and is *kind*; charity *envies not*; charity *vaunts not itself*, is *not puffed up*,

5 Does *not behave itself unseemly*, seeks not her (Sam, read *its*) own, is *not easily provoked*, *thinks no evil*;

6 *Rejoices not in iniquity*, but *rejoices in the truth*;

7 *Bears all things, believes all things, hopes all things, endures all things.*

---

12. https://theexplanation.com/gender-equality-gender-inequality-or-gender-compatibility/

Imagine a man juggling these PREEMINENT RULERSHIP balls perfectly, Image his wife balancing these EMINENT RELATIONAL HELP balls perfectly. That's love. Imagine any two people, business partners, mother and adolescent, co-workers, workers, and management, balancing these rulership and relational balls properly. Say goodbye to strife, bickering, fighting, and killing.

Humans, men, and women, whoever we are, will never have all the balls up in the air, perfectly juggling them at all times. BUT, if we tried a little harder, teaching ourselves and our children from the youngest age, that's the responsibility of parents. How to juggle the balls of *not easily provoked*, *bearing all things*, the right approach to *iniquity* and *truth*, etc., then, and only then would we have better rulership and relations between members of the complementary sexes[13]. Remember, they're NOT opposite; we need the attributes of EACH gender.

It's only when the male and female play their respective roles and NEGED mirrors side-by-side OR CORRECTLY in-front OR behind each other, that harmony can be instituted.

Don't misread what I'm saying here. Some women have better *masculine* skills than men (plumbers, pilots). Some men have better *feminine* skills than women. (nurses, teachers). That's part of life and to be expected. We need to accept these special amazing people for what they are. We'll never have, nor should we strive to have a 50/50 break in plumbers and nurses. The genders are equal but different[14]; this is what NEGED shows us. We have to occupy the right position based on each's talents and skills. We all have to make an effort to fit ourselves into the WHOLE GAME. And each of us must allow others to fit themselves into the WHOLE GAME.

---

13. https://theexplanation.com/parenting-father-mother-have-essential-complementary-roles/

14. https://theexplanation.com/gender-equality-gender-inequality-or-gender-compatibility/

Women have played essential roles in all of humankind's undertakings. Katherine Johnson is an example of a mathematical genius mind[15]. Her whole story is the movie, *Hidden Figures*. Whether it's outer space or marriage, there's a great woman in the thoughts of every great man, and there's a great woman beside (not behind) every great man.

A marriage relationship as with inter-gender relationships can be heaven or hell. It depends on the whereabouts of NEGED. Daily we hear and read about heavenly and hellish relationships[16]. Here is a smattering of both positive (correct *neged* placement) and negative (INcorrect *neged* placement) articles[17]. Men, women, husbands, wives, sex, harassment, #metoo, clergy, and public immodesty have all become subjects of controversy, as to what is allowed and what is not allowed. Genders are not positioning themselves correctly one to the other.

Women have a tremendous role in the professional world, as we saw in Proverbs 31[18]. Women have a predominant role in sexuality, as we saw in the Song of Solomon[19]. But both these roles have to be played BESIDE (neged) their partner and the male gender in general, likewise with men assuming their positions of leadership.

Motherly love and fatherly authority. The counterpart is fatherly love and maternal authority. In the absence of the father, for whatever reason, the mother should and must exercise her motherly authority. In this case, she is rightfully in front of (neged) the father. In the absence of the mother, the father should and must exercise his fatherly love. In this case, he is rightfully in front of (neged) the mother.

---

15. https://youtu.be/4rT8-gbkqCE

16. https://theexplanation.com/audit-of-the-universe-hashtags-that-corroborate-the-explanation/

17. https://theexplanation.com/audit-of-the-universe-hashtags-that-corroborate-the-explanation/

18. https://theexplanation.com/proverbs-31-feminism-and-womens-rights-what-mix/

19. https://theexplanation.com/song-of-solomon-friends-and-lovers-love-and-sex/

Women make a difference. They are bridges connecting the members of their family together. They cement relationships and make organizations work[20]. They have incredible empathy and communication skills with the ability to use language adroitly and compassionately. The female gender is overflowing with feelings, imagination, intuition, rhythm, holistic thinking; they have dreams, take initiatives, and reach success[21].

At the foundation of each home is a woman. Their essential role in society is indisputable. Men and women, husbands and wives, parents, and children live together. It can be side-by-side (neged) or face-to-face (neged). God created a female *helpmeet* for the lonely male; the *meet* (neged) can be suitable or unsuitable, appropriate or inappropriate, heaven or hell. The Biblical Hebrew allows for both. God has given free will[22] to males and females for them to be side-by-side or face-to-face.

Living a lifelong twosome relationship, with men and women responsibly taking their respective positions, one with the other is what the Bible recommends. In the next chapter, we'll see that positive *neged* brings the two together to form one.

---

20. http://women-initiative-foundation.com/

21. https://www.fondationorange.com/-Coups-de-coeur-O-Feminin-?lang=en

22. https://theexplanation.com/free-will-we-all-possess-it-but-we-cant-always-utilize-it/

One Flesh, Inseparable, Together Forever

One flesh is a two-word description of marriage. The Biblical Hebrew and the context reveal so much more. It's the ultimate goal of humankind.

One flesh, in Genesis, is traditionally associated with the marriage union. Two human beings, biblically, a male and a female, joined together. It's definitely that. But that's only the tip of the iceberg; this is the finality of the Creation week. One flesh points to the culmination of God's plan. Here's the more profound meaning.

We're approaching the end of *The Explanation* of Genesis 2. The entire chapter is the expansion of Genesis 1:27. It reveals the details of the creation of man and woman and the physical relationship between them. We tend to focus on the translation, which points to marriage. Rightfully so, but this is only a minor aspect of the infinite plan of God.

Genesis 1 and 2 reveal the Bible plot, God's entire story of humankind; this is the first five minutes of the play, and God is setting the stage.

Consider this:

Genesis 1:27

So God created man (H120, this is NOT the gender this is humankind, all humans) in his own image, in the image of God created he him (humankind); male and female created he them.

The above verse teaches us that humans have God's image. God's image comprises BOTH male and female. When God created the male and the female, He took His UNIQUE Image and separated it into TWO parts, two separate, compatible human beings, male and female. Each with a different PART of His image. Together, they possessed the WHOLE image.

Genesis 2, with the detailed creation of the male and the female, gives vivid details of Genesis 1:27, concluding with verses 22-24.

Genesis 2:22-24

22 And the rib, which the Lord God had taken from man, made he a woman, and **brought her to the man.**

23 And Adam said, This is now bone of my bones, and flesh of my flesh: she shall be called Woman, because **she was taken out of Man.**

24 Therefore shall a man leave his father and his mother, and shall cleave to his wife: and **they shall be one flesh.**

I've already expounded on the rib made into a woman[1], bone of my bone, and flesh of my flesh[2]. Now, step back and look to the whole picture of Gen. 1:27 and Gen. 2:24. First, God SEPARATES His image into TWO (male and female). Then He brings the female to the male, and they are to CLEAVE together and become ONE FLESH.

I want you to see the order of events in the above three verses. God SEPARATES them only to COMBINE them again. Why would you want to separate something and then combine it again? Outwardly, it doesn't make sense, leave it as it is, combined in ONE Image, the image of God.

Understanding the answer to that question tells us the ENTIRE PLAN of God. WHY He created HUMANKIND. WHY He created MALE and FEMALE, it goes far beyond the admirable institution of marriage, which, of course, it includes.

Male and Female = Christ and Church

I've already pointed out the relationship between the male and female to Christ and the Church[3].

Ephesians 5:31-32

31 For this cause shall a man leave his father and mother, and shall be joined to his wife, and they two shall be one flesh.

32 This is a great mystery: but I speak concerning Christ and the church.

---

1. https://theexplanation.com/god-created-woman-and-reveals-humankinds-future/

2. https://theexplanation.com/
bone-of-my-bone-flesh-of-my-flesh-whats-the-relation-to-womanhood/

3. https://theexplanation.com/one-of-a-kind-woman-man-couple-yahveh-elohim-lesson/

The profoundness of this sacred text reveals that Adam was the first imperfect man who prefigured Christ, the second perfect man. Eve was the first imperfect female who prefigured the made-perfect Church. The Father presents the bride, the Church, to Christ at His Second Coming. And the TWO are JOINED TOGETHER to become ONE. Genesis 1:22-24 prophecies the incarnation of Christ (the man), His FIRST coming to Earth, some two-thousand years ago. It further prophecies His establishment of God's Church (the woman). And, ultimately, the marriage of Christ and His Church.

I cannot get into all the details of these momentous, astounding events: the culmination of God's plan for humankind. A vital, but intermediary step will occur when all of God's people (both, those who have died and those who are alive at Christ's Return) will inherit IMMORTALITY (1 Corinthians 15:51-54), like Christ. They will have the IMAGE of GOD.

That's why Christ said they would NOT marry but be like the angels. (Luke 20:35-36, "But they which shall be accounted worthy to obtain that world, and the resurrection from the dead, neither marry, nor are given in marriage: 36 Neither can they die any more: for they are equal to the angels; and are the children of God, being the children of the resurrection.") God's sons and daughters will have God's COMBINED IMAGE, the perfect balanced image of male and female described in Genesis 1:27. The mystery is grandiose.

Let's verify this by taking a closer look at the Biblical Hebrew and corroborating this scenario with New Testament theology. There's NO difference between the profound message of God in what we call the Old and New Testaments. There are different circumstances and situations; the Old is a precursor of the New. But, the underlying message of both is identical just as Adam and Eve (Old Testament) are precursors of Christ and the Church (New Testament). Physical and

Spiritual representing TWO sides of ONE, and ONLY ONE coin. There are continuity and corroboration.

Taken out of man but bone of his bone

Bone of my bones, flesh of my flesh has become such an idiomatic expression that many might not even realize what its origin is. Even if they do, do they grasp the implication or rather imbrication, of how they *fit together?* To describe this enmeshment, we have two couples of words: male + female, man + woman. If you go back and re-read the explanation of zachar[4] (male) and nekava[5] (female) you'll see that this reveals two separate independent entities. Each equal before God, and united with each other, let's say two meshed into one.

From the formation of the latter pair, we have, issuing from the one-man the second individual, one becoming two. When you put this together, male and female, man and woman are interwoven, interlaced, interlocked together, in a communal adventure. Mutually, in concert, man with woman, woman with man forge ahead as a single unit. Together they are the overseeing human masterpieces of God's creation, in the adventurous voyage their Creator has in store for this inseparable couple. Here are the unity and indivisible nature of the man and the woman.

1 Cor 11:8-12

8 For the man is not of the woman; but the woman of the man.

9 Neither was the man created for the woman; but the woman for the man.

---

4. https://theexplanation.com/male-gender-its-significance-and-why-god-created-it/

5. https://theexplanation.com/female-gender-significance-why-god-created-it/

10 For this cause ought the woman to have power on her head because of the angels.

11 Nevertheless neither is the man without the woman, neither the woman without the man, in the Lord.

12 For as the woman is of the man, even so is the man also by the woman; but all things of God.

The Lord brought her to the man

The Lord God brought her to the man (Gen 2:22). It's akin to a father walking his daughter down the aisle to present her to her future husband. In New Testament language, God presents the Church to Christ. Once again, we find Genesis projecting us into the future.

Revelation 21:2

2 And I John saw the holy city, new Jerusalem, coming down from God out of heaven, prepared as a bride adorned for her husband.

Rev. 19:7-8

7 Let us be glad and rejoice, and give honour to him: for the marriage of the Lamb is come, and his wife has made herself ready.

8 And to her was granted that she should be arrayed in fine linen, clean and white: for the fine linen is the righteousness of saints.

God's plan starts in Genesis and culminates in Revelation with both books combining to present the same events. The first on a physical plane to prefigure the second on a spiritual plane. The woman brought to the man. The righteous saints (the Church also representing New Jerusalem) presented, as the bride, by God to the Lamb, Jesus Christ.

Leave and cleave to Church alone!

I used to be a diamond cleaver. The idea is to SPLIT a raw stone right through an impurity so you'd have two smaller but purer stones. In the context of Genesis and Revelation, cleave means exactly the opposite. In modern Hebrew, the word in Genesis 2:24 is used for *glue*. That translates the concept of husband and wife, Christ and the Church glued together in total oneness. You can verify these references at UnlockBibleMeaning.com[6].

H1692

דָּבַק dâbaq, daw-bak'; a primitive root; properly, to impinge, i.e. cling or adhere; figuratively, to catch by pursuit

KJV: abide fast, cleave (fast together), follow close (hard after), be joined (together), keep (fast), overtake, pursue hard, stick, take.

Again, we see the parallel between physical marriage and spiritual marriage; this leads to the ONE flesh. This parallel is so real; it helps us understand a couple of other points.

1. The Lord, in the Old Testament, the future Jesus Christ, was MARRIED to Old Testament Israel. If you haven't heard this concept before, here it is in Isaiah 54:5, "For your Maker is your husband; the Lord of hosts is his name; and your Redeemer the Holy One of Israel; The God of the whole earth shall he be called."

---

6. http://unlockbiblemeaning.com

That verse carries a lot of explanation. Your Maker means Creator. Very relevant to Genesis 1 and 2, where we're talking about Creation. His name is the Lord, that is YAHVEH[7]. And YAHVEH is the husband of Israel. That is a marriage relationship, and marriage is binding until death (1 Corinthians 7:39). Since that's marriage law, under those circumstances, the Lord could NOT marry the New Testament Church, that would be bigamy. But, when Christ died, His former marriage ENDED. He is now free to marry the Church.

His death liberated Him from that former union so He could take His new Bride, the Church. Old Testament Israel had been a *neged-against*[8] wife. His new bride is to be an azer-neged, a helpmeet, a suitable helper[9], a *neged-beside*[10], at His right side for all eternity. We could go much more in-depth about this, but not now.

2. **The idea that Christ married Mary Magdalene is nonsense**. Spurious books, including some that are considered sacred, refer to Jesus in a marital state with Mary, even with children. The Da Vinci Code, among other works of fiction, popularized this idea. It is false information. As Isaiah says above, Christ was ALREADY married to ancient Israel. He could not marry anyone during His lifetime on Earth.

The Lord was *glued* to the Old Testament nation of Israel. He will be married and glued to the New Testament Church.

One Flesh

How glued is glued? The last two words of verse 24 answer that question.

---

7. https://theexplanation.com/yahweh-yahveh-meaning-identity-gods-name/

8. *https://theexplanation.com/marriage-relationship-man-woman-in-front-beside-or-behind/*

9. https://theexplanation.com/helpmeet-the-surprising-god-given-role-of-woman/

10. *https://theexplanation.com/marriage-relationship-man-woman-in-front-beside-or-behind/*

Genesis 2:24

Therefore shall a man leave his father and his mother, and shall cleave to his wife: and they shall be *one* (H259) *flesh* (H1320).

Here's the understanding of the Biblical Hebrew for *one*.

H259

אֶחָד 'echad (ekh-awd'); a numeral from OT:258; properly, united, i.e. one; or (as an ordinal) first:

KJV - a, alike, alone, altogether, and, any (-thing), apiece, a certain, [daily-], each (one), eleven, every, few, first, highway, a man, once, one, only, other, some, together,

H258

אָחַד 'achad (aw-khad'); perhaps a primitive root; to unify, i.e. (figuratively) collect (one's thoughts):

KJV - go one way or other.

H259 is the word for the cardinal number 1 (one), that's togetherness, it can neither be added to nor divided.

Strong does not associate the next words with echad (H259), but I'm taking the liberty of doing so. Why? Because the aleph (א) of H259 and the yod (') of H3161 are interchangeable letters, (like vowels). While the other two consonants (חד) are common to both words, the key to understanding is the meaning — notice, particularly H3173, *darling*, and *solitary*. Being *Christ's darling* is the epitome of the positive sense of *one flesh*. That is a manner of speech, but you see what I mean.

On the other hand, the second key to mastering Biblical Hebrew[11] comes into full play here with the word *solitary*. The total opposite of *darling*, it means being estranged from, cut off from Christ. Now, the translation of H258 makes even more sense, *go one way or other*. Humans have one of two choices. Becoming Christ's darling OR being alone and solitary. Think about it. That's the story of the two Trees, the choice between Life and Death.

H3161

יָחַד yachad (yaw-khad'); a primitive root; to be (or become) one:

KJV - join, unite.

H3162

יַחַד yachad (yakh'-ad); from OT:3161; properly, a unit, i.e. (adverb) unitedly: -alike, at all (once), both, likewise, only, (al-) together, withal.

H3173

יָחִיד yachiyd (yaw-kheed'); from OT:3161; properly, united, i.e. sole; by implication, beloved; also lonely; (feminine) the life (as not to be replaced):

KJV - darling, desolate, only (child, son), solitary.

Christ and the Church are well imbricated, as you can see. Here are some of the explicit Words of Christ:

"At that day you shall know that I am in my Father, and **you in me**, and **I in you**" (John 14:20). "He that eats my flesh, and drinks my blood,

---

11. https://theexplanation.com/each-biblical-hebrew-word-is-a-precious-jewel-to-be-discovered/

dwells in me, and **I in him**" (John 6:56). "I am the vine, you are the branches: He that **abides in me**, and **I in him**, the same brings forth much fruit: for without me you can do nothing" (John 15:5).

God's people are IN Christ, and Christ is IN them. You can't get any more ONE and unified than that.

Flesh

We already discussed *flesh* when we elaborated flesh of my flesh[12]. But let's remind ourselves of the root or basis for the Biblical Hebrew word *flesh*.

H1320

בָּשָׂר basar (baw-sawr'); from OT:1319; flesh (from its freshness); by extension, body, person; also (by euphem.) the pudenda of a man:

KJV - body, [fat, lean] flesh [-ed], kin, [man-] kind, nakednessself,, skin.

H1319

בָּשַׂר basar (baw-sar'); a primitive root; properly, to be fresh, i.e. full (rosy, (figuratively) cheerful); to announce (glad news):

KJV - messenger, preach, publish, shew forth, (bear, bring, carry, preach, good, tell good) tidings.

Notice: preach, publish GOOD TIDINGS. Yes, that's old English, but you understand it. *One flesh* means the good news of being Christ's

---

12. https://theexplanation.com/

   bone-of-my-bone-flesh-of-my-flesh-whats-the-relation-to-womanhood/

helpmeet. It's an excellent message published from the beginning of Creation. It's the fabulous outcome of the creation of man and woman, the advent of Christ and His Church. What could be better news than that? It's the Gospel - the Good News of what God has planned for all humanity.

Only through the UNION of Christ and the Church, His Church, the One He founded, of which He's the Cornerstone, which He nurtures, betroths and marries, can God's plan be accomplished.

Creation story Ending: Naked and Not Ashamed

The Conclusion of the Creation Story
is NOT simply:

Naked and not Ashamed

Genesis 2:25 says:

**They were both,
the man and his wife,**

Wise and not Confused

TheExplanation.com

The Creation story ends with the male and the female being naked and not ashamed. This translation is only partially correct. It's a total letdown.

The Creation story is the narration of God creating the Universe and everything in it down to the male[1] and female[2] and the marriage union[3]. A unique undertaking, even for God. This incredible project ends by discussing nakedness and shamefulness. Really?! Think, this is totally out of place. It's like completing the story of the modernization of Saudi Arabia with "it shined in the sun and was not overheated."

---

1. https://theexplanation.com/male-gender-its-significance-and-why-god-created-it/

2. https://theexplanation.com/female-gender-significance-why-god-created-it/

3. https://theexplanation.com/marriage-relationship-man-woman-in-front-beside-or-behind/

Genesis 2 details the creation of the man[4] and the woman[5]. It goes to great lengths to explain the relationship of the woman to the man[6] and particularly their oneness[7]. The last two words of verse 24 are one flesh; this appears to be the culmination of the Creation story. Then, we read:

Genesis 2:25

And they were both naked, the man and his wife, and were not ashamed.

What an anticlimax, even a disappointment. Imagine being present and witnessing what took place during the entire Creation week. Seeing Earth take shape with its ultramarine oceans[8], lush land, colorful plants[9], populated with roaming animals[10] and finally a couple of human beings. Would you have exclaimed in wonderment, "Wow, they're both naked and not ashamed." You might have thought as much, but this is far short of the entirety of the scene before you.

The key to unlocking the meaning of this concluding phrase resides in Biblical Hebrew. In English, with "naked and not ashamed," we receive a true, but very very limited picture of the conclusion of the Creation story. Let's dig for the gold nuggets of understanding.

H6174

4. https://theexplanation.com/god-breathed-nostrils-dust-man/

5. https://theexplanation.com/i-will-build-my-church-yahweh-built-the-woman/

6. https://theexplanation.com/
   bone-of-my-bone-flesh-of-my-flesh-whats-the-relation-to-womanhood/

7. https://theexplanation.com/one-flesh-ultimately-inseparable-together-forever/

8. https://theexplanation.com/
   dry-land-seas-and-flora-why-this-combination-on-day-3-of-creation/

9. https://theexplanation.com/
   dry-land-seas-and-flora-why-this-combination-on-day-3-of-creation/

10. https://theexplanation.com/creation-day-5-and-6-god-created-fish-fowl-and-fauna/

עָרוֹם `arowm (aw-rome'); or `arom (aw-rome'); from OT:6191 (in its original sense); nude, either partially or totally:

KJV - naked.

H6191

עָרַם `aram (aw-ram'); a primitive root; properly, to be (or make) bare; but used only in the derivative sense (through the idea perhaps of smoothness) to be cunning (usually in a bad sense):

KJV - very, beware, take crafty [counsel], be prudent, deal subtilly.

H6195

עָרְמָה 'ormâh or-maw'; feminine of H6193 (עָרֵם); trickery; or (in a good sense) discretion:

KJV – guile, prudence, subtilty, wilily, wisdom.

I've added H6195 to this context. You'll notice that the three root letters[11] of H6195 and H6174 are identical in Hebrew (the מ becomes a ם when it is the final letter of a word, it merely changes format, but it's the same letter). H6195 translates to *prudence* (the translations in the King James Bible follow the *KJV* above). Note the synonym, *wisdom*; that is a more modern, easily understandable version of *prudence*. It is the reason for using the word *wise* in the translation in the image that accompanies this chapter.

---

11. https://theexplanation.com/biblical-hebrew-roots-to-anchor-your-bible-comprehension/

Also notice Strong's comment[12], referring to *cunning*, "usually in a bad sense." We shall see this bad side of *aram* much more in Genesis 3:1. In Genesis 2:25, the focus is on the GOOD side of *aram*. Here's how we can know this without a doubt. Yes, I add without a doubt, because what we are discovering is vital information for the understanding of the Creation story and what God accomplished. Here's God's climactic conclusion, all His effort (if I may call it that) was to reach this pinnacle.

Proverbs 15:5

A fool despises his father's instruction: but he that regards reproof is *prudent* (H6191).

Pro. 19:25

Smite a scorner, and the simple will *beware* (H6191): and reprove one that has understanding, and he will understand knowledge.

Both the man and his wife, the woman, were in this positive state of prudence, simplicity, and bewareness. We'd call this, their mental state or frame of mind. Remember, Genesis 2:7 God breathed the breath of life into the man[13] (only humans on Earth possess this). The *breath of life* is a poor translation of neshama[14], the essence of God's life, the human mind[15] on our physical level. (God also possesses neshama, hence His ability to transmit it).

---

12. http://unlockbiblemeaning.com

13. https://theexplanation.com/god-breathed-nostrils-dust-man/

14. https://theexplanation.com/neshama-meaning-god-given-human-mind/

15. https://theexplanation.com/human-mind-mind-power-neshama-ruach/

Nakedness is referring to the purity of the male and female mind. They were naked, bare of any mud or dirt or anything that remotely reflected a speck of dirt. Their minds were pristine clean.

There are two points to retain from the man's and the woman's nakedness. Firstly, this has to do with their MINDS[16]. Considering this is the culmination of the Creation story, it means that God's ultimate interest in humans is the state of their minds. No room for details here, but New Testament theology confirms this: "Let this mind be in you, which was also in Christ Jesus" (Philippians 2:5).

Secondly, *nakedness* refers to a PURE mind. Throughout the teaching of the New Testament, the emphasis is on this point, "I stir up your pure minds" (2 Peter 3:1), "every man that has this hope in him purifies himself, even as he is pure" (1 John 3:3). As an aside, purity of the mind was also an emphasis in the Old Testament (Psalm 24:3-5, 51:10). But, remember, they did not have the Holy Spirit and what God required of them was the purity of body and actions, NOT thoughts. Hence the 10 Commandments, which refer mainly to physical acts, "you shall not kill." It does not say; you shall not hate. The New Testament says, "you shall not hate," and therefore INCLUDES, "you shall not kill." Enough said, you understand the concept. In Genesis 2:25, the man and the woman had NEW TESTAMENT PURE MINDS.

The result was they were NOT ASHAMED. Here's the deeper meaning.

H954

בּוּשׁ bûwsh boosh; a primitive root; properly, to pale, i.e. by implication to be ashamed; also (by implication) to be disappointed or delayed:

KJV – (be, make, bring to, cause, put to, with, a-) shamed(-d), be (put to) confounded(-fusion), become dry, delay, be long.

Shamed means *confounded* or *confusion*. Look at these verses.

Psalm 22:5

They cried to you, and were delivered: they trusted in you, and were not *confounded* (H954).

Psalm 35:4

Let them be *confounded* (H954) and put to shame that seek after my soul: let them be turned back and brought to confusion that devise my hurt.

Psalm 71:1, 13, 24

In you, O LORD, do I put my trust: let me never be put to *confusion* (H954). 13 Let them be *confounded* (H954) and consumed that are adversaries to my soul; let them be covered with reproach and dishonour that seek my hurt. 24 My tongue also shall talk of your righteousness all the day long: for they are *confounded* (H954), for they are brought to shame, that seek my hurt.

It is logical that if the man and woman had a WISE GODLY MIND, they were NOT CONFUSED.

Put yourself in the first man's and the first woman's shoes (oops, they didn't have shoes! but you know what I mean). They were in a gorgeous, bountiful garden[17]; they were in the presence of tame animals[18] and

---

17. https://theexplanation.com/garden-of-eden-represents-much-more-than-a-garden/

the pleasure of each other's company. They received instruction from their Creator. This teaching was the first they received; they could not compare it, contradict it, or debate it with anything or anyone. It was clear and concise. At this point, the conclusion of the Creation story, there is no confusion.

Both the wisdom and the absence of confusion are MENTAL ATTRIBUTES. Of course, all the other events and items, including the animals, were in a perfect state of *order*. The New Testament teaching confirms this absence of confusion "Wherefore also it is contained in the scripture, Behold, I lay in Sion a chief cornerstone, elect, precious: and he that believes on him shall *not be confounded*" (1 Peter 2:6). Believers become mentally *naked* and *not ashamed*, wise, and not confused. That is the result of being a follower, a son or daughter of God.

From "tohu ve bohu" to "naked and not ashamed."

The Creation story takes us from Gen. 1:1-2 "without form and void" to Gen. 2:25 "wise and not confused." Do you see the juxtaposition of tohu and bohu leading to naked and not ashamed? Everything in between goes crescendo until they reach that climactic conclusion. The in-betweens are stepping-stones in God's plan to reach His ultimate goal.

In these first two chapters of Genesis, we have the ENTIRE plan of God. This plan is not just the PHYSICAL creation (summed up with "naked and not ashamed"); it is the SPIRITUAL Creation of Human Beings, ALL human beings, MALES and FEMALES. We are in this together, each having an equal opportunity to reach that state of wisdom and absence of confusion.

---

18. https://theexplanation.com/rain-falls-on-earth-entirely-because-yahveh-initiated-it/

We could add much here, and I will return to this subject. For now, let me observe that this statement concluding Gen. 2:25 is the climax of *It was good* declared after each of the first five days. Then, *It was very good* at the end of the sixth day. Then, the ultimate, *they were wise and not confused*. Do you see this steady increase in intensity? Again, I can't detail it here, and I can't corroborate what I'm about to say with a specific verse but, remember the seventh day[19]. The meaning of that day of rest includes wisdom and no confusion. It takes the seventh day, the day of God, working with humans (read that chapter)[20] to develop the spiritual purity that characterizes His people. Indeed, you cannot have wisdom and absence of confusion without the Sabbath day.

It starts as tohu and bohu. Throughout the Bible narrative, there are ups-and-downs, as I pointed out in the chapter Confusion > Order > Confusion[21]. Then, in the Creation story, there's the chapter about Christ and the founding of His Church, with His people, and that will end in the future with wisdom and no confusion. This story is *it is Very Good,* multiplied in power by let's say 1,000,000 times; this is the meaning of ONE FLESH[22], the unity of Christ and the Church, the marriage of the Bride and Groom. That is the comprehension of good, very good, excellent tidings[23], another meaning of *flesh* H1319.

The Highest of High Points

The statement, "naked and not ashamed," "wise and not confused" is one of those benchmark declarations that speckle the Bible narrative.

19. https://theexplanation.com/
    god-pursued-his-work-resting-with-adam-and-eve-whom-he-created-to-make/
20. https://theexplanation.com/
    god-pursued-his-work-resting-with-adam-and-eve-whom-he-created-to-make/
21. https://theexplanation.com/ups-and-downs-order-confusion-order-bible-cycle/
22. https://theexplanation.com/one-flesh-ultimately-inseparable-together-forever/
23. https://theexplanation.com/one-flesh-ultimately-inseparable-together-forever/

You'll find them at the beginning and the end of outstanding events or episodes in the Creation story. Here are a few to whet your appetite.

The establishment of the founding father of spiritual humanity: Abraham. "And the Lord said, Shall I hide from Abraham that thing which I do; 18 Seeing that Abraham shall surely become a great and mighty nation, and all the nations of the earth shall be blessed in him? 19 For I know him, that he will command his children and his household after him, and they shall keep the way of the Lord, to do justice and judgment; that the Lord may bring upon Abraham that which he has spoken of him. (Gen. 18:17-19)

You can find such benchmark statements for the beginning of Christ's Ministry, "This is my beloved Son, in whom I am well pleased" (Matthew 3:17). And the end, just before His Crucifixion, "I have glorified you on the earth: I have finished the work which you gave me to do. And now, O Father, glorify you me with your own self with the glory which I had with you before the world was" (John 17:4-5).

And the clincher of all for humankind. The curtains-down conclusion of the entire narrative of humanity; this is the ultimate counterpart to *tohu va bohu*, just as *wise and not confused* is an intermediary benchmark. "And there shall in no wise enter into it (New Jerusalem) any thing that defiles, neither whatsoever works abomination, or makes a lie: but they which are written in the Lamb's book of life" (Revelation 21:27). That's wisdom, oneness and no confusion.

Each one of these statements is a piece in the ongoing assembly of the puzzle picture of the Creation story. You guessed it, or hopefully, I could say, you're beginning to understand that the Creation story is NOT the creation of PHYSICAL humans but the creation of SPIRITUAL CHILDREN, the very SONS, and DAUGHTERS of GOD. The time when every single human being will have had the opportunity to become *wise and not confused* as to the plan of God for themselves individually, and ourselves collectively as humankind, God's creation, that's the real spiritual Creation story.

4. Genesis 1 and 2 – God's Plan for Humans

Sapiens, The Brief, but True Story of Humankind

Sapiens means wise. Only humans have wisdom, be it positive or negative. Only Humans have a history and a story.

Homo Sapiens are the only living creatures who have a dynamic story. Animals live identical lives from generation to generation. Not so with homo sapiens. Their wisdom, (where does that originate?!) allows them to modify their environment in every shape and form. They can choose their destiny, be it the person they live with, their profession, their dwelling, their leisure activities, etc. Of course, not all humans have the same liberty of choice, but that's another matter. Genesis 2 is the story of Sapiens, Homo Sapiens, Wise Man, Wise Humans.

Over the last 60 chapters in two books, *The Explanation* has expanded Genesis 2. We mastered the Biblical Hebrew[1] to unlock the depths of Bible meaning. We now have the full story of God's intention for Sapiens, Humankind. We don't have all the account. For that, we have to continue our study into Genesis 3, and add the role of a paramount character, the Serpent, the Devil. Yes, it exists, more about it, and its devious ways in *Agony of Humankind, and the Antidote*[2], book 7 of *The Explanation* series.

This expounding or commentary on Genesis 2, entitled, *Origin of Woman*, represents book 6 in *The Explanation* series. It follows Inventory of the Universe and Humankind[3], Audit of the Universe[4], Audit of Humankind[5], Origin of the Universe[6], and Origin of Humankind[7]. Even If you're a subscriber to *The Explanation* and read each article weekly, it would be hard to join all the dots. This chapter does just that. It takes all 60 segments, with the links to each one, and relates the coherent completeness of the Story of Sapiens. The whole, unadulterated story of humankind, past, present, and future, told in Genesis 2; this is part of the first five minutes, a full story in itself. It needs Genesis 1 and Genesis 3 to be complete. The rest of the Bible gives the graphic details of Genesis chapters 1-3, from *tohu va bohu* to *naked and not ashamed*, from *chaos and turmoil* to *wisdom and no confusion*.

---

1. https://unlockbiblemeaning.com

2. *https://theexplanation.com/read-all-the-content-of-agony-of-humankind-online/*

3. https://theexplanation.com/inventory/
   read-all-the-content-of-inventory-of-the-universe-online/

4. https://theexplanation.com/read-content-audit-universe-online/

5. https://theexplanation.com/read-all-the-content-of-audit-of-humankind-online/

6. https://theexplanation.com/read-content-origin-universe-online/

7. https://theexplanation.com/read-content-origin-humankind-online/

Sapiens is generally associated with homo, homo sapiens. Wise man, or preferably, *wise human*. There are fundamentally two schools of thought as to how we obtain wisdom and become wise. There's the do-it-yourself method[8]. Or, the get-help from someone who knows-better-than-you[9] method. *The Explanation* adopts the second method. Hence the Story of humankind in Genesis 2.

Our story has eight sections over two books. *Origin of Humankind* (1-5), and *Origin of Woman* (1-3 plus the overviews of God's plan). The narrative takes us from creation through to the ultimate union with God, coherent completeness[10], and one flesh[11]. That's the good news for the future. Here's the entire story; use the links for the details.

Origin of Humankind – The Book

1. Creation of Human Beings

The story of humankind starts in Genesis 1:28 by answering the big question of the real origin of humanity. Were Humans Created, or did Humans Originate? Creation Day 6[12] (*Origin of Humankind* chapter 1.1). Right from this starting point, human reasoning that stands on observation, philosophy, and science parts company from believers in God. The development of Humankind takes two distinctly separate directions.

The Bible indicates Humans have the Likeness of God – What that Means[13] (1.2). When you scrutinize humankind, you can see Godly

---

8. https://theexplanation.com/observation-first-way-human-reasoning/

9. https://theexplanation.com/religion-solution-world-peace/

10. https://theexplanation.com/coherent-completeness-is-the-logical-reasoning-of-the-ssource/

11. https://theexplanation.com/one-flesh-ultimately-inseparable-together-forever/

12. https://theexplanation.com/were-humans-created-or-did-humans-originate-creation-day-6/

13. https://theexplanation.com/humans-have-the-likeness-of-god-what-that-means/

features. Made in the Image of God – The Definition[14] (1.3). Humans are kin to God, not to animals. Humans were created in the image of God, in His Likeness[15] (1.4). They have all the singularities of God, on a human level, of course, like having the ability to plan, create, turn their thoughts and actions into projects and accomplishments. Human Beings – God Created them Equal but Different[16] (1.5), of the seven billion people on Earth, no two are alike, even identical twins. Yet, before God, each one has and especially will have an equal opportunity to become His son or daughter.

Male Gender – Its Significance and Why God Created it[17] (1.6). From his genitalia to his role, males have the preeminence. The significance is that the male represents Christ, and He had and has Preeminence. In Hebrew, *male* is *zachar,* which also means to *remember.* Men are to remember their origin, from God, and also that Christ's Preeminence is that He came to serve (Luke 22:26-27). Likewise, with men.

The Female Gender - its Significance and Why God Created it[18] (1.7). The Hebrew *nekava* signifies *hole,* her genitalia, which, along with her sexual processes, are complementary to the male preeminence. This same hole gives birth and is the only natural way to multiply the population of God's future sons (males) and daughters (females). Males depend on females in that area and many others. The female, as such, *saves* humankind; and occupies a prominent position. The two genders are equal before God; each gender endowed with the complementary masculine and feminine characteristics of God their Father.

---

14. https://theexplanation.com/made-in-the-image-of-god-the-definition/

15. https://theexplanation.com/humans-were-created-in-the-image-of-god-in-his-likeness/

16. https://theexplanation.com/human-beings-god-created-them-equal-but-different/

17. https://theexplanation.com/male-gender-its-significance-and-why-god-created-it/

18. https://theexplanation.com/female-gender-significance-why-god-created-it/

God gave the male and female dominance over all the inanimate and animate creation. Their goal is to Rule Earth – To Rule the World is God's Purpose for Humans[19] (1.8). In *Audit of the Universe,* we asked the question, is the glass of peace and prosperity getting fuller or emptier? It's up to you to answer that question. Consider the state of rulership of this Earth. That is the barometer of how humans are accomplishing their God-given purpose.

There's a second all-important role God has given humankind. God Blessed the Male and the Female – Here's the Meaning[20] (1.9). It is marriage; the underlying key is relationships. The relationship is the beginning, middle, and end of a marriage. If there's no relationship between the man and woman, the marriage will not succeed; this is true, not only in marriage but in every aspect of life, personal, professional, and leisure. Relationships bring happiness and fulfillment, not so, with money and fame.

2. Why Create Humankind?

God created humans to Rule the World. Humankind is on Earth for that Purpose[21] (2.1). Genesis 1 Reveals Basics: Social Relations & Rulership[22] (2.2). Genesis 2 continues to expand and flesh out the fundamentals of Genesis 1. Immediately after creating the man and the woman on the sixth day, On the Seventh Day, God Continues Finishing His Work[23] (2.3). There's no record of the origin of the seven-day week, except in the Bible. Creation Week Reveals God's plan. Remember it[24] (2.4). The restoration of Earth and its preparation for

---

19. https://theexplanation.com/rule-earth-to-rule-the-world-is-gods-purpose-for-humans/

20. https://theexplanation.com/god-blessed-the-male-and-the-female-heres-the-meaning/

21. https://theexplanation.com/rule-the-world-humankind-is-on-earth-for-that-purpose/

22. https://theexplanation.com/genesis-1-reveals-basics-social-relations-rulership/

23. https://theexplanation.com/on-the-seventh-day-god-continues-finishing-his-work/

24. https://theexplanation.com/creation-week-reveals-gods-plan-remember-it/

humankind, which now consumes 21 000 000 000 meals a day (what planet has that type of resources?) allows us to establish the Timeline of History, The Universe, Earth, and Humankind[25] (2.5).

At the beginning of Genesis 2, another VIP Figure appears on the scene, Yahweh or Yahveh. Meaning & Identity of God's Name[26] (2.6). Within the Oneness of Elohim, there's a plurality of Spirit Beings; One Being carries the name Yahweh Elohim. Discover This Inseparable Relationship[27] (2.7). Why the Bible narrative digresses to water: Rain falls on Earth Entirely Because Yahveh Initiated It[28] (2.8). That's the introductory background for what most, even believers, consider a figurative or even fictitious story of creation. However, elsewhere, the Bible shows us The Foolishness of God's Word is True Theology[29] (2.9).

Get ready for Sapiens, the brief but true story of humankind.

3. Creation of Man and the Role of Neshama

The real origin of humanity started when God Created Man. Why the Bible says, God Formed Man[30] (3.1). The composition of a human physical body is commonplace earth From Dust You Came. The Biblical Hebrew Meaning[31] (3.2). The spark of life to animate the lump of clay came when God Breathed into the Nostrils of His Dust Man[32] (3.3). The result of *animated dust* is a Soul, Nephesh, in Biblical Hebrew. Here's the Definition[33] (3.4). The *Breath of Life* God breathed

---

25. https://theexplanation.com/timeline-history-universe-earth-humans/

26. https://theexplanation.com/yahweh-yahveh-meaning-identity-gods-name/

27. https://theexplanation.com/yahweh-elohim-inseparable-relationship/

28. https://theexplanation.com/rain-falls-on-earth-entirely-because-yahveh-initiated-it/

29. https://theexplanation.com/foolishness-gods-word-true-theology/

30. https://theexplanation.com/god-created-man-bible-god-formed-man/

31. https://theexplanation.com/from-dust-you-came-biblical-meaning/

32. https://theexplanation.com/god-breathed-nostrils-dust-man/

into the first man is Neshama Reveals Humankind's Relationship with God[34] (3.5). Only God and humans (not animals) possess *nishmat chayim*. That's plural for Many lives for You and Me? What the Bible Says[35] (3.6).

Can science vanquish the anguish of death? Life and Death are Major Issues. Which One Prevails?[36] (3.7). Life prevails because it's plural and because God has a future for each human, but that's another story. You and I, who can read and understand this, are unique creatures for the following reason: Neshama and Ruach Together Make Humans Human[37] (3.8). And so, we arrive at the biggest mystery with which both religion and science grapple. Neshama Meaning? The God-Given Human Mind[38] (3.9). The mind, not the brain, is the key to the story. Genesis 2 and the creation of man is only ONE VERSE. But from the perspective of answering the question, WHO and WHAT is a human, Genesis 2:7 alone, contains the essential answer, neshama.

4. God's Spirit and Man's spirit

Animals and humans do have a unique *spirit* in common, Ruach, The Core Senses of Sentient Beings[39] (4.1). God's spirit. The ruach Animates all Living Beings[40] (4.2). Just as the understanding of *neshama* is vital, so is that of *ruach*. Two spirits. God's Spirit and the spirit in Humans[41] (4.3). The opening verse of the Bible presents the

---

33. https://theexplanation.com/soul-nephesh-biblical-hebrew-definition/

34. https://theexplanation.com/neshama-humankinds-relationship-god/

35. https://theexplanation.com/many-lives-you-i-bible-says/

36. https://theexplanation.com/life-and-death-major-issues/

37. https://theexplanation.com/neshama-ruach-make-humans-human/

38. https://theexplanation.com/neshama-meaning-god-given-human-mind/

39. https://theexplanation.com/ruach-core-senses-sentient-beings/

40. https://theexplanation.com/gods-spirit-ruach-animates-living-beings/

41. https://theexplanation.com/two-spirits-gods-spirit-spirit-in-humans/

nature of the Spirit of God. The Spirit of God MOVED on the Face of the Waters. Meaning?[42] (4.4).

These are the first five minutes of the movie, the presentation of the characters and forces in play. A Spirit God is the Author, Producer, and Director. Here's the understanding of His role compared to the human part, The Spirit Realm & the Physical Realm Interconnection[43] (4.5). And, the powers at work that put puny universal powers to shame, Fluctuation, or Frequency of the Power of the Spirit[44] (4.6). Yet, human dust people in a dust universe have their role in this cosmic story, Material World, Spiritual World. Are They Compatible?[45] (4.7). Genesis 2 tells us explicitly, WHO WE ARE, Human Person; this is What Defines You as Human[46] (4.8).

5. Mind and the Theory of Everything

Solving the mystery of the human mind. Genesis 2 is down-to-earth. It answers the big questions in life. What confers on homo sapiens their intelligence? Human Mind and Mind Power. Neshama and Ruach[47] (5.1). God is a hands-on caring Creator, The Holy Spirit of God. Its Interrelationship with Humans[48] (5.2). Animals are in the equation, they do have capacities but nothing like humans, here's why, Animal Spirit is Not Spirit Animal, But They are Related[49] (5.3).

---

42. https://theexplanation.com/spirit-of-god-moved-face-waters-meaning/

43. https://theexplanation.com/spirit-realm-physical-realm-interconnection/

44. https://theexplanation.com/fluctuation-frequency-power-spirit/

45. https://theexplanation.com/material-world-spiritual-world-compatible/

46. https://theexplanation.com/human-person-what-defines-you-as-human/

47. https://theexplanation.com/human-mind-mind-power-neshama-ruach/

48. https://theexplanation.com/holy-spirit-of-god-interrelationship-humans/

49. https://theexplanation.com/animal-spirit-not-spirit-animal-but-they-are-related/

The reality of what God gave humans at the instant of their creation, Human Software – God Breathed Neshama into Adam[50] (5.4). Science naturally focuses on the brain, but what about the unseen and immeasurable? Human Brain. Its Role in Consciousness and Mind[51] (5.5). Beyond the mathematical formulas of the physical forces that hold the Universe together, lies something which clenches the physical and spiritual into a tightly knit unit, The Theory of Everything. Universe and Consciousness[52] (5.6). In the end, the physical decays; that's not God's emphasis, the material is a means to the end. That end is spiritual and involves the spirit component in humans. Understanding the Human Mind. Key to God's plan[53] (5.7).

Origin of Woman – The Book

1. In the Garden of Eden

The Garden of Eden, myth, or reality? God had and has a special place for humans. Garden of Eden. Represents Much More than a Garden[54] (1.1). And along comes Evil. God Deliberately Allowed it in the Garden of Eden. Here's Why?[55] (1.2). But there's also a refreshing River of Living Water. The Profound Spiritual Meaning[56] (1.3). That river is the head of the Four Rivers of Eden. Beginning of World Geography[57] (1.4). Not only world geography, but especially the spiritual satiation and nourishment of the entire world.

---

50. https://theexplanation.com/human-software-god-breathed-neshama-adam/

51. https://theexplanation.com/human-brain-role-consciousness-mind/

52. https://theexplanation.com/the-theory-of-everything-universe-consciousness/

53. https://theexplanation.com/understanding-the-human-mind-key-to-gods-plan/

54. https://theexplanation.com/garden-of-eden-represents-much-more-than-a-garden/

55. https://theexplanation.com/evil-god-deliberately-allowed-it-in-garden-of-eden-heres-why/

56. https://theexplanation.com/river-of-living-water-profound-spiritual-meaning/

57. https://theexplanation.com/four-rivers-of-eden-beginning-world-geography/

In this sumptuous Garden, God places the man and woman and a question arises, Dress and Keep Garden of Eden. Man Destined to be a Gardener?[58] (1.5). Why the emphasis on trees? Trees in Eden – Significance of Biblical Hebrew "Tree"[59] (1.6). Amazingly, immediately at the beginning, in the paradisiac Garden of Eden, there's evidence of evil, The Tree of Knowledge of Good and Evil. The Meaning[60] (1.7). Whether it's the tree or the imminent arrival of the Serpent, Bible readers wonder if God Created Evil. NO, He didn't; God Only Creates Good[61] (1.8).

2. Creation of Woman

The last eight verses of Genesis 2 (compared to only one verse for the man) throw the limelight on the creation of woman, Women in the Bible, the Strangest Creation story. Why?[62] (2.1). Without the woman, God's plan is dead in the water. Her arrival is not only complementary to the man but has significant other meaning. One of a Kind: Woman, Man, Couple, Church, Yahveh, Elohim. Lesson?[63] (2.2). God Created Woman and Reveals Humankind's Future[64] (2.3). She is both the complement to the man and Christ as representing the Church. But, like the man, she has a specific place on the chessboard, Helpmeet, The Surprising God Given Role of Woman[65] (2.4).

To fulfill this role, she has been very specially endowed. God Made a Woman. The Feminine Moment. Discover the Meaning[66] (2.5). We're

---

58. https://theexplanation.com/dress-keep-garden-of-eden-man-destined-to-be-a-gardener/

59. https://theexplanation.com/trees-in-eden-significance-of-biblical-hebrew-tree/

60. https://theexplanation.com/the-tree-of-knowledge-of-good-and-evil-the-meaning/

61. https://theexplanation.com/god-created-evil-no-he-didnt-god-only-created-good/

62. https://theexplanation.com/women-in-the-bible-the-strangest-creation-story-why/

63. https://theexplanation.com/one-of-a-kind-woman-man-couple-yahveh-elohim-lesson/

64. https://theexplanation.com/god-created-woman-and-reveals-humankinds-future/

65. https://theexplanation.com/helpmeet-the-surprising-god-given-role-of-woman/

talking about the woman, but there's also something vastly superior taking place. I will Build My Church = Yahweh Built the Woman[67] (2.6). Genesis 2 and the Old Testament are not outmoded. They teach the balanced view of what it means to be feminine, Proverbs 31, Feminism, and Women's Rights. What Mix?[68] (2.7). A good home, with a good husband and wife who can procreate, is the epitome of what relationships and rulership are all about, Song of Solomon, Friends, and Lovers, Love and Sex[69] (2.8).

3. Ultimate Union

The conclusion of Genesis 2 is grandiose. The closeness and unity of the man and woman are bound indelibly, Bone of my bone, flesh of my flesh. What's the Relation to Womanhood?[70] (3.1). The man and the woman are in step with each other. They've learned to walk side-by-side as a bound twosome, Marriage Relationship. Man & Woman. In Front, Beside, or Behind?[71] (3.2). This unity goes far beyond the physical relationship of marriage. It is the good news of the binding of Jesus Christ, the Second Man, with His Wife, the Bride, the Church, to live eternally, One Flesh – Ultimately, Inseparable – Together Forever[72] (3.3).

This phase of God's plan involving humans has the most positive ending. Creation story Conclusion: Naked and Not Ashamed. That's It?![73] (3.4). This correct, but inadequate translation, hides the *Wisdom*

---

66. https://theexplanation.com/god-made-a-woman-the-feminine-moment-discover-the-meaning/

67. https://theexplanation.com/i-will-build-my-church-yahweh-built-the-woman/

68. https://theexplanation.com/proverbs-31-feminism-and-womens-rights-what-mix/

69. https://theexplanation.com/song-of-solomon-friends-and-lovers-love-and-sex/

70. https://theexplanation.com/
    bone-of-my-bone-flesh-of-my-flesh-whats-the-relation-to-womanhood/

71. https://theexplanation.com/marriage-relationship-man-woman-in-front-beside-or-behind/

72. https://theexplanation.com/one-flesh-ultimately-inseparable-together-forever/

and *No Confusion* this verse epitomizes. The story of homo sapiens, wise man, wise humans, will take them from the dust people they are, counting on their wisdom, on a trajectory to Deus Sapiens, Wise Gods. The conclusion is Sons and Daughters endowed with God's Wisdom, Ruling in a perfect Godly Family Relationship.

The rest of the Bible Story gives us the details of that pathway.

Genesis Reveals Who, Why, Where, What, When

God's plan for humankind is revealed in the first two chapters of the Bible. Don't misunderstand the beginning! You won't grasp the rest of the book.

God's plan, His plot is laid bare in Genesis chapters 1 and 2. The first five minutes of the famous TV detective series, Colombo, reveals the intrigue, the instigator, and the protagonist. The rest of the program explains what's going on. Similarly, with the Bible, the first two chapters reveal all the answers to the big questions in life.

No other book[1] and no human reasoning like observation[2], philosophy[3], science[4], or religion[5] have revealed and explained these phenomena.

As we finish *Origin of Woman*[6], we're in a position to answer a good part of all those why questions[7]. Those nagging questions that terminate in endless debates and often, in hot disputes. In Genesis 1 and 2, in a neatly written, tight story, we have real answers to fundamental questions about life.

Further crucial answers to questions like, why is there such confusion in the world? are forthcoming. The answer is in the book *Agony of Humankind and the Antidote*, which is the title of the seventh book in *The Explanation* series. It details the relationship between the three main characters, Yahveh Elohim, the Serpent, and Humanity. It will answer questions like, how can a good God allow such evil to exist? Why situations generally get worse before they get better? Why is humankind so stubborn? And many others.

Theology, Bible, Logical Reasoning, Coherent Completeness

As we answer the why questions in establishing God's plan, or the 5W1H questions, the Who, Why, Where, What, When, and How questions I'd like you to ponder another subject we discussed at the beginning of *Origin of the Universe*. The Sacred Book, Could it be the

---

1. https://theexplanation.com/the-sacred-book-if-it-exists-could-it-possibly-be-the-bible/

2. https://theexplanation.com/observation-first-way-human-reasoning/

3. https://theexplanation.com/philosophy-love-wisdom-whose-wisdom/

4. https://theexplanation.com/science-world-savior-human-reasoning/

5. https://theexplanation.com/religious-belief-mighty-motor-human-reasoning/

6. *https://theexplanation.com/read-all-the-content-of-origin-of-woman-online/*

7. https://theexplanation.com/why-questions-are-the-first-questions-to-ask-about-the-universe/

Bible?[8] As well as the definition of Theology, Coherent Completeness is the Logical Reasoning of the Source[9]. You'll notice that I left out the s/ on s/Source. God's plan, as expounded in Genesis 1 and 2, can only come from the Source.

I believe there's solid evidence for God and the veracity and authenticity of the Bible.

I believe that the Source of the Sacred Book reveals and develops His Plan therein.

I believe that God's plan is made visible and clear through the Biblical Hebrew.

We've developed all these themes in *Origin of the Universe*[10] and *Humankind*[11], and *Origin of Woman* which are Commentaries on Genesis 1 and 2. Please, also note that we have used no exterior, third-party commentaries, or explanations. The Bible, in particular, the Old and New Testaments, totally different eras, totally different objectives, yet so complementary, are the foundation for corroborative texts.

I receive emails with objections to what I write, like flat Earth or Young Earth, the definition of One God. It might be well-meaning, but they are short on coherent completeness. These objections twist the puzzle pieces, and it is impossible to establish ONE picture from the multitude of millions of parts that compose the image.

Genesis 1 and 2 encompass all the pieces in the most coherent way.

---

8. https://theexplanation.com/the-sacred-book-if-it-exists-could-it-possibly-be-the-bible/

9. https://theexplanation.com/coherent-completeness-is-the-logical-reasoning-of-the-ssource/

10. *https://theexplanation.com/read-content-origin-universe-online/*

11. *https://theexplanation.com/read-content-origin-humankind-online/*

The first verse of the Bible reveals the Instigator-God, His Spirit, and the Protagonist-Serpent. The WHO. The first two chapters of Genesis tell the entirety of God's plan for humankind. The WHY, the WHERE, the WHAT, the WHEN, and the HOW. That's the reason you've got to start by understanding the beginning of the book.

The Questions

The following questions and mainly the answers are in short-form. You won't understand the answers unless you read more detailed accounts of the Biblical Hebrew meanings of words in the context of the story. Please use the links to do just that.

Who?

Genesis1:1-2 establish who is involved, with additional characters mentioned a little later.

1. Elohim[12]: In the beginning, God (Elohim) created the Heaven and the earth.
2. The Serpent[13]: the earth was without form and void;
3. God's Spirit: the Spirit of God moved[14] on the face of the waters. Read the article to see the Spirit is not a WHO, but certainly a critical player in this scenario.
4. Humans, male and female[15]: God made, created, them in Genesis 1:27
5. Yahveh Elohim[16]: Working individually with the details of

---

12. https://theexplanation.com/yahweh-elohim-inseparable-relationship/

13. https://theexplanation.com/the-serpent-in-the-bible-is-it-reality-or-some-fairytale-created-by-and-foisted-on-humans/

14. https://theexplanation.com/spirit-of-god-moved-face-waters-meaning/

15. https://theexplanation.com/were-humans-created-or-did-humans-originate-creation-day-6/

16. https://theexplanation.com/yahweh-yahveh-meaning-identity-gods-name/

Creation in the entirety of Genesis 2.

John 1:1-3[17], which is a parallel context with Genesis chapters 1-3, corroborates the cast.

1. In the beginning was the **Word**, (Yahveh Elohim[18]) and the Word was with **God** (Elohim), and the Word was God. 2 The same was in the beginning with God. 3 All things were made by him; and without him was not any thing made that was made.
2. John 1:32 I saw the **Spirit** descending from heaven like a dove. A dove moves like the Spirit in Genesis 1:2[19]
3. John 1:37 Two disciples heard Christ speak. **Humans** are frequently mentioned in John. Christ's mother at the wedding and the bridegroom represent the **genders** and **marriage** mentioned throughout the Gospels.
4. Matthew 4:1 Then was Jesus led up of the Spirit [20]into the wilderness to be tempted of the **devil (the Serpent)**.

In just a few verses in John, we understand the reason for the plural *Elohim* and the singular bara[21] (created) in Genesis. Elohim (plural): The Word was WITH God, and the Word WAS God. Two Beings, BOTH GOD = Elohim plural. Bara (singular): All things were made by HIM, the Word = bara singular = Yahveh Elohim.

Why?

---

17. https://unlockbiblemeaning.com

18. https://theexplanation.com/yahweh-yahveh-meaning-identity-gods-name/

19. https://theexplanation.com/spirit-of-god-moved-face-waters-meaning/

20. https://theexplanation.com/river-of-living-water-profound-spiritual-meaning/

21. https://theexplanation.com/heaven-does-it-exist-yes-in-fact-there-are-three-heavens/

Here's the reason why God is doing what He's doing, the way He's doing it.

We are His physical family with the potential of joining His Spirit Family. He is in the process of multiplying His Family, which will reach numbers that defy the imagination, similar to the number of stars in the sky.

God made humans in His image and likeness[22]. Males and females alike[23], around the world, past, present, and future, are God's kin[24]. We are His sons and daughters, His family, now physical with the potential of being spirit beings. PLEASE, remember, this last sentence is the briefest of resumes. GO and READ the details at the links.

Here's a verse that sums up what God has in mind. Why He created humans. Notice the promise God made to Abram, not Abraham. The nuance in names is vital information. Abram was his UNconverted name representing the ENTIRETY of humankind. God made ABRAM the promise of multiplying humanity, of which AbraHAm would become the Father of the Faithful; this means the UNconverted multitude would become a CONverted multitude.

Gen. 15:3, 5

3 And Abram said, Behold, to me you have given no seed: and, lo, one born in my house is mine heir.

5 And he brought him forth abroad, and said, Look now toward heaven, and tell the stars, if you be able to number them: and he said unto him, So shall your seed be.

---

22. https://theexplanation.com/humans-were-created-in-the-image-of-god-in-his-likeness/

23. https://theexplanation.com/human-beings-god-created-them-equal-but-different/

24. https://theexplanation.com/were-humans-created-or-did-humans-originate-creation-day-6/

God plans to expand His Family.

Where?

Earth is man's abode. Humankind is on a small eccentric planet, in a small eccentric galaxy. God has given humans rule over the whole planet. Notice that we are not on Earth by coincidence. This orb and its biodiverse resources and minerals were created and handed to us. They essentially become our training ground.

Genesis 1:28

28 And God blessed them, and God said to them, Be fruitful, and multiply, and replenish the earth, and subdue it: and have dominion over the fish of the sea, and over the fowl of the air, and over every living thing that moves upon the earth.

Ps 115:16

16 The heaven, even the heavens, are the Lord's: but the earth has he given to the children of men.

I think we can safely say, if we, as the human race, can't make it on Earth with the resources and know-how we possess, we're not going to make it on another planet! Not that we'll ever get to another planet, let alone setting up a colony on the moon.

God's plan gives Earth to humankind. Let's do our best on Earth. That in itself is already a challenge humankind is having difficulty with, as I pointed out in *Audit of the Universe*[25] and *Humankind*[26].

---

25. *https://theexplanation.com/read-content-audit-universe-online/*

26. *https://theexplanation.com/read-all-the-content-of-audit-of-humankind-online/*

What?

What are humans supposed to accomplish during their life on Earth? Were they created to be idle, or did God give them specific instruction as to what their human occupation was to be? Yes, He did. Genesis 1:28 reveals human orientation. Be you fruitful, and multiply, and replenish the earth, and subdue it; this is the two-part reason God placed humankind on Earth.

1. Relationships
2. Rulership

Relationships can be summed up by the *marriage*, and *multiply* directives God gave the man and woman. In other words, develop the family. We know this is foundational and worldwide. Adult and infant mental health and development depend on the state of relationships in the family environment. That's WHAT humankind, worldwide, is supposed to be accomplishing. *Audit of Humankind* tells us WHAT kind of a job we're doing.

Rulership of Earth is our second calling. We have another more common term for that today, *ecology*, how we manage all the resources of our planet home. In a nutshell, this is what we do with our professional and leisure lives. The first five minutes of the story of humankind indicate WHAT humankind is to do with their time on Earth.

God's plan is for each human being to have an abundant life with brimful relationships and fulfilling occupations and careers.

When?

Too many people and organizations focus on signs, dates, and interpretations of events. Prophecy seems to be the focal point of many

Biblical scholars. And misinterpretations follow. Yes, we are to keep an eye on the signs of the times (Matthew 16:3), but remember, there have always been ups and downs in world history[27], and many have been caught up in wrong predictions. *The Explanation* does not play that game.

Genesis 1 and 2 do reveal a timeframe and give us a framework for knowing the sequence of events God has in mind. *The Explanation* has not devoted a lot of space to these points in particular. That is an upcoming project. There is a timeline of seven thousand years, six thousand of which are now history[28]. During that 7,000-years-plan, God has set benchmarks, which, in the Old Testament, were called Moadim[29], or Seasons and Feasts; this was established on Day 4 of Creation week by the movements of the Sun, Earth, and moon, which are the basis of our calendar year. Genesis 1:14 states, "Let there be lights in the firmament of the heaven to divide the day from the night, and let them be for *signs* (H226), and for *seasons* (H4150-moadim), and for days, and years."

That allows us to answer the question, WHEN was the length of days and nights, months, and years established? WHEN was the calendar set in motion?

Another enigma is WHEN was the SEVEN-day week established? Generally, nobody asks this question, Why? Because, whereas there are astronomical phenomena to calculate the day, month, and year, there is NO such cosmic movement whatsoever to establish a 7-day week. WHEN was it founded? At Creation as Genesis 2:2-3 states, "And on the seventh day God ended his work which he had made; and he rested

---

27. https://theexplanation.com/ups-and-downs-order-confusion-order-bible-cycle/

28. https://theexplanation.com/timeline-history-universe-earth-humans/

29. https://theexplanation.com/day-4-of-creation-sun-and-moon-establish-calendar/

on the seventh day from all his work which he had made. 3 And God blessed the seventh day, and sanctified it."

The seven-day week is God-originated, and the seventh day is unique. No details now, for lack of space. Consider the parallel between the 7-day week and these two periods:

- Seven day week: 6 for humankind, 1 for and to develop Godkind
- Seven thousand years: 6,000 for humanity, 1000 for and to develop Godkind

As you ponder this, keep in mind God's plan. To take humankind and the Earth from tohu and bohu to nakedness, from chaos to no confusion and proper wisdom[30].

How?

How is God going to accomplish His plan? How is God going to multiply humans and take them through a process from turmoil and chaos to peace and prosperity with no confusion? How is He going to enlarge His Family with righteous, loving children?

Genesis 1 and specifically chapter 2 answer this HOW question. It starts and revolves entirely around neshama. Neshama is the critical ingredient with which God is concerned. Neshama is the human mind[31], the counterpart of God's mind, that God conferred on humankind when He created the first man in Genesis 2:7.

That neshama endows each human being, worldwide with an identical group of singularities[32] which sets them aside as the human species.

---

30. https://theexplanation.com/sapiens-the-brief-story-of-humankind/

31. https://theexplanation.com/neshama-meaning-god-given-human-mind/

32. http://theexplanation.com/rule-life-responsibly-the-key-human-singularity/

Humans are not animalkind; they are Godkind. Two Human Singularities are the possession of a dual nature[33], the ability to do good and bad, and free will[34]. Combined, they lead to the third human singularity: behavior[35]. Each human being has their behavior. And therein is the essence of confusion on a personal, community, national, and international level. Humans cannot harmonize their behavior. In Biblical terms, this misbehavior is called sin.

God's plan consists of helping humankind become aware of their sin. I cannot go into details here. Genesis 2 refers to rain[36], which God uses to test humanity and develop their spiritual stamina. He also provides for forgiveness[37] symbolized by the death of Adam[38] (putting him to sleep) and the creation of a helpmeet, a Church to nurture his physical and later spiritual born children.

The entire Bible is the recital of HOW God is working through this 7000-year process with humankind. His methodology is symbolized by both the Sabbath and God's Moadim, His Feasts.

- Ceasing from sin.
- Resting with Christ's yoke. Matthew 11:29-30, "Take my yoke upon you, and learn of me; for I am meek and lowly in heart: and you shall find REST unto your souls. 30 For my yoke is easy, and my burden is light."

The pathway from sin to righteousness is the same as tohu and bohu to not ashamed.

---

33. https://theexplanation.com/20_mans-singularity-dual-nature/

34. https://theexplanation.com/free-will-we-all-possess-it-but-we-cant-always-utilize-it/

35. https://theexplanation.com/human-behavior-is-the-expression-of-human-nature-and-free-will/

36. https://theexplanation.com/rain-falls-on-earth-entirely-because-yahveh-initiated-it/

37. https://theexplanation.com/forgiveness-the-healing-bond-for-humans-to-function-peacefully/

38. https://theexplanation.com/god-created-woman-and-reveals-humankinds-future/

Colossians 1:21-22

21 And you, that were sometime alienated and *enemies* (tohu and bohu) in your *mind* (the primary focus) by wicked works, yet now has he reconciled

22 In the body of his flesh through death, to present you *holy* and *unblameable* and *unreproveable* (this is NAKED[39]) in his sight:

That is the story of Genesis 1 and 2; this is God's plan; this is the story of the Bible. It is the narrative of what God is doing with neshama, the mind. It is the account of what God is accomplishing with each human being who walks the face of this Earth; this is the story of humankind.

---

39. https://theexplanation.com/creation-story-conclusion-naked-and-not-ashamed-thats-it/

Genesis 1 and 2 = Science, Sociology, Society

Genesis 1 and 2 are the basis for understanding contemporary society. They convey the foundation for individual and collective living.

Genesis 1 and 2 are the introduction to the story of humankind. They set God's stage of fundamental knowledge for establishing a stable society and worldview. These two initial Bible chapters indicate the basis on which to build a firm personal and community life. Yhe choice is left to each one, to follow or not follow.

In chapter 4.3 of *Audit of Humankind*[1], *The Explanation* expanded on Government for the People is Also Concern for the Poor[2] and listed the Ministries for suitable and moral government. Rulership is

---

1. *https://theexplanation.com/read-all-the-content-of-audit-of-humankind-online/*

2. https://theexplanation.com/government-for-people-concern-for-poor/

one of the most contemporary issues with which communities and nations grapple. Look around; government leadership worldwide is in shambles. We've removed ourselves from the fundamental realities to focus on the personalities and personal aspirations of influencers.

Genesis 1 and 2 are down-to-earth reminders of what's crucial in the 21st century; this is not archaic, mythical, ignorant literature. Indeed, these two chapters, believe them or not, are the most relevant expertise that society, worldwide, could heed.

The reason is, the fundamentals of society have not changed during the millennia humankind has been present on Earth. Yes, technology, knowledge, progress, science, etc., have made tremendous strides and thrust us into the Space Age, and the Artificial Intelligence era. But the underlying functions, operations, and reasoning of humankind have not changed over those millennia.

Human beings worldwide, regardless of their politics or beliefs, are characterized by seven essential singularities[3]. Genesis 1 and 2 allude to all of them, which need to be satisfied to reach a stable society.

As we complete *Origin of Woman*, a commentary on the end of Genesis 2, one of the goals of *The Explanation* has been to relate the content of the Bible to present-day affairs. This Book is not historic, anachronic literature. The Bible is a living, dynamic manual, applicable to modern-life with all its intricacies. Maybe, more so than at any time in the past. Society is modern, but living has become too complicated. We're not looking for simplistic answers; we are looking for uncomplicated solutions.

Let's see what Genesis 1 and 2 have to offer. We'll survey governmental ministries and associated branches of Science. Science and technology

---

3. https://theexplanation.com/love-is-the-most-distorted-english-word-heres-why/

are the motors of modernity. Below is a graphic summary of the fascinating branches and fields of this discipline.

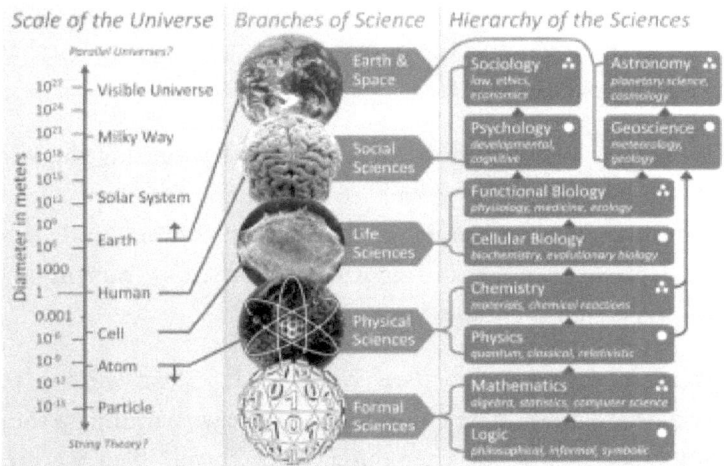

Please, particularly notice *Formal Sciences*, at the bottom of the schema. It has two hierarchies: Mathematics and Logic, algebra, and philosophy. That's quite a mix. Theology, as a *science*, places itself alongside this latter category, together with informal and symbolic. *The Explanation* has already defined theology[4]; it has nothing to do with philosophy, nor informalism[5] and symbolism. Notice, the chart ties *Logic* closely to *Mathematics;* this is interesting because some scientists believe mathematics can explain the Universe[6], even consciousness.

This surprising combination of Mathematics and Philosophy is said to explain the most intimate secrets in and of human beings. These two are the sole Sciences not joined with the physical universe (the blue column). Here's the paradox of *measurable* math and ***unmeasurable***

---

4. https://theexplanation.com/deity-and-sound-reasoned-words-are-the-crux-of-theology/

5. https://www.britannica.com/topic/Western-philosophy/The-informalist-tradition

6. https://www.livescience.com/42839-the-universe-is-math.html

consciousness, both on this chart, and in Science today. Are they two peas in a pod? Or, two separate issues? In chapter 9.5 of *Audit of the Universe*[7], we discussed the clash between artificial computer intelligence (mathematics) coupled with transhumanism (material biological technology) and the human mind (non-material neshama[8]). They are two separate entities.

Science is facing two significant frontiers, understanding the vastness of and mastering space travel to colonize other planets, and understanding and reproducing the human brain/mind through artificial intelligence and algorithms. There's nothing more contemporary than these subjects.

Genesis 1 and 2 give us focused vision and real answers as to the viability of these modern, profound quests. Are we barking up the right or wrong tree? Can we master outer space travel? Can we create a human mind?

Do you see a problem with the organization of the above diagram? They've evaluated all the sciences based on SCALE, from the massive *visible universe* at the top down to the minuscule *physical particles* at the bottom.

The problem is *sociology* and *psychology,* DO relate to humans but they do NOT have a sizeable SCALE. In this chart, they should be associated with the formal sciences at the bottom. Specifically, with philosophy, which, similarly, does not have a measurable SCALE.

Sam's Reflections

If SCALE of the Universe (the blue column on the left) is NOT the yardstick for comparing BRANCHES of Science

---

7. https://theexplanation.com/the-illusion-of-artificial-intelligence-and-transhumanism/

8. https://theexplanation.com/neshama-meaning-god-given-human-mind/

(the second, green column), then what is? FREQUENCY is the answer. With its ability to reason, the human mind, be it scientifically, philosophically, or spiritually, cannot be compared to such physical sciences as mineralogy or paleontology. We already discussed the interface between the material and the non-material world[9], which I suggest you revise. We also established the significance of God's Spirit MOVING over the face of the Earth[10] in Genesis 1.

The common denominator, and hence the instrument of measurement, is FREQUENCY[11]. We know the frequency of the human brain. We don't know the frequency of the human mind, logic, philosophy, nor of the Holy Spirit. However, what we do know is their frequencies put these non-material sciences in a non-material Hierarchy of Science[12] (the third brown column of the above chart). Let's compare apples with apples, not apples with pears.

Mathematics, and everything associated with that discipline, although not having physical *size,* is all about measurement. Scientists use it to express all modes of physical science.

But, you can NOT express psychology, sociology, ethics, philosophy, religion, and theology in mathematical terms. This science, if we can call it that, is an entirely different field. They are not physical sciences. They are non-physical. Some would say, non-material, mind, or even spiritual affairs.

---

9. https://theexplanation.com/material-world-spiritual-world-compatible/

10. https://theexplanation.com/spirit-of-god-moved-face-waters-meaning/

11. https://theexplanation.com/fluctuation-frequency-power-spirit/

12. https://theexplanation.com/the-theory-of-everything-universe-consciousness/

This distinction is vital. Logic has to do with the human mind and consciousness[13]. Without this understanding, first of all, it is impossible to understand human beings truly. Secondly, it becomes challenging to comprehend the difference and the relationship between Genesis 1 and 2.

- Genesis 1 primarily presents the creation of the PHYSICAL ENVIRONMENT and its MANAGEMENT.
- Genesis 2 presents the creation of HUMANKIND (the man and woman) and their SPIRITUAL MANAGEMENT.

God hands management of the world over to humankind[14], "subdue and have dominion over all the living creatures" (Genesis 1:28). For humankind's personal development, God tells them of which Tree they may eat and the one of which it is forbidden to eat. (Genesis 2:9, 16-17) In other words, there are do's and don'ts. There's discipline[15], which is something we don't like to hear much about nowadays. There are respective consequences for our behavior[16] concerning our attitude and application of God's injunctions.

God does NOT force us into any decision. The first created man and woman have free will[17], just as you and I do. They make their own decisions[18], and justice[19] is applied based on behavior[20]. The way I'm

13. https://theexplanation.com/
   consciousness-and-human-mind-you-cant-have-one-without-the-other/

14. https://theexplanation.com/rule-earth-to-rule-the-world-is-gods-purpose-for-humans/

15. https://theexplanation.com/the-tree-of-knowledge-of-good-and-evil-the-meaning/

16. https://theexplanation.com/social-behavior-an-audit-of-human-nature-coupled-with-free-will/

17. https://theexplanation.com/free-will-we-all-possess-it-but-we-cant-always-utilize-it/

18. https://theexplanation.com/your-choices-tell-us-who-you-are-in-fact-they-identify-you/

19. https://theexplanation.com/justice-goes-hand-in-hand-with-ethics-to-obtain-peace/

20. https://theexplanation.com/
   ethics-are-the-blueprint-for-behavior-how-humanity-should-function/

expressing the personal spiritual management addressed in Genesis 2 might sound harsh to some people. Sorry about that, but it's not Sam telling you this, it's *The Explanation* of God's Words right here in Genesis.

Let's look at Genesis 1 and 2. To show how contemporary and practical these opening chapters of the Bible are. I've added the SCIENCES and government MINISTRIES that would have jurisdiction over these fields along with some practical applications. Genesis 1 and 2 are not archaic mythologies; they are useful foundational knowledge and the basis of solutions for the 21st century.

Genesis 1 establishes the Physical Sciences and their management

The Creation in Genesis 1 lists the entirety of Space and Earth sciences and human management.

- Creation Day 1: Space (in beginning[21])—Sciences: Cosmology, Astronomy, Physics, Chemistry
    - Ministry of Science
        - Space, Artificial Intelligence, Development
- Creation Day 2: Atmosphere (a firmament[22])—Sciences: Meteorology
    - Ministry of Environment (atmosphere, pollution) and Energy
        - Meteorology, solar, wind, atomic issues
- Creation Day 3: Sea (waters[23])—Sciences: Oceanography

---

21. http://theexplanation.com/what-on-earth-is-humankind-doing-in-beginning-there-were-no-humans/

22. http://theexplanation.com/earths-firmament-is-its-atmosphere-or-sky/

23. http://theexplanation.com/dry-land-seas-and-flora-why-this-combination-on-day-3-of-creation/

- - Ministry of Water, Maritime Affairs (Oceans),
    - Canals, water supply, water cycle, protection and sustainability
    - Sanitation, civil protection (fire-fighting & detection)
- Creation Day 3: Land (dry land[24])—Sciences: Geology, Geography, Chronology
  - Ministry of Land, Natural Resources and Energy
    - Mineral resources, mining, petroleum
  - Ministry of Works
    - Infrastructure, housing, construction, and maintenance of buildings roadworks, highways, roads, canals, bridges
  - Ministry of Transport and Networks,
    - Cars, trains, trucks, physical communications (computers, telephones)
- Creation Day 3: Flora (grass[25])—Sciences: Botany, Mycology, Phytology
  - Ministry of Agriculture:
    - Food, Farms
    - Forestry
- Creation Day 4: Seasons (seasons[26])—Sciences: Ecology
  - Ministry of Environment
    - Global warming
- Creation Day 5: Marine and Atmospheric Life (whales[27], fowl[28])—Sciences: Ichthyology, Ornithology

---

24. http://theexplanation.com/dry-land-seas-and-flora-why-this-combination-on-day-3-of-creation/

25. http://theexplanation.com/dry-land-seas-and-flora-why-this-combination-on-day-3-of-creation/

26. http://theexplanation.com/day-4-of-creation-sun-and-moon-establish-calendar/

27. https://theexplanation.com/creation-day-5-and-6-god-created-fish-fowl-and-fauna/

- ○ Ministry of Fisheries and Avarians
- Creation Day 6: Animal Life (cattle[29])—Sciences: Zoology, Embryology
  - ○ Ministry of Terrestrial life
    - ▪ Cattle, Wildlife
- Creation Day 6: Human Life (hu-man[30])—Sciences: Biology
  - ○ Ministry of Human Affairs
    - ▪ Healthcare

Genesis 2 establishes the Social Sciences and their management

- Creation Day 6: Man, Dust, Neshama-Human Mind (dust[31], neshama-mind[32])—Sciences: Anatomy, Cellular Biology, Medicine, Psychology
  - ○ Ministry of Health
    - ▪ Body, Mind
- Creation Day 6: Woman, Family, Humankind (woman[33], humanity[34])—Sciences: Sociology, Gynecology
  - ○ Ministry of Womanhood and Family Affairs
    - ▪ Families, Women, Children, Adolescence, Seniors
    - ▪ Dating, Marriage, Childbirth, Child-education
- Creation Day 6: Relationships (bone of my

28. https://theexplanation.com/creation-day-5-and-6-god-created-fish-fowl-and-fauna/

29. https://theexplanation.com/creation-day-5-and-6-god-created-fish-fowl-and-fauna/

30. https://theexplanation.com/were-humans-created-or-did-humans-originate-creation-day-6/

31. https://theexplanation.com/from-dust-you-came-biblical-meaning/

32. https://theexplanation.com/neshama-humankinds-relationship-god/

33. https://theexplanation.com/god-created-woman-and-reveals-humankinds-future/

34. https://theexplanation.com/god-made-a-woman-the-feminine-moment-discover-the-meaning/

bones[35])—Sciences: Sociology, Behavioral Sciences
- ○ Ministry of "Love your neighbor"
  - ▪ Gender, inter-racial, community, national, international relations
- Creation Day 6: Rulership—(subdue[36]) Sciences: Leadership
  - ○ Ministry of Personal Development
  - ○ Ministry of How to Govern, Personal, Community, National and International levels
- Creation Day 6: Tree of Life and Death (Two Trees[37])—Sciences: Law, Justice
  - ○ Ministry of Justice
    - ▪ Law and Order, Police
    - ▪ Courts, Prisons, Reinsertion
- Creation Day 6: Till the ground (dress and keep[38])—Sciences: Workmanship
  - ○ Ministry of Trade and Industry
  - ○ Ministry of Labor, relations, apprenticeships, advancement, training
  - ○ Ministry of Commerce, Business, import, export
  - ○ Ministry of Economy and Finance
    - ▪ Inland revenue, taxation, budget
- Creation Day 7: Day of Rejuvenation (seventh day[39])—Sciences: Theology
  - ○ Ministry of Education
    - ▪ Role of God
    - ▪ Role of Yahveh

35. https://theexplanation.com/bone-of-my-bone-flesh-of-my-flesh-whats-the-relation-to-womanhood/

36. https://theexplanation.com/rule-the-world-humankind-is-on-earth-for-that-purpose/

37. https://theexplanation.com/the-tree-of-knowledge-of-good-and-evil-the-meaning/

38. https://theexplanation.com/dress-keep-garden-of-eden-man-destined-to-be-a-gardener/

39. https://theexplanation.com/on-the-seventh-day-god-continues-finishing-his-work/

- Role of Spirit (Interface spirit and physical), Spiritual Life
  ○ Ministry of Ethics
    - Information, Media

These opening two chapters of Genesis cover all the major contemporary subjects in Science[40], sociology[41], and society[42]. The above is simply an outline that is the solid foundation of the rest of the Bible.

It's like when a couple gives birth to a new baby. Genesis 1 is the preparation of the PHYSICAL room, the decoration, the crib, the dimmed lighting, the diapers, the bottles, baby food, even a baby-friendly pet, everything necessary for the newborn's welfare.

Genesis 2 is the birth of the baby. We're no longer dealing with objects. We're dealing with a human being, and one of the first things new parents learn is: A baby, from its first day, has a mind of its own. It cries when it wants; it eats when it wants, it poops when it wants. It develops its character and personality as it wants. That is the baby's neshama functioning. That neshama is the heart and soul of the baby.

The role of parents is to keep that baby clean and not confused. That's the meaning of naked and not ashamed[43]. The baby comes into the physical world with a pure and unconfused mind, a clean slate, as we'd say. Genesis 2 focuses on maintaining that slate as clean as possible. Developing and protecting that little mind as it grows and matures. Directing it spiritually and psychologically to the Tree of Life, not the Tree of Death.

---

40. https://theexplanation.com/science-world-savior-human-reasoning/

41. https://theexplanation.com/observation-first-way-human-reasoning/

42. https://theexplanation.com/social-behavior-an-audit-of-human-nature-coupled-with-free-will/

43. https://theexplanation.com/creation-story-conclusion-naked-and-not-ashamed-thats-it/

Nature and Human Nature

Let's describe Genesis 1 and 2 another way. For instance, nature and human nature. *Inventory of the Universe*[44] is an overview of Nature, from space, through the atmosphere down to Earth with its Oceans and Land, Flora, Fauna, and Human Beings. The take-away of Life[45] on our planet is not that we can manipulate molecules and genes to obtain Life. The take-away is that we have millions of just-in-time processes[46] that are thoroughly and intricately interwoven to not only generate Life but to sustain it in such an orderly fashion.

Genesis 1 is *The Explanation* of this enmeshed ensemble. Genesis 1 is the only literature, the only Sacred Book[47] that assembles all the pieces of the puzzle to give humankind an overview of nature. This opening chapter of the Bible spells out why humanity is on Earth and our rulership role[48] concerning the inventory of resources God has given us. It is the coherent completeness[49] of the logical reasoning of the Logos[50], the Word, Christ[51].

Likewise, with Genesis 2. It reveals succinctly, but surely, every part of the human nature of humankind[52]. From the neshama-mind[53] to our dual nature[54] coupled with free will[55] (Two Trees and Choice). Then,

---

44. *https://theexplanation.com/inventory/read-all-the-content-of-inventory-of-the-universe-online/*

45. https://theexplanation.com/life-is-complex-simplicity-perfectly-interlaced/

46. https://theexplanation.com/apoptosis-programmed-cell-death-even-before-birth/

47. https://theexplanation.com/the-sacred-book-if-it-exists-could-it-possibly-be-the-bible/

48. https://theexplanation.com/rule-earth-to-rule-the-world-is-gods-purpose-for-humans/

49. https://theexplanation.com/
social-media-hashtags-comprising-the-coherent-completeness-of-the-universe/

50. https://theexplanation.com/coherent-completeness-is-the-logical-reasoning-of-the-ssource/

51. https://theexplanation.com/deity-and-sound-reasoned-words-are-the-crux-of-theology/

52. https://theexplanation.com/focus-on-human-behavior-study-how-humans-function/

53. https://theexplanation.com/neshama-meaning-god-given-human-mind/

the discipline and justice[56] of our decisions (Life or Death depending on our choice of Trees). This chapter includes God's RELATIONSHIP with humankind[57] and His entire plan of Salvation[58] through the Man and the Woman[59] representative of Christ and the Church[60]. The outcome of which is one flesh[61] and human nature transformed into naked and not ashamed[62]. In other terms, our human nature will be transformed into divine nature. The human mind is the focus of God's attention and has been, is, and will be His transformative work throughout human existence[63]. Humankind will be dressed in the image and likeness[64] of their Creator God.

Genesis 1 is a contemporary description of sustainable ecology that the world is clamoring about, without much progress. Genesis 2 is the foundation of the nurturing process of humankind based on family relationships. The human family in the image of the divine family, mirroring the way God works with humanity. This chapter reveals the principal roles and the inter-relationship of preeminent leadership[65] and the eminent relational helpmeet[66]. It shows how the two genders[67]

---

54. https://theexplanation.com/20_mans-singularity-dual-nature/

55. https://theexplanation.com/free-will-we-all-possess-it-but-we-cant-always-utilize-it/

56. https://theexplanation.com/justice-goes-hand-in-hand-with-ethics-to-obtain-peace/

57. https://theexplanation.com/neshama-humankinds-relationship-god/

58. https://theexplanation.com/god-made-a-woman-the-feminine-moment-discover-the-meaning/

59. https://theexplanation.com/marriage-relationship-man-woman-in-front-beside-or-behind/

60. https://theexplanation.com/i-will-build-my-church-yahweh-built-the-woman/

61. https://theexplanation.com/one-flesh-ultimately-inseparable-together-forever/

62. https://theexplanation.com/creation-story-conclusion-naked-and-not-ashamed-thats-it/

63. https://theexplanation.com/understanding-the-human-mind-key-to-gods-plan/

64. https://theexplanation.com/humans-were-created-in-the-image-of-god-in-his-likeness/

65. https://theexplanation.com/male-gender-its-significance-and-why-god-created-it/

66. https://theexplanation.com/helpmeet-the-surprising-god-given-role-of-woman/

67. https://theexplanation.com/god-blessed-the-male-and-the-female-heres-the-meaning/

are to work together in harmony for their own well-being as well as that of their children, which they birth.

Genesis 1 and 2 explain our PHYSICAL world and ALL HUMAN BEINGS that populate it. These two chapters establish the foundation for living a wholesome life with proper rulership and right relations. Are we hearing or disdaining the Bible's opening instruction?

Creation story: From Tohu & Bohu to One Flesh

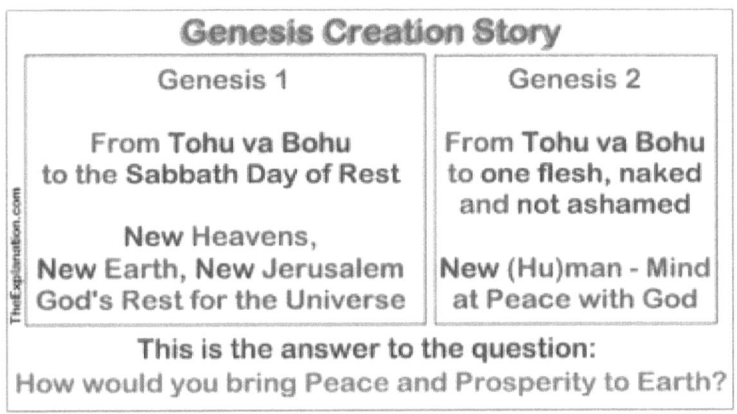

Genesis Creation story: starting with tohu and bohu, we terminate with one flesh. That is the good news of the coherent completeness of a perfectly assembled puzzle.

The Genesis Creation story has covered a lot of Biblical ground. With this final chapter of *Origin of Woman*, we're in a position to give an overall picture of Genesis 1 and 2. These two chapters in Genesis represent the end of the beginning. The end of the introduction of God's plan, but the beginning of the accomplishment of the story of humankind, the story told in the rest of the Bible.

In the last chapter we saw that Genesis 1 relates to the physical sciences of the Universe, and Genesis 2 to the life sciences of humankind. That chapter covers the material, worldly relationship of the Bible to the 21st century.

To terminate *Origin of Woman*, *The Explanation* gives you the spiritual overview of the whole story of the Universe and Humankind expounded in Genesis 1 and 2. Here is God's plan of Salvation for humankind; this is the assembly of the coherent completeness of the entire theological puzzle.

The Genesis Creation story establishes the framework for the story of the Universe. It starts general, with the heavens and the Earth, and gets specific with the Sabbath day of rest, in chapter 1. Then, chapter 2 focuses on the role of humankind. They become one flesh with God through the marriage of humankind with Christ (Husband and Bride, Christ and Church). That process is the purification, the cleansing, and justification of the human mind. That's the spiritual transformation into naked and not ashamed, the Godly wisdom and absence of confusion.

Genesis 1 from tohu va bohu to the Sabbath day of rest

Let's see where the story in the New Testament leads to its conclusion. Here's how the Apostle Paul refers to Genesis with *The Explanation*'s comments in brackets. Paul expounds on the labor necessary to enter the Sabbath rest. He gives the in-depth spiritual version of the Genesis Creation story, the process of ceasing from tohu va bohu and moving to the Sabbath rest.

Hebrews 4:4-11

4 For he spake in a certain place of the seventh day on this wise, And God did rest the seventh day[1] from all his works. (read *The Explanation* of Gen. 2:3 here[2])

---

1. https://theexplanation.com/

   god-to-do-with-his-work-to-make-them-on-7th-day-to-take-care-his-creation/

2. https://theexplanation.com/

   god-to-do-with-his-work-to-make-them-on-7th-day-to-take-care-his-creation/

5 And in this place again, If they shall enter into my rest (*shevet, Shabbat* means rest, sitting still in Biblical Hebrew[3]).

6 Seeing therefore it remains that some (those called during the New Testament era) must enter therein, and they to whom it was first preached (the Old Testament era) entered not in because of unbelief:

7 Again, he limits a certain day, saying in David, To day (New Testament era), after so long a time; as it is said, To day if you will hear his voice, harden not your hearts.

8 For if Jesus had given them rest, then would he not afterward have spoken of another day.

9 There remains therefore a rest (the Shabbat of Genesis 2:3[4]) to the people of God.

10 For he that is entered into his rest, he also has *ceased* from his own works, as *God did from his.* (a specific reference to the Shabbat of Genesis 2:3[5]. Remember that Shabbat ALSO means cease[6]. The Sabbath represents both the process (ceasing) and the end result (rest) of the plan of God).

11 Let us labour therefore to enter into that rest, (Note verse 10, cease from one's *own works* = works of tohu va bohu[7] to labor and replace them with transformation and the renewing of one's mind, putting on the mind of Christ[8]).

---

3. https://theexplanation.com/biblical-hebrew-amazing-language-both-simple-deep-same-time/

4. https://theexplanation.com/
   god-to-do-with-his-work-to-make-them-on-7th-day-to-take-care-his-creation/

5. https://theexplanation.com/
   god-to-do-with-his-work-to-make-them-on-7th-day-to-take-care-his-creation/

6. https://theexplanation.com/biblical-hebrew-amazing-language-both-simple-deep-same-time/

Only human beings can follow this Godly spiritual pathway from tohu va bohu to the Sabbath rest. Only human beings possess neshama[9], which gives us the understanding to choose, apply, and be thankful for this spiritual trajectory. For those of you who already have a deeper understanding of God's plan for ALL of humankind, the possibility to enter HIS REST extends to the 1000 years and the Last Great Day, AFTER Christ's Return. That encompasses the ENTIRETY of humankind, who will have their opportunity to follow the process of tohu va bohu (ceasing from one's own works) to the Sabbath (the rest referred to by Paul). It's all there in Genesis 1.

That said, in the book of Romans, Paul also personifies the pathway to REST for the entire PHYSICAL Creation of Genesis 1. The heavens and Earth are crying out for rest. The COP25 Climate Change Conference takes place in Madrid[10] amid worldwide indifference. Paradoxically, attending European members flew in because it's cheaper than taking the train. Besides, in France trains are on strike as I write. Creation has never been in worse a state as it is today in the so-called enlightened 21st century.

Romans 8:22-23

22 For we know that **the whole creation groans and travails in pain (a direct reference to tohu va bohu[11])** together until now.

---

7. http://theexplanation.com/

   tohu-va-bohu-signifies-confusion-and-void-a-horrible-state-to-be-in/

8. https://theexplanation.com/understanding-the-human-mind-key-to-gods-plan/

9. https://theexplanation.com/human-software-god-breathed-neshama-adam/

10. https://www.euractiv.com/section/climate-environment/news/

   cop25-news-and-views-whats-happening-in-madrid/

11. http://theexplanation.com/

   tohu-va-bohu-signifies-confusion-and-void-a-horrible-state-to-be-in/

23 And not only they, but ourselves also, which have the firstfruits of the Spirit, even **we ourselves groan within ourselves**, waiting for the adoption (to be the sons and daughters of God), to wit, the *redemption* of our body.

Redemption means God's plan for saving, humankind, and the planet. The creation is groaning in its tohu va bohu because of humankind's rulership mismanagement[12]. In Genesis 3, I show you why and how humankind ended up, or rather started in tohu and bohu, and is responsible for that same state of the planet. That's the next book, *Agony of Humankind and the Antidote*[13], in *The Explanation* series.

God's process alone will restore peace and prosperity to this planet and its inhabitants. The Genesis Creation story outlines that plan, as we're seeing. The ultimate Sabbath rest for the Creation is the New Heavens, the New Earth, and New Jerusalem.

Revelation 21:1-3

1 And I saw a *new* heaven and a *new* earth: for the first heaven and the first earth were passed away; and there was no more sea.

2 And I John saw the holy city, *new Jerusalem*, coming down from God out of heaven, prepared as a bride adorned for her husband.

3 And I heard a great voice out of heaven saying, Behold, the tabernacle of God is with men, and *he will dwell with them*, and *they shall be his people*, and *God himself shall be with them*, and be their God.

---

12. https://theexplanation.com/governance-structure-important-role-in-rulership/
13. *https://theexplanation.com/read-all-the-content-of-agony-of-humankind-online/*

God's Creation plan, as outlined in Genesis 1 and 2, is the only answer to the questions, How can we bring Peace and Prosperity to Earth? How can we transform tohu va bohu into the Sabbath rest? After the process of ceasing, which is a meaning of the Biblical Hebrew Shabbat, from human ways, comes rest. The rest for the groaning physical creation is the NEW Heaven, the NEW Earth, and NEW Jerusalem.

The difference between Genesis 1 and 2 Creation story is an illusion. These two chapters tell the same story from a complementary point of view — the first focusing on the Universe, the second on Humankind.

Genesis 2 from tohu va bohu to One Flesh, which is Naked and Not Ashamed, Wise and Not Confused

Genesis 2 is a total makeover of the body and mind. To be the Bride of Christ, which is the goal of the Church, its members must become like Christ. That is to say; the end result is they will have spiritual bodies and spiritual minds.

This concept, of course, flies in the face of *artificial intelligence* (creation of the perfect brain and mind) and *transhumanism* (creation of the perfect human body). Human science is proposing its solutions to today's dilemmas. God's Sacred Book has offered the answer to the human predicament for millennia. The *new man* is not Superman or Superwoman or Iron Man or Spiderman. The new human is a transformed being who will be composed of Spirit and endowed with Godly wisdom. A new body and a new mind. Nothing to be ashamed of, to the contrary, this Godly Individual will be wise and not confused.

Paul explicitly refers to their bodily transformation. In the following passage, understand that for all of Paul's references to weakness, dead (because we've eaten from the Tree of Knowledge of Good and Evil), dishonor, living soul, earthy, natural, corruption, first man, image of the earthy, you can substitute and read *tohu va bohu*. Likewise, for incorruption, glory, power, spiritual body, quickening spirit, last Adam, from heaven, image of the heavenly, you can substitute and read *naked and not ashamed* or, better yet, a more suitable translation, *wise and not confused.*

1 Corinthians 15:42-49

42 So also is the resurrection of the dead. It is sown in corruption; it is raised in incorruption:

43 It is sown in dishonour; it is raised in glory: it is sown in weakness; it is raised in power:

44 It is sown a natural body; it is raised a spiritual body. There is a natural body, and there is a spiritual body.

45 And so it is written, The first man Adam was made a living soul; the last Adam was made a quickening spirit.

46 Howbeit that was not first which is spiritual, but that which is natural; and afterward that which is spiritual.

47 The first man is of the earth, earthy: the second man is the Lord from heaven.

48 As is the earthy, such are they also that are earthy: and as is the heavenly, such are they also that are heavenly.

49 And as we have borne the image of the earthy, we shall also bear the image of the heavenly.

Between the Bible context above and those below, Paul expresses God's Creation story as outlined in Genesis 1 and 2. Humans are dust. We have physical life with a mind and free will. The human dual nature makes wrong choices, which lead to bad behavior, the result of which is (slow) death. Through Christ and His Church (the man who *sleeps/dies* and woman who gave birth to the Saviour), we can be one flesh, united to Christ, and become naked (rid ourselves of the tohu va bohu) and not ashamed (not confused), and partake of the Tree of Eternal Life.

New man (human), New mind

As there is no discrepancy between Genesis 1 and Genesis 2, likewise, there's no discrepancy between the Old Testament and the New Testament. There's continuity and more in-depth understanding as we progress.

Genesis 2 and the entire New Testament are about the RENEWAL of the NESHAMA God breathed into the first man. Christ is the example of this NEW Neshama in action. His whole LIFE on Earth revealed the result of this NEW Neshama, this NEW GODLY mind at work.

2 Corinthians 5:17-21

17 Therefore if any man (God's plan is inclusive of ALL humans) be in Christ, he is a **new creature** (a new creation, a new mind, becoming wiser in God, less confused): old things are passed away; behold, all things are become new (the old tohu and bohu in the process of becoming naked and not ashamed).

18 And all things are of God, who has reconciled us to himself by Jesus Christ. (Christ and the Church becoming One Flesh and in the future being presented to God the Father).

19 To wit, that God was in Christ, reconciling the world to himself, not imputing their trespasses to them, (The rest

of the Bible is the story of turning human confusion into Godly order, that's the meaning of *reconciliation*. Taking humankind and turning them into Sons and Daughters, Children of God).

21 For he (God the Father) has made him (Jesus Christ) to be sin for us (humankind), who knew no sin (Christ was naked and not ashamed, Godly wise and not confused); that we might be made the righteousness of God in him (All humanity is being MADE, (remember what God did on the seventh day[14]) UNashamed, pure of heart and mind, not confused, in a right relationship to be able to rule with Christ).

Genesis 2 is humans (males and females, made in the image and likeness of God), with their neshama, the Godly ingredient possessed only by human beings. It is the mind and consciousness that endow us with the singularities that define humankind[15]. Humans alone have a dual nature with free will that allows them to choose between good and bad. Humans alone have good and bad behavior, and every single human has done bad things (sin), whether in their body or mind. We've all broken the rules of life, God's rules, and need forgiveness and rehabilitation; this is the whole story of the woman who represents the Church, the assembly of broken humankind, presented to the (second) man, Jesus Christ, and the two becoming ONE FLESH. That's reconciliation.

Paul and the teachings of the New Testament are the continuation and expansion of the Genesis Creation story.

Ephesians 2:12-22

---

14. https://theexplanation.com/

   god-to-do-with-his-work-to-make-them-on-7th-day-to-take-care-his-creation/

15. https://theexplanation.com/love-is-the-most-distorted-english-word-heres-why/

12 That at that time you were without Christ (tohu va bohu), being aliens from the commonwealth of Israel, and strangers from the covenants of promise, having no hope, and without God in the world:

13 But now in Christ Jesus you who sometimes were far off are made nigh by the blood of Christ.

14 For he is our peace, who has made both one, and has broken down the middle wall of partition between us;

15 Having abolished in his flesh the enmity, even the law of commandments contained in ordinances; for to make in himself of twain **one new man,** so making **peace**; (this is the only way to peace. This whole context is an allusion to making the descendants of the original helpmeet[16] (the first woman) one flesh with Christ)

16 And that he might reconcile both unto God in one body (bone of my bone[17], one flesh[18]) by the cross (remember, God put the first man to sleep symbolizing Christ's death[19]), having slain the enmity thereby:

17 And came and preached peace to you which were afar off, and to them that were nigh.

18 For through him we both have access by one Spirit to the Father.

---

16. https://theexplanation.com/helpmeet-the-surprising-god-given-role-of-woman/

17. https://theexplanation.com/
   bone-of-my-bone-flesh-of-my-flesh-whats-the-relation-to-womanhood/

18. https://theexplanation.com/one-flesh-ultimately-inseparable-together-forever/

19. https://theexplanation.com/god-created-woman-and-reveals-humankinds-future/

19 Now therefore ye are no more strangers and foreigners, but fellowcitizens with the saints, and of the household of God;

20 And are built upon the foundation of the apostles and prophets, Jesus Christ himself being the chief corner stone;

21 In whom all the building fitly framed together grows unto an holy temple in the Lord (the process of transformation from tohu va bohu > naked and not ashamed):

22 In whom you also are built together for an habitation of God through the Spirit (one flesh).

The new (hu)man is a transformed mind. The human mind is the central focus of God's attention in the Bible from Genesis to Revelation.

Ephesians 4:22-24

22 That you put off concerning the former conversation the old man, which is corrupt according to the deceitful lusts (tohu va bohu);

23 And be renewed in the spirit (spirit in man[20] - ruach) of your mind (neshama[21], the God-given software[22] that makes us human with all the human singularities[23]);

---

20. https://theexplanation.com/gods-spirit-ruach-animates-living-beings/

21. https://theexplanation.com/human-mind-mind-power-neshama-ruach/

22. https://theexplanation.com/human-software-god-breathed-neshama-adam/

23. https://theexplanation.com/rule-life-responsibly-the-key-human-singularity/

24 And that you put on the **new (hu)man** (the human plasticity of the mind[24] with the help of the Holy Spirit), which after God is created in righteousness and true holinesss (naked and not ashamed)

Each human being follows this process of *tohu va bohu* to *shevet*, resting in God's abode, New Jerusalem, as part of the one flesh, the Bride, the Church married to Christ. The whole plan for the entire Universe and especially the HUMAN component, is in Genesis 1 and 2.

Colossians 3:8-10

8 But now you also put off all these; anger, wrath, malice, blasphemy, filthy communication out of your mouth (the tohu va bohu).

9 Lie not one to another, seeing that you have put off the old man with his deeds;

10 And have **put on the new man**, which is renewed in knowledge (the process of becoming naked and not ashamed) after the **image** (G1504 - the image and likeness of God) of him that created him (Genesis 1 and 2):

Go over to UnlockBibleMeaning.com[25] G1504 and verify the meaning and origin of this Greek word. Eikon (i-kone'); from G1503; a likeness, i.e. (literally) statue, profile, or (figuratively) representation, resemblance: KJV - image; This harks back to Genesis 1:27 the image and likeness of God. With the creation of the male (Gen. 2:7) and female (Gen. 2:22), each possessing their respective side of God's male and female character.

---

24. https://theexplanation.com/understanding-the-human-mind-key-to-gods-plan/

25. https://unlockbiblemeaning.com

Genesis 2 focuses on creating the FIRST PHYSICAL (Gen. 2:7) and the SECOND, NEW Man! (Gen. 2:24-25 UNashamed humans). It's all about the NESHAMA[26]. That is the key. And psychology and religion don't know what this is all about! They do NOT have the KEY. How can you expect to UNlock a mystery if you do NOT possess the key? Impossible.

There is continuity in the story from Genesis 1:1 to 2:25. There is NO break of progression between Genesis 1 and 2. It is the same story that takes us from utter destruction to the restoration of planet Earth. And on to this planet, the epitome of God's Creation, the man and the woman in a bound marriage with a wise and not confused husband and wife.

The PHYSICAL restoration to wisdom and no confusion is the story of the rest of the Bible and culminates in Revelation 21-22 with the NEW Heavens and the NEW Earth and especially with wisdom and absence of confusion. It's not humankind anymore, but the transformation into Godkind when all humans will inherit the Image of God. The last words of the Bible confirm the inclusion of all those with a converted mind. And the exclusion for those who have fixed their minds in a contrary way, to the Tree of the Knowledge of Good and Evil.

Revelation 22:13-15

13 I am Alpha and Omega, the beginning and the end, the first and the last.

14 Blessed are they that do his commandments, that they may have right to the tree of life, and may enter in through the gates into the city.

---

26. https://theexplanation.com/understanding-the-human-mind-key-to-gods-plan/

15 For without are dogs, and sorcerers, and whoremongers, and murderers, and idolaters, and whosoever loves and makes a lie.

We started with billions of pieces all jumbled. In *Inventory of the Universe and Humankind,* all we did was turn the pieces right side up. *The Explanation* gave you a look at the isolated images of each piece and their basic diverse shapes. None of these pieces has either the same image or the same shape. Yet, they assemble perfectly to form the Universe and Humankind.

The Creation story from Tohu va bohu to the Sabbath, with its *cease and rest,* reveals how God will turn our present civilization around. It is the entire story of the present Universe, Heavens, Earth, and Humans, changed into the New Heavens, New Earth, and New (Hu)mans with a new world capital, New Jerusalem. In that Kingdom, God's Kingdom, there will reign a New Rulership and New Relationships.

Genesis 1 and 2 denote God's Creation narrative. We have the beginning to the end story of humankind.

Epilogue

Genesis 1 and 2. Significance for Today's World

Genesis chapters 1 and 2 reveal the foundation of knowledge for the big questions in life. Why is there Space and Time? What does it mean to be Human? What is Mind? Why are Humans on Earth?

Genesis chapters 1 and 2 are fundamental literature. The Biblical Hebrew reveals all the reasons for Human presence on our planet. This narrative answers all the big questions Science, Philosophy, and Religion, haggle over. This profound introduction to the Sacred Book plots the coherent completeness of God's plan for humankind.

The epilogue of *Origin of Woman* gives you an overview, a worldview, even a universeview, of the main issues dealt with in this narrative. We are going to assemble all the major pieces of the puzzle. In so doing, they answer the question, How would you bring peace and prosperity to Earth? We're going to step back and visualize the assembled whole puzzle, 20/20 vision of the Universe and Humankind.

These two chapters are the starting point for all the journeys we wish to make with our individual lives; this is the robust framework on which we can hang all our ideas, plans, hopes, dreams, and future. At the same time, this is what should be the rock-solid foundation of Science, Philosophy, and Religion; this is real Theology.

Here are the overall highlights of Genesis chapters 1 and 2. These keys are the essentials to remember. They are the foundation and skeleton of a correct worldview. These are the roots of the rest of the Bible, Human Life, Peace, and Prosperity.

1. **Space** - Creation of living space (resources to sustain life) for Humans. Creation Days 1-3
2. **Time** - Creation of the calendar with seasons. Creation Day 4
3. **Life** - Creation of Fauna Life on Earth. Creation Day 5-6
4. **Humans** - Creation of Male and Female in God's Image. Creation Day 6
5. **Mind** - The KEY factor. Neshama sets humankind apart from animalkind and makes us Godkind. Creation Day 6
6. **Relationships**, **Rulership**. The goal of what humankind is to achieve on Earth. Creation Day 6
7. **Sabbath** - Day of Peace of Mind. Real theology, presence of Godly wisdom, and absence of confusion. Ceasing from Human ways. Resting in God's ways. Creation Day 7

The Explanation series has outlined this 7-step schema. The first three books, *Inventory of the Universe, Audit of the Universe,* and *Audit of Humankind,* went in-depth to paint a realistic worldview. These books focus on a human point-of-view. They tell the story of humankind from a HUMAN viewpoint (observation, philosophy, science, religion). The fourth, fifth, and sixth books, *Origin of the Universe, Origin of Humankind,* and *Origin of Woman* developed Genesis chapters 1 and 2, based on the meaning of Biblical Hebrew[1]. They tell the story of humankind from a GODLY viewpoint (Theology). The first three books ASK all the unanswered why questions. The last two books ANSWER all the why questions.

Below is a chart outlining a more detailed eighteen-steps of God's plan with references to the chapters in each of the six books. The links to the relevant sections for consultation are online in the Epilogue to *Origin of Woman*[2]. This schema paints the coherent completeness of the plan of God for humankind. It tells us our past, present, and future. It gives us the solid outline by which each human being worldwide can guide their lives.

The key points to grasp are 10 and 11 A, B, C. They reveal the difference between animals, humans, and God and show that humans are Godkind, not animalkind. The reason for this is that ONLY humans and God possess NESHAMA, which endows humankind with consciousness and the human mind.

In the table below, the six books are *Inventory of the Universe* (1). *Audit of the Universe* (2). *Audit of Humankind* (3). *Origin of the Universe* (4 - a commentary on Genesis 1). *Origin of Humankind* (5 - a commentary

---

1. https://unlockbiblemeaning.com

2. https://theexplanation.com/
genesis-chapters-1-and-2-their-meaning-significance-for-todays-world/

on the beginning of Genesis 2). *Origin of Woman* (6 - a commentary on the end of Genesis 2).

6 Books – The Explanation series

Giant Steps for Humankind	1 Inven Univ	2 Audit Univ	3 Audit Hum	4 Orig Univ	5 Orig Hum	6 Orig Wom	Creat ion Day	Genesis chapters 1 and 2 Bible verses Creation Events
1 Space	1	1		6+7 8.1 5			1	Big Bang – Gen. 1:1 Let there be light – Gen. 1:3
2 Atmosphere	2	2		8.6			2	Firmament, heaven – Gen. 1:6
3 Water	3	3		8.7			3	Seas, freshwater - Gen. 1:9
4 Land	4	4		8.7			3	Dry land – Gen. 1:9
5 Flora	5	5		8.7	2.8		3	Grass, fruit trees – Gen. 1:11 First 3 days = Creation of Resources for Life on Earth – Space
6 Sun, moon Measure time				8.8			4	Time: Seasons, calendar. – Gen 1:14 4th day = Creation of Time
7 Fauna	6	6		8.9			5+6	Fish, fowl, animals – Gen. 1:24-25
8 Life	7	7	1		1.1		5+6	What is Life?
9 Body – Brain	8	8	2		1.5-7 3.1-4		6	Male, Female, Humans = Godkind – Gen. 1:26-27 Man = dust – Gen. 2:7

6 Books – The Explanation series

Giant Steps for Humankind	1 Inven Univ	2 Audit Univ	3 Audit Hum	4 Orig Univ	5 Orig Hum	6 Orig Wom	Creat ion Day	Genesis chapters 1 and 2 Bible verses Creation Events
10 Brain – Mind	9	9	3		3.5-5.7		6	**Neshama** = Consciousness, Mind, Gen. 2:7 Brain – Mind issue solved
11A Animal-Human comparison	10				1.4		6	Animals after their kind – Gen. 1:25,28 Humans after Godkind – Gen. 1:27
11B Who is God				4&5	2.6-7		6	Intro to Relationships: God-Humans-Serpent Elohim – Yahveh
11C Human-God Comparison					1.2-4		6	Humans in God's image & likeness – Gen. 1:26-27 **Animalkind-Humankind-Godkind comparison** >> Key to Understanding
12 Singularities of Humans - Result of possessing neshama – mind			4				6	**9 Singularities that characterize humans alone:** 1. Dual nature 2. Mastering our time and space 3. Creativity 4. Imagination 5. Learning 6. Choice 7. Progress, improvement 8. Challenges with courage 9. Rule life responsibly

6 Books - The Explanation series

Giant Steps for Humankind	1 Inven Univ	2 Audit Univ	3 Audit Hum	4 Orig Univ	5 Orig Hum	6 Orig Wom	Creat ion Day	Genesis chapters 1 and 2 Bible verses Creation Events
								7 Steps for humans to reach peace with themselves and others: 1. Human nature 2. Free choice 3. Behavior 4. Ethics 5. Justice 6. Self-reproach 7. Forgiveness
13 How Humans Function			5			1.1-8	6	> Humans in Garden of Eden, 2 trees, 4 rivers - Gen. 2:8-14 > Dress and keep it, (love God, do His will) – Gen. 2:15 (human nature: ethics + choices = behavior) > Freely eat – Gen. 2:16 (choice) > Eat of wrong Tree and surely die (justice) – Gen. 2:17 > Creation of Woman through whom Humanity is saved. (self-reproach/repentance, forgiveness)
14 How Humans Socialize			6		2.2	2.1-8 3.1-3	6	**Relationships** > In God's image and likeness, male and female - Gen. 1:26-27 > Not good alone (social being/mankind-ONE family) – Gen. 2:18-20 companion for man, helpmeet, bone of my bones, one flesh, cleave

6 Books - The Explanation series

Giant Steps for Humankind	1 Inven Univ	2 Audit Univ	3 Audit Hum	4 Orig Univ	5 Orig Hum	6 Orig Wom	Creat ion Day	Genesis chapters 1 and 2 Bible verses Creation Events
15 How Humans Rule			7		1.8 2.1-2		6	**Rulership** > Human Government, national & international peace & prosperity > Subdue, Dominion – Gen. 1:27-28-2,1,18 1Corinthians 13:4-7
16 How Humans Reason			8		4.1-3		6&7	**4 Reasoning Methods** used by the human mind 1. Observation 2. Philosophy 3. Science 4. Religion
17 How God Reasons				1 > 5				> **Real Theology** – To REASON God's way, not the human way. > Bible = knowledge and wisdom, mind and God's Word
18 Sabbath cease and rest				5.4	2.3	3.4 4.4	7	> **God rested with creation** to do, to make humans - Gen. 2:2-4 > Sabbath Rest Restored, Unity with God through Christ – Gen. 2:24 > Naked, not ashamed, Wise mind, no confusion – Gen. 2:25 > **Establishment of Humans at Peace with God & Earth** > **Godkind animated by Godly Relationships & Rulership**

Yes, it will take time to fathom the schema of Genesis chapters 1 and 2 concerning the real world in which we live. But such a study will be worth every moment of your valuable time. The foundation covers vast but essential subjects. In a day and age when data tweets, scanty social media, TV, and radio coverage represent the mainstream of information you need coherent completeness. First, we need to plant the trunk of the tree with its roots BEFORE we haggle over twigs and leaves.

If we can't answer the why questions, how can we expect to answer the what and how? The above schema is designed to answer the why questions. The column on the right directs you to the fundamental understanding of coherent completeness. Space lacks to detail the finer points. For instance, the seven-step process of how humans function is not a *shot-in-the-dark* list of characteristics. It is the outline of the Feast Days elaborated in the Old Testament, which needs to be developed and amplified.

Where is Humankind Today?

The seven points below are the most fundamental issues that face humanity today. Observation, Science, Philosophy, and Religion pour over these subjects jostling for positions of preeminence. But they are not bringing viable applicable solutions to the table.

1. **Space** - Sustainment of life resources of the planet. Ecology, sustainable economy.
2. **Time** - Climate change has upset our seasons. We no longer govern how we use our time.
3. **Life** - While we promote AI and transhumanism, human bodies and minds are in a state of anxiousness.
4. **Humans** - #MeToo is the visible tip of the melting iceberg of understanding genders and their respective roles.
5. **Mind** - The KEY factor. We flounder around with patchwork ideas about the enigma of all times.
6. **Relationships, Rulership. We are witnessing the disintegration of Family, Government, and Society worldwide.**
7. **Sabbath** - Less and less peace of mind. More and more *instant-solutions* (pills, technology, yoga, books of rules, etc.) from the thinkers and gurus.

Society is further and further removed from the reality of Genesis chapters 1 and 2. The basis for knowing how to live happy and prosperous lives.

The bottom-line is Humankind is following a path opposed to ALL of the above seven fundamentals. We, on Earth, are putting every effort into doing the opposite of point 7. Instead of God's Word (real theology, wisdom, and order), we're establishing human words, were following human ways, and frowning on God's principles. Result: Instead of *Peace of Mind,* we're the generation of *Stress of Mind.* And saying *stress of mind* is probably the understatement of the year.

Relationships and Rulership are in shambles. It's a worldwide plague, and the world population is paying a massive physical and mental price for this mismanagement. The world tries to apply its solutions, AI, transhumanism, drugs, mind manipulation. Yes, they'll give short term relief, but like infected sores patched with band-aids, they'll come back to haunt us with a vicious bite. This vicious bite is the crux of Genesis 3, the next book in *The Explanation* series, *Agony of Humankind and the Antidote.* We're in this agony in the 21st century.

In the two *Audit* books, *The Explanation* has outlined our world of relational, governmental, scientific, philosophical, and religious cacophonic confusion. They took each one of those pieces and analyzed its state. How is it doing at the beginning of the 21st century? Is the glass of peace and prosperity for each of these pieces getting fuller or emptier?

An interviewer asked Jared Diamond[3], do you think humanity is going to make it to the next level? He answered, there's a 51% yes and 49% no chance for humankind pulling it off. Today, an *Audit of the Universe* changes those odds 51% against and 49% for humanity pulling it off.

---

3. https://youtu.be/sDdf0qc6Q-Y

The doomsday clock[4] is at two minutes before midnight. Scientists will announce a new time, but the year has not been a good one for the cohesiveness of our planet. In fact, it was advanced to one minute and forty seconds before midnight in 2020.

It sounds like bad news. Well, from a purely human point of view, I can understand that. But *The Explanation* does NOT come from that point of view. It presents a theological outlook, which, of course, throws a curveball at Jared Diamond, Yuval Harrari, Steven Pinker, and similar types of approaches.

The world has a semblance of order, granted. There is good, plenty of good in the world. There is progress, as Diamond says in the above video[5]. Nobody denies that, but there's an underlying state of tohu and bohu. Daily news and headlines scream out these examples. Humankind hasn't, can't and won't accept that we're in a downhill slide of our values and morals.

You can find relief and refuge in the coherent completeness of Genesis chapters 1 and 2, explained in the three *Origin* books.

In conclusion, remember this. The first human created was the male, in Biblical Hebrew *zachar*, which means REMEMBER. Humankind is to recognize its ORIGIN, its Creation. As well as its FUTURE, the meaning of the seventh day of the week, the Sabbath day. Our ORIGIN is God; Our FUTURE is to CEASE from human ways and REST in God's ways. REMEMBER that Humankind ORIGINATED from God and will FINISH with God. Humanity has a difficult time seeing that finish-line, but Genesis chapters 1 and 2 state that it is present. Humankind is still running the race and will get there. For your physical, mental, and spiritual well-being, REMEMBER and

---

4. https://thebulletin.org/doomsday-clock/

5. https://youtu.be/sDdf0qc6Q-Y

mediate on the Sabbath. It is the finish-line of peace and prosperity of humankind with God.

www.TheExplanation.com

Join The Explanation Newsletter[6] – no spam, total privacy

Sam's latest blog post notifications and information about The Explanation

---

6. https://mailchi.mp/theexplanation/7keystomasterbiblicalhebrew

Annex

Biblical Hebrew – What a Language

Limited vocabulary, but so expressive

In comparison to Biblical Hebrew with about eight thousand words, the 20 volume Oxford Dictionary exposes 171,000 English words in current use. Quite a difference. One might think that with an infinitely smaller vocabulary, Biblical Hebrew would be easier to understand. To the contrary, there's much less controversy with the millions and millions of words in the Oxford Dictionary than the entire 419,687 words of the Old Testament, mainly in Biblical Hebrew.

We are going to make a brief incursion into an exciting aspect and complexity (or simplicity) of Biblical Hebrew. I expound this significantly in *Origin of the Universe*, the third book of *The Explanation* series and the online course *7 Keys to Master Biblical Hebrew*.

It's these complexities/simplicities which open the way for the multitude of *interpretations* of the biblical texts – the cacophonic confusion that surrounds the most printed, and probably the least understood book of all times.

As one of my Hebrew teachers said, "every translation is an interpretation." Simple and profound, each language has its vocabulary that often doesn't have an identical counterpart in another language. So, how do you decode it? A translator's sensitivity, culture, education, and even belief or non-belief come markedly into play.

Keep in mind that I'm not asking you to believe or accept any of this, what I'm saying, what you might think the Bible says or doesn't say, whether the Bible is true or false. All of that is neither here nor there. We're dealing with the literary best-seller of all times that was originally written in Hebrew. All we're doing is analyzing some vocabulary.

Let's jump into the deep end of Biblical Hebrew

Here are four biblical texts from the Kings James Bible. Notice the highlighted, *italicized words*.

Exodus 21:19

If he rise again, and walk abroad upon his staff, then shall he that smote him be quit: only he shall pay for the *loss* of *his time*, and shall cause him to be thoroughly healed.

Proverbs 20:3

It is an honour for a man *to cease* from strife: but every fool will be meddling.

Isaiah 30:7

For the Egyptians shall help in vain, and to no purpose: therefore have I cried concerning this, Their strength is to *sit still*.

Obadiah 3

The pride of your heart has deceived you, you that dwell in the clefts of the rock, whose *habitation* is high; that says in his heart, Who shall bring me down to the ground?

In the image below, even if you do not know Biblical Hebrew whatsoever, it is easy to see that the 4 Hebrew words from excerpts of the four verses above have three identical letters: *shin, beth, taf.* (We write Hebrew from right to left that's why the English is *jumbled* and also needs to be read, in blocks, from right to left).

What I submit to you is this: From reading these four verses in English – or in any and other translations – you'd never guess or know in 1000 years that these four phrases come from ONE ORIGINAL Hebrew word *shevet*. And you'd be hard-pressed to find the relationship between these phrases if any.

What, if anything, do these four English words, from the single Hebrew word *shevet* have in common?

Loss of time

Ceasing

Sitting still

Habitation / cease

This short expose is not intended to give answers. It is simply to explain that the four options: Observation, Philosophy, Science, and Religion, exposed in the final chapter of *Audit of Humankind*, are not the only ways humans can use their minds to reason. There's a fifth option: Theology. That possibly hasn't been properly explored to find out about what makes our world tick.

If I go to the crux of the matter and give you a little challenge, go and ask a well-known political or another experienced leader, go and question a philosopher, go and quiz a scientist, go and query a religious representative about those four verses above. Ask them what, if any, relationship there is between the four different translations of the unique Hebrew word.

Can they enlighten us? I wonder, maybe. Well, proper theology can and will inform us.

In conclusion, this is just a hint, an inkling of what Biblical Hebrew is all about. You don't have to read Biblical Hebrew; you don't have to memorize it, you don't have to learn its vocabulary to deepen your comprehension of theology.

I'm not going to give you the answer now to the above puzzle, but I will provide you with the tools and show you the METHOD so you can Unlock Bible Meaning for yourself, and find the answer to this enigma, and many others. Help and more in-depth understanding of Biblical Hebrew and ultimately, the sacred book – the Bible – is not far away.

Your Language Can't Translate Biblical Hebrew

Just **ONE** Biblical Hebrew word:

דָּבָר

translated into **FIFTY** native language words in the Bible:

act, advice, affair, answer, because of, book, business, care, case, cause, certain rate, commandment, counsel, decree, deed, due, duty, effect, errand, evil favored, hurt, language, manner, matter, message, thing, oracle, portion, promise, provision, purpose, question, rate, reason, report, request, sake, saying, sentence, some (uncleanness), somewhat to say, speech, talk, task, thing (concerning), thought, tidings, what(-soever), which, word, work.

Why?

TheExplanation.com

Languages fall short of the Bible text's richness

Let's start at the beginning. You might have little or no knowledge of the Bible, that's fine. You might consider the Bible to be a bunch of fables of no particular interest other than tales to tell kids. Frankly, that's fine too. You might even believe that the Bible is full of lies and is a *negative book*. Well, you're entitled to your viewpoint.

All of that said, one point remains. The Bible is the best-seller of all times and one way or another; it is *a piece of literature*. If not for any other reason, but general knowledge, it behooves you to have even a cursory understanding of its contents. Let's take a closer look. I guarantee you it is going to be very revealing.

Bible Translations

The vast majority read the Bible in their native language. That's normal. Because the Bible has such a broad audience, it has been translated into 636 languages. The New Testament into 1442 tongues and portions of the Bible into yet another 1145 dialects, making it the most translated book of all times with new translations still appearing.

In a nutshell, Bible translations (which have taken a lot of effort and scholarship) are constructive, but they are incomplete for one excellent reason. The original words, mainly in Hebrew and Greek, have more meaning than what can be rendered in any one translated word or phrase. How can I affirm this? Simply because if you take any translation, you'll see that a SINGLE original word – let's say in Hebrew – has been translated with MULTIPLE words in the translation, no matter what the language.

If it were so simple, every single Hebrew word would have just one translated word. But each Hebrew word has more than one – some have fifty different translations. Yes, you read that correctly – 50 different renderings for the same Hebrew word as we'll shortly see.

You need to ask the fundamental question: How can ONE Hebrew word have FIFTY different translations? These are expert linguists and Bible scholars who are doing their utmost to stay faithful to the original text.

The answer to that question is why I wrote this e-book and developed a free video course:

> 7 Keys to Master Biblical Hebrew – A Study Method to Unlock Bible Meaning, with no fuss.

Biblical Hebrew is the original language of the Bible. You need to understand why a single Biblical Hebrew word can be rendered *correctly* with up to 50 words in your native language. The vast majority of the original language words have multiple translations. With that understanding in mind, I think you can easily and quickly realize that when you read ONE word or ONE short phrase in your native language you are getting understanding, but your understanding is INcomplete.

Don't misunderstand what I'm saying here. Your native language translation in 99.99% of cases is correct. You can understand what the a/Author of those words is saying even if sometimes it is difficult. What I'm saying is that understanding of the Bible in any of the 636 or thousands of translations is only PARTIAL understanding.

And partial understanding can lead to erroneous comprehension of the text. Just like incomplete understanding of any subject, be it, science, history, geography, or mathematics, can lead to error. Especially when we think we are drawing conclusions based on complete comprehension – because that's what we believe or have been given to understand.

Following is just a short answer to the above fundamental question regarding multiple native language translations for one Biblical Hebrew word. It is a preview of the online course with the same title where you'll discover several unspoken characteristics of Biblical Hebrew. If you want to understand the Bible, you need to be aware of these principles.

You may not be aware of some of the examples I evoke here – all the more reason to join the course and increase your general knowledge. A friend of mine told me recently that he was playing a quiz game with some friends and a Bible-related question came up which he answered to the surprise of everyone there! He told me he knew the answer because of a conversation we'd had. You never know when this information is going to come in handy. Not that that's your main motivation.

I'll even go so far as to say that most people with some knowledge and interest in the Bible are not aware of these seven keys and indeed not of this study method to unlock Bible meaning.

Here's an overview of the seven keys:

1. Biblical Hebrew words have Various Meanings

I've already mentioned this one. Here's an example that I think everyone is aware of because of *The Ten Commandments*. Again, remember, I'm not asking you to believe that this story ever took place or even that Moses existed and received the Ten Commandments from God. Just consider this as literature, written originally in Biblical Hebrew, if you want. The Hebrew word used in this context for *commandment* (Exodus 24:38) is *davar*. It's used about 1400 times in the Hebrew Bible. Here is a simple list of over 50 words and phrases used as translations in the English language King James Bible:

Act, advice, affair, answer, because of, book, business, care, case, cause, certain rate, commandment, counsel, decree, deed, due, duty, effect, errand, evil favored, hurt, language, manner, matter, message, thing, oracle, portion, promise, provision, purpose, question, rate, reason, report, request, sake, saying, sentence, some (uncleanness), somewhat to say, speech, talk, task, thing (concerning), thought, tidings, what(-soever), which, word, work.

Why can *a straightforward word* have so many different translations? What is the implication of this?

It means that sometimes when you read the KJV and come across one of these 50 words, in fact, it is the same word as *commandment* like in the Ten Commandments; this is only one example of how translation affects comprehension. Think about this: practically EVERY SINGLE word in Biblical Hebrew has MULTIPLE translations in your native language. This Biblical Hebrew course will explain why this is so.

Each Biblical Hebrew Word is a Precious Jewel

Biblical Hebrew words are thrilling discoveries

Each Biblical Hebrew word is like a rough stone to be dug up, cleaned off, and viewed under a magnifying glass to reveal its glitter and perfection. Let's continue with four more principles to master Biblical Hebrew: Keys 2-5

2. Words can have Opposite Meanings

Here's a word most people are aware of: elohim. If you asked someone for its translation, I think 100% of the time you'd hear *God* and that is correct. But it can also refer to angels, judges, gods, and goddesses.

In Genesis 31:30, the translation gods refers to idols. Exodus 12:12 talks about the *gods* of Egypt using the word elohim; this has nothing to do with *God* (whether you believe in idols and God or not). Even the context shows that the *gods of Egypt* are the opposite as the verse says the *Lord* will smite their *gods-elohim*.

In Psalms 82.6, human-beings are called elohim. How do you explain that? As an added interesting biblical fact, in the New Testament we see the term *god of this world* (2 Corinthians 4:4) with the Greek *theos*, which refers to god but in this verse, *god* is in opposition to *God*. Do you know who this god of this world is (even from a literary point of view)?

Thinking that *elohim* is *God* is correct, but that comprehension is not complete. Not understanding the total opposition of the meaning of Hebrew words can lead to significant misunderstandings; this is just one point in what I refer to as coherent completeness[1]. Elohim = God is correct but INcomplete.

Furthermore, these *oppositions* go further, in that they teach us lessons about life. Here's another translation example among dozens that I'll show you how to spot in the Bible course. The biblical Hebrew word for *eat* and *war* is *lacham*, the common word used in modern Hebrew today for *bread* derives from this: lechem. We all eat, basically every day, even multiple times in a day. It is one of the most common human activities. Why is the same Hebrew word also used for *war*?

Why did the author leave such ambiguity? What is the implication of this?

3. Words can have Concrete & Abstract meanings

How would you express hand on a piece of paper or stone? You'd draw its outline: ? A *hand* is very concrete you can see and touch it, you can easily picture it and envision its shape. Now, how would you represent the concept of *success* or the idea, *you did it*. Well, you could

---

1. http://theexplanation.com/coherent-completeness-is-the-logical-reasoning-of-the-ssource/

use a variation of something concrete to denote a notion, sentiment or feeling, like this: ?*victory*. Just like the sentiment of love is expressed with a concrete and tangible heart ♥. We're even using the word *concrete* (cement and gravel) here in an abstract way.

Today we use all sorts of pictograms, icons, and smileys thinking this is a *modern* form of expression. It goes back to the origins of written language itself when the formation of alphabets began.

Biblical Hebrew goes back to those origins when letters and root words represented concrete, tangible, visible items like a: hand, house or a head ☺ Biblical Hebrew is replete with the concrete expressing the abstract. Here are just a few examples:

- Breath represents spirit
- Head designates the beginning
- Eyes point to understanding
- A lion pictures strength
- Sleep suggests torpor

Like today we use a light bulb to depict a bright idea or that Eureka, eye-opening, aha moment. The real and visible representing the conscious and invisible.

The English word *head* translates from the Hebrew *rosh*. Here's how rosh is rendered in various places in the King James Version of the Bible: band, beginning, captain, chapiter, chief(-est place, man, things), company, end, excellent, first, forefront, (be-)head, height, (on) high(-est part, (priest)), principal, ruler, sum, top. No less than seventeen different English words.

Did you know that the first word of the Bible, in the book of Genesis, is this word *head, beraisheet,* with a slightly different pronunciation which I'll explain later? In Genesis 1:1 it is translated by probably the best known Bible quotation: *in the beginning*.

Understanding some of the 17 translated words above in your native language helps comprehend that this *beginning* is somehow related to the notion *excellent*, another rendering of this same Hebrew word. I won't get into the association of these two variant translations for the same Hebrew word now, suffice to say, there's a relationship.

But this is important considering the very next verse in Gen 1:2, which states: the earth was *without form and void*. If the beginning is associated with *excellent,* how do we explain the presence of this chaos? Do you see what I mean by grasping partial meaning from a translation, but not full comprehension? As a result, Genesis 1:1 has more interpretations than ever. If you get the first sentence in a story wrong, how can you understand the rest? You've missed a critical point.

For now, retain this third key: That the concrete, tangible, physical words that your hands can reach out and touch like *head* represent abstract conceptual ideas that emanate from the mind like *excellent*. We shall see the relevance of this key shortly when I get into Genesis 1:1.

4. Words can have Literal and Figurative meanings

Dual meanings are not unique to Hebrew; we find it in English and other languages too. For example, *night* literally is the twelve hours of darkness, but figuratively we use it in expressions like *a long night for the survivors*. Night can also be metaphorically referring to *dark, evil,* or *confusion*. Translations only render one of those meanings, generally the most obvious, and without getting into it here, but I do in due course, it is mainly only the literal meaning.

Case in point: Genesis 1:2 where we read: *darkness was upon the face of the deep*. I will show you, and you can check it for yourself, but not only was there an *absence of light* but darkness figuratively means to *destroy*, and *make a noise.*

If all you grasp from this verse is the literal darkness, you've missed at least half the meaning which is not transmitted by the translation. And it's entirely possible that the figurative comprehension might be equally if not more important than the literal translation. What have *destruction* and *noise* got to do with creation? What is the implication of this? What does it do for comprehension when we miss fifty percent of the author's meaning?

5. Names of men and women have significance

Just one example. *Noah*, as you know, was instrumental in the story of the worldwide flood that covered even the mountains. I'm just repeating what the book of Genesis says. Whether you believe it's true, a legend, a lie or if you've never read it or can't make up your mind, don't matter at this time. There are numerous statements in the Bible that say there was a flood.

What I want to draw your attention to is that the word *noah*, with a small *n,* is first and foremost a derivative of a Biblical Hebrew word *nooach* – not just a name. This word *nooach*, and its other derivatives, are used over 70 times, and they have been translated, among others, by *cease, be confederate, lay, let down, (be) quiet, remain, (cause to, be at, give, have, make to) rest, set down.*

When you understand just this one point, you can realize that a recent blockbuster film which depicts God and Noah as putting a definitive end to all of humankind is incorrect. Yes, God destroyed humanity, at that time, according to the Bible story (it doesn't matter now whether you believe this piece of literature or not) but, if you understand the meaning of Noah's name you realize that somewhere in this story, there are *quiet* and *rest.*

Maybe you don't understand how and where the *quiet* and *rest* fit in (that's where *Unlock Bible Meaning* comes into play) but, if you know the meaning of Noah's name, the central figure in this account, that should give us some comfort. It also should make us wonder why a man named *quiet* and *rest* was the key figure in massive destruction.

Two major questions that are misunderstood, about the flood episode, are:

How can a righteous and peaceful God put people to death?

The whole question of death and afterlife is a concern for all of us.

Coupled with this is the concept from point 3 that these names can have both literal and figurative aspects to them. The point being that one name, identity, descriptive for a man or woman can have multiple meanings.

Translations *capitalize* the word identifying an individual (Noah), and we tend to take it solely as a name. Well, in Biblical Hebrew, there is no capitalization! It's just another word like all the others, including all the nuances that these 7 Keys to Master Biblical Hebrew will unlock for better Bible understanding.

For now, incredible as it might sound, whether you believe it or not, the meaning of *noah* – referring to *comfort*, and that whole episode, as gruesome, as you might consider it, has some incredibly comforting lessons.

But you'll have to be a little patient until we reach Genesis 6. There is so much to unlock before then to put the Bible story in context and give its theological perspective.

Biblical Hebrew Roots Anchor Comprehension

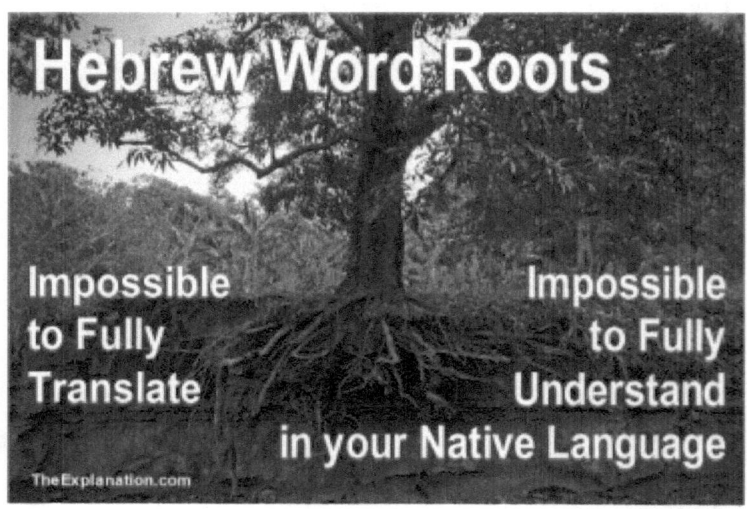

Roots are the writing base of the Bible.

Biblical Hebrew roots and Hebrew word stories are the final two keys of our series to master Biblical Hebrew. Both of these principles are basic, especially the latter. Most Bible readers are not aware of them. Even religious and theological (as differentiated from *intellectual*) Bible scholars are unaware of the most crucial seventh key.

6. Biblical Hebrew construction is based on Roots

Each biblical Hebrew word builds upon a *base*, a common denominator. Here's an English example of a family of words with a common thread: ocular, utrocular (I hadn't heard of that one either), monocle, monocular, binoculars, oculus, oculist. You might not know the meaning of all these words, but you can spot the common denominator: oculus – about the *eye*.

In English we practically never refer to the *common root* of words but, in Biblical Hebrew (and in modern Hebrew) we do. Roots are a fundamental key to understanding meanings and relationships.

The Hebrew Bible only contains about 8600 different words repeated over and over to compose the text. These 8600 words build-up from approximately 2000 roots, or fundamental building blocks like *oculus*. There's a root, a single trunk, from which other words branch out. Understanding this, helps us grasp the relationships between words, some, even most, of which are not evident at first sight.

We've already seen examples of this with *rosh* (head, beginning) and *noah* (quiet, rest) as well as with *lechem* (eat, war). Every word in Biblical Hebrew is either a root or the derivative of a root. It is impossible to see this in your native language where different unrelated translated words, like the three examples above: head/beginning, quiet/rest and eat/war, cannot render full meaning when taken separately.

Another factor to do with the 2000 roots is that some of them are inter-related, further enhancing the relationships and meanings. I can't get into it here but, for those who know a little Hebrew, here's the transliteration of three words: *yashav, shevet, shoov*. Their underlying meanings include: *sit, Sabbath,* and *return*. I say underlying meanings because, as we saw with *noah,* there are multiple native language translations for each of these three roots.

When you read any of these three words in your native language, there's absolutely no way of even knowing they have a common root, let alone realizing there's a definite relationship between those three concepts.

I'll even go so far as to say that for most scholars who read and study Biblical Hebrew, this relationship is unknown or not apparent.

For those not aware of this, the common denominator of *yashav*, *shevet*, and *shoov* consists of the two letters *shin* and *beth* (pronounced here as *vav*). It is impossible to see these roots and hence, these intricate and revealing relationships in any translation. I repeat, the native language translations of these words are correct. But they reveal a very, very limited amount of information. It is impossible to have a complete understanding.

If you reread the above points, you'll now realize that each Biblical Hebrew word: elohim, rosh and noah is either a root (rosh is the only one here) or a derivative of a root. The point is you're beginning to see fundamental concepts in Biblical Hebrew that open up a complete understanding of this best-seller, the Bible. Whether you believe the Bible or not, it's full of words that will open up this literary marvel as never before.

I'll show you how to easily and quickly identify Biblical Hebrew word roots and find all the derivatives and their meanings. We'll be discussing this in the Hebrew course, and soon you'll be able to get a much more complete understanding of full Biblical Hebrew word meanings.

7. Biblical Hebrew Words tell Stories

Stories take us full circle back to point 1. The King James translators (and other translators for all different translated versions in all languages) ended up using MULTIPLE words in English to render ONE Biblical Hebrew word. The result is that sometimes we end up with a jumble of *foreign language* words that don't seem to make sense.

Somewhere, somehow, there's a relationship between them. I call that association of words a *story*. Yes, practically every word, and especially the roots, have a tale to tell. It is these accounts that unlock Bible meaning. There's an exciting story behind shevet, noah, rosh, lechem and hundreds of other words and roots.

Understand that we're not talking about *counting letters* or *hidden code* or *deciphering symbols* or anything of that nature. While I'm on the subject, when I refer to Hebrew roots, I am in no way referring to the *Hebrew Roots movement* which proposes a return to first-century Hebrew Roots Christianity. What I'm talking about here has nothing to do with these organizations and concepts with which I am not associated in any way, shape, or form.

We're talking about Biblical Hebrew vocabulary and the dictionary meaning of words. Just like in your native language, if you don't understand a word, you take a dictionary and look it up. That's what we'll be doing. Looking at the meaning, the FULL meaning of Biblical Hebrew roots and words. It's this full meaning that is the word story.

I will say bluntly, you've never heard these stories before. Without these word stories, it is impossible to grasp a full understanding of what the A/author of what we call the Old Testament has in mind.

I'll conclude this section by bringing us back to another fundamental principle. As mentioned in point six, there's a relationship between the three roots *yashav*, *shevet*, *shoov;* they are interconnected, each telling its own story and each being a part of a larger story; this is what I call *coherent completeness.*

Well, coherent completeness goes much further than that: The 2000 roots are interconnected, not grammatically but figuratively. The 8600 Biblical Hebrew words are interconnected. In the end, I believe, they all tell ONE story. *Each Biblical Hebrew word is a puzzle piece.*

In *Inventory of the Universe* and *Audit of the Universe*, I turned over all the pieces that constitute our physical and non-physical Universe. Turning them right-side-up, giving you an overview of what this Universe is all about and what state it's in right now. In *Origin of the Universe*, we're going to turn the Biblical Hebrew words of Genesis over, one by one. We're going to see their relationship with each other as well as their relationship with our Universe.

We're going to turn Biblical Hebrew words right-side-up and make *coherent completeness* out of all this information. The combined and interrelated stories of the Biblical Hebrew roots will tell us the story of our Universe. They will reveal to us the *Origin of the Universe*.

Bonus – The 8th Key: Active – Passive Verbs

Here's a short example to illustrate this point: In English, we could say, "the teacher taught a course to the students or learners."

Think about what's happening here: a teacher is tutoring a subject, let's say math.

One person is *giving* the math, and the others are *receiving* the math. The first, the teacher, is the active element. The others, the learners, are the passive elements. In English, we use two separate words *teach/learn* for the *active/passive*. In Hebrew we can use the same root with interspersed modifications, like vowels, to express this: *melamad* and *talmid*. The root being the three letters: *lamed*, *mem*, and *daled* (lmd).

One Biblical Hebrew root expresses both the active and the passive.

Once again, translations are a great introduction to begin to understand the Bible. But it is impossible to see the word roots and hence the various concrete and abstract, literal and figurative meanings as well as the word relationships and therefore their stories. Translations are limited in their scope; this is something that Bible readers are not aware of and is one point that leads to incomplete comprehension.

In the course *7 keys to master Biblical Hebrew, a study method to Unlock Bible Meaning* I'll expand each one of these keys that I've evoked in this annex, by using real Biblical Hebrew word examples.

There'll be Biblical Hebrew word mysteries that you'll solve; I'll help you, using the freely accessible online Bible tools[1]. But, the goal of this course is for YOU to ACQUIRE a STUDY METHOD so you can unlock Bible meaning yourself. All I want to do is help you study your Bible better.

Here's the challenge

Here's the first mystery you'll crack it's the first puzzle that I ran across in Biblical Hebrew some 30 years ago that helped me develop this master-course to Unlock Bible Meaning applying Biblical Hebrew. Remember that we're not focusing on Biblical Hebrew per se, Biblical Hebrew is only a means to understand what the Bible is telling us.

In the book of Genesis, the Bible states that Adam and Eve were *naked* (Genesis 2:25, 3:1), in the following verse it indicates that the serpent was *subtil* (old King James English spelling where we'd put *subtle*). The *mystery* is that in Biblical Hebrew, both these words are practically identical (I'd even say identical and I'll explain why during the course) and come from the same root (aram). You can use the Interlinear Bible at www.UnlockBibleMeaning.com[2] to verify this.

The question is, what's the full story being told by this word and its use in this context in Genesis immediately after the Creation story. Again, I

---

1. http://www.unlockbiblemeaning.com/

2. http://www.unlockbiblemeaning.com/

repeat, whether you believe the Creation story or not, it doesn't change the way this story was recorded; however, long ago it was written.

When you solve this mystery, which we'll do during the first lessons of the course, you'll have an answer to one of the most asked worldwide questions about today's society. I guarantee you'll be amazed. But at least as important as the answer is the Bible study method you'll begin to incorporate for your ongoing studies.

Enroll in this course here and solve the mystery of naked and subtil[3]. Very revealing.

---

3. http://theexplanation.com/courses/unlock-bible-meaning-via-biblical-hebrew-no-fuss/

www.TheExplanation.com

Join the Explanation Newsletter[4] ... no spam, total privacy

Sam's latest blog post notifications and information about The Explanation

---

4. https://mailchi.mp/theexplanation.com/7keystomasterbiblicalhebrew

Don't miss out!

Visit the website below and you can sign up to receive emails whenever Sam Kneller publishes a new book. There's no charge and no obligation.

https://books2read.com/r/B-A-GZZJ-PXFHB

BOOKS 2 READ

Connecting independent readers to independent writers.

Also by Sam Kneller

Watch for more at https://www.TheExplanation.com.

About the Author

Sam started learning Hebrew at the age of 10. Little did he know how that would serve him half a century later. At the age of 20, a statement challenged him: *You can prove God exists*. He found the answer, not in *proofs*, but as evidence from the Bible. In a simple but profound way, he saw that there was more to the Bible than what any single or group of authors could pen. His fascination with the Bible story and its Authorship has continued, unabated.

As his Ministry in France progressed, he began to refer more and more to the Biblical Hebrew. He realized there was additional information that the almost word-for-word native-language translations do NOT translate. For instance, he saw that some Hebrew words can have double, even opposite meanings. As an example, the word translated *breath* can be to give or take life. Sometimes *breath* (ruach), translated *blast*, refers to its destructive powers. You cannot see this in English or any other language.

Sam wondered whether his Biblical Hebrew study method to deepen Bible comprehension was correct. Was he deforming the scriptures? He followed two years of online Biblical Hebrew studies with *The Israel Institute of Biblical Studies*, in Jerusalem, to put this question to the test. The method is valid.

The outcome is a unique study method, *Unlock Bible Meaning with 7 Keys to Master Biblical Hebrew.* He developed online Bible tools so anyone can do their independent study and verification of the explanations he proposes. He encourages you to check what he suggests. There's free access to an online King James Version of the Bible, Strong's Concordance, Interlinear Bible and Hebrew-Greek Concordance.

Each week Sam adds a chapter online at TheExplanation.com. He's completed Genesis 3. There is so much in the Biblical Hebrew that you cannot grasp in any other language.

He continues to be captivated, more than ever, with the Bible narrative. This book, and the rest of his works, are his desire to share this foundational knowledge with readers. May you learn and have a better understanding of the Word of God.

Read more at https://TheExplanation.com.